Imtiaz Ahmed Cajee has relentlessly struggled to see that his dear uncle Ahmed Timol's personal sacrifices to attain a just and equitable society were not in vain. He continued to tirelessly collect information and stories that helped to shape Timol's fascinating life story. Imtiaz should be commended for having produced a very enthralling readable publication; a book that not only complements his earlier one but one that brings to light fresh information. He places before the reader a set of information that offers one a clear insight into, among others, the apartheid SB's dirty tricks. He also provides the readers with his close readings of the second inquest, and his interpretation and understanding should cause readers to rethink what 'transitional justice' truly means during this post-apartheid period.
— IMAM HARON FOUNDATION

Ahmed Timol was a revolutionary, a freedom fighter and a true South African who loved life and his people. He lived his life in the pursuit of freedom and died a martyr by the hands of tyrants. His life was an inspiration to the members of the Ahmed Timol MK unit. Unlike many recent struggle publications that trade on the life sacrifices of our martyrs for the writers own glorification, this story speaks truth to power. Even if that power happens to be from within the ranks.
— JAMEEL CHAND, AHMED TIMOL UNIT

Imtiaz reminds us in this book that his uncle, Ahmed Timol, gave the best of himself for our liberation. Therefore, I believe that we owe Timol (and all other martyrs of our struggle) the best of ourselves too. It is now up to us, (as Imtiaz so ably demonstrates) to realise the society that his uncle died for. One that's anchored on justice, love and equality. A luta!
— LUKHANYO CALATA, SON OF FORT CALATA AND AUTHOR OF
MY FATHER DIED FOR THIS

The Murder of Ahmed Timol
My Search for the Truth

Imtiaz A. Cajee

Foreword by Nkosinathi Biko

First published by Jacana Media (Pty) Ltd
First and second impression 2020

10 Orange Street
Sunnyside
Auckland Park 2092
South Africa
+2711 628 3200
www.jacana.co.za

© Imtiaz Cajee, 2020

All rights reserved.

ISBN 978-1-4314-2963-9

All royalties accrued on the sale of books are to be donated to the Ahmed Timol Family Trust.
www.ahmedtimol.co.za

Cover design by publicide
Editing by Sahm Venter
Proofreading by Lara Jacob
Set in Ehrhardt 11.5/15.5pt
Printed and bound by ABC Press, Cape Town
Job no. 003674

See a complete list of Jacana titles at www.jacana.co.za

I was five years old when my uncle, Ahmed Timol, was killed in police detention. I have never claimed to have known him. That opportunity was afforded to his siblings, his contemporaries, his comrades and others. It is not for me to judge how they preserved his legacy. The views expressed here are my own and do not represent those of the family, and I take full responsibility for any inaccuracies. This is my story.
— IMTIAZ AHMED CAJEE

*To my late wife Kay, who stood beside me throughout my journey.
Your intuition was always correct. You are sorely missed and will always
remain a part of my life.*

*To the late Mrs Amina Desai (Mummy); Aunty Rookaya Saloojee
(the widow of Suliman 'Babla' Saloojee); the late Comrade Tony
Seedat; the late Yusuf Akhalwaya and Prakash Napier of the Ahmed
Timol Unit; and the unsung heroes and heroines of the struggle against
apartheid and the families of all other apartheid-era victims.*

*Lest we forget the voiceless – those who were lynched in the farms
and country towns, those that were gunned down by the police for
misdemeanours, the many that were denied treatment and left by the
roadside to die due to the lack of available ambulances and medical
services for people of colour, the children who were murdered by the
police in 1976, the deaths from the abject poverty and subjugation as a
consequence of the apartheid system, the many indirect deaths of innocent
people, with no one held accountable for their deaths.*

*My personal journey is to right the wrongs and hold those
responsible for my uncle's murder accountable, but also to ensure we
remember the many voiceless victims whose families have long suffered in
silence at the hands of a brutal and murderous regime.*

Contents

Foreword..xi
Preface..xv

PART I: *Ahmed Timol's Journey*
   I Shaping my life..3
   II A painful past..13
   III Getting involved..23

PART II: *Capture*
   IV Taken..41
   V 'Detainee dies in police custody'...........................53
   VI Reawakening..71

PART III: *My Investigation*
   VII Gathering intelligence....................................85
   VIII Interrogation..103
   IX The first inquest...123

PART IV: *The Second Inquest*
   X Culture of torture...145
   XI A different picture.......................................161
   XII Police witnesses..179
   XIII He was murdered..179
   XIV The wheels of justice turn slowly........................207

Ahmed Timol timeline...221
Acknowlegements..225
Endnotes...227

Foreword

On 12 October 2017, Judge Billy Mothle read a historic ruling at the Gauteng North Division of the High Court of South Africa, which had led an inquest into the death of Ahmed Timol. Rejecting the findings of an initial judicial cover-up under apartheid, the judge stated categorically that Timol had been murdered during his detention at John Vorster Square in 1971 in what the perpetrators cold-heartedly chronicled as suicide. This progressive ruling meant that after more than four decades, the falsehoods about Timol's murder began to crumble as the wheels of justice creaked into motion.

Evading accountability for the deaths of thousands of freedom fighters in South Africa and the frontline states was rampant under apartheid. A few years ago, the Steve Biko Foundation commissioned research to examine the category of apartheid victims who were tortured and subsequently killed while detained under state security laws. Bantu Stephen Biko, who was killed five years after the murder of Timol, is a member of this class and is listed as number 49. The names of victims that we have uncovered thus far are listed on a commemorative wall in the permanent exhibition at the Steve Biko Centre in King William's Town. Their names also appear on an external wall in the commemorative garden – a tranquil space at the bottom of the property. As far as we know it has for years been the furthest reaching attempt to ensure that this class of freedom fighters is not expunged from history.

A closer scrutiny of the records betrays the despicable morality of apartheid. Almost without fail the official explanation of the death of the victims is either 'suicide by hanging' or 'jumped out the window'. Alternatively, it is 'slipped on a bar of soap'. In short, not only were perpetrators responsible for torturing chained defenceless activists, but once they were done visiting the worst atrocities on their bodies, they were also determined to deprive them of a place of honour that is commensurate with their heroism.

That even under a democratic South Africa the courage of these freedom fighters continues to be befogged by the veil of denialism jumps at me every time I gaze at this list. The testimony of Rodrigues at the inquest was incredibly elusive. In the multiple subsequent applications with the intent of avoiding trial, he went further by being so bold as to argue that the failure of the democratic government to pursue these cases timeously is an injustice to him.

Although such an argument may possibly hold in law, in ethics it bears no trace of the obligation that he has, due to the freedom he now enjoys, to do right by the Timols. Unfortunately, many in his position have similarly evaded justice and scorned attempts to attain the truth and achieve reconciliation. Thus as Judge Mothle extended his ruling recommending the reopening of the Timol matter to include other inquests in this class of murders, I felt that only with the passing of time shall we come to fully appreciate just how much he moved the needle.

Two years ago, the founders of Black Consciousness Movement gathered at the Steve Biko Centre to celebrate 50 years since the establishment of the South African Student Organisation. Founded in 1968, SASO was the first of what became a wide network of Black Consciousness structures. On the last day of the reunion the group visited Kei Road police station at which the late activist Mapetla Mohapi was murdered in 1976. Mohapi was one of the founders. I am told that his death had a huge impact on members of this group, including Bantu Stephen Biko. As a result they began to reflect on the serious probability of death in detention and to talk about how to handle interrogation. The article Biko penned titled 'On Death' is an outcome of the reflections of that era.

Foreword

Travelling with the reunion group was Thenjiwe Mthintso, who was also arrested and tortured at Kei Road police station a week after the death of Mohapi in 1976. I noticed that restlessness hung over her as we waited for the commander to open the facility. Then, completely unscripted, she began to share with the group the brutal nature of her torture in the same cell. During the interrogation her tormentors referenced what they had done to her colleague in the same room a few days before. As she told her story in the cell with us was one of Mohapi's daughters, Mothiba Mohapi. Mothiba was visiting the cell for the first time, having previously been refused access by the station commander, even in a democratic South Africa. Thus, for the first time in 42 years she was witnessing a first-hand account of what happened to her father. I suspect that such accounts, painful as they are, are a necessary step towards closure for many people in her position.

It is for the renewed promise of such possibilities that we must be beholden to the ultimate protagonists on this journey. The relentless quest by Imtiaz Cajee to seek justice for the murder of Ahmed Timol has gifted the nation with the opportunity to give back a voice to the silenced. Perhaps, put more accurately, we stand to raise the voice of the silenced, for although many of them died lonely deaths in silence the forensic evidence that explains their deaths is their definitive word. Until now, we have simply refused to hear it. Collectively, their forensic files speak volumes about what happened in the respective torture chambers that were police headquarters. The time for their stories to be heard has come. One hopes that many more such stories will be told.

This book provides us with the story of Timol and the journey of Imtiaz Cajee. In giving us this gift, I am acutely aware of how much Imtiaz has had to give of himself, for the act of giving is as draining as it is fulfilling. May he take a well-deserved turn to lean on the emboldened shoulders of his fellow travellers as we all walk the rest of the road to justice.

Nkosinathi Biko

Preface

Ahmed Timol was killed in police detention on 27 October 1971. A year later, an apartheid-era inquest found that he had committed suicide by jumping out of the window of Room 1026 on the the tenth floor of John Vorster Square, where he had been interrograted.

Nearly 25 years later, as I watched his frail mother, my grandmother, plead for information about what really happened at the Truth and Reconciliation Commission (TRC) without much outcome, I made a silent vow to do everything possible to have Uncle Ahmed's case reopened. In 2009 I called for the reopening of the inquest and finally, 46 years after his death, a new inquest found that Ahmed Timol had been murdered.

João 'Jan' Anastacio Rodrigues, a former security policeman and the last person to see Uncle Ahmed alive, was informed on 30 July 2018 that he would face trial for murder and defeating the ends of justice. He lost his application for a permanent stay of prosecution and has appealed the decision. As we await the outcome of the appeal to the Supreme Court, this is the story of my journey to expose the truth.

The first time I saw him was in a black-and-white official police photograph of the crime scene. Taken from behind, it shows a man dressed in Afrikaner male fashion of the day: knee-length socks and a light-coloured safari suit with short pants. He was facing an open window. It was the window from which he claimed that my uncle jumped to his death.

The first time I saw Rodrigues in the flesh I was taken aback by his size. Nudging 80 years old and walking with a cane after a recent surgery, he showed no signs of a shuffle or a stoop. At 1.88 metres tall, he appeared as fit, erect and strong just as he did in the photograph, taken nearly 50 years before. I had had decades to ponder the events that took place in that room on the top floor of the security police headquarters in Johannesburg. I had imagined my uncle's last moments over and over again. The bullying, humiliation, assault and, finally, the murder of my beloved uncle by hefty policemen.

I grew up with a hole in my close-knit and devoutly Muslim family that I could not initially understand. It was a hole that the passing of time could not heal because it was poisoned by the web of lies the police created to cover up my uncle's death. Their version that he had killed himself remained falsely noted in the record books – for close to half a century.

Ahmed Timol was not the first or the last person to die at the hands of the brutal apartheid police, and ours is not the only family to have suffered the double injustice of loss and a lack of accountability.

We thought that when apartheid ended, South Africa's democratically elected government would go out of its way to shine a torch of truth on the deaths, the disappearances and the cover-ups, and that it would bring justice to bear on the perpetrators – not least because they were the people who had laid down their lives for our freedom. But this has not been the case. Instead, the administration seems to have gone out of its way to find excuses for not investigating the crimes of the past.

In April 1996, two years after our political liberation, the TRC held its first public hearings. Victims of politically motivated crimes testified about their experiences before a spellbound nation. Among the first witnesses was Uncle Ahmed's mother, Hawa Timol, and it was on that day, 30 April 1996, that I vowed never to give up my quest for justice, however long it took.

While the TRC was an important forum for victims of human rights violations to tell their stories – and for the nation to listen and learn about its past – arguably more significant was its amnesty mechanism.

Perpetrators were invited to apply for amnesty from prosecution, which they would receive if they could prove that their actions had been politically motivated and commensurate with their objectives, and that they had made a full and truthful disclosure. Critically, the commission did not insist on the perpetrators clearing their consciences. Amnesty was the carrot, but there was also meant to be a stick. Those who chose to take their chances and evade the commission and those who were refused amnesty would be prosecuted for their crimes. The commission's final report to the nation on its findings and recommendations, released on 21 March 2003, recommended that more than 300 cases should be further investigated. That required political will.

The Truth and Reconciliation Commission was designed as part of a restorative justice process, but the government lost its appetite for the process, and it came to a juddering halt once the final report was released. Nobody applied for amnesty in respect to my uncle's death, which the 1972 inquest court had ruled as suicide and decided that nobody was to blame. It had become apparent to me, that unless I took up the investigation, that would be the last word on the matter.

It took me 21 years to fulfil the oath I made to my grandmother at the commission. It took 21 years of begging and cajoling – and in their minds, harassing – prosecutorial authorities to reopen the apartheid inquest. Twenty-one years of bureaucratic delays; of doors being slammed in my face; of having to engage in lengthy and costly processes to force the government to reveal information that victims of apartheid security forces should have been free to access. It was 21 years in which I watched both perpetrators and the loved ones of their victims succumb to old age, without accountability or closure. It was as if someone up there had made a conscious decision that if they could delay long enough, until everyone was dead, then the problem would miraculously disappear. As if the families could ever forget. My 21 years of perseverance led to the courtroom appearance of this giant-like man, who, 46 years before, had claimed to have been the only eye witness to what was called my uncle's suicide.

João Rodrigues was the state's star witness at the 1972 inquest.

A white South African of Portuguese descent, he was working as an administrative clerk at the security police headquarters in Pretoria at that time. After more than 10 years of service, he had ascended just one step up the police hierarchy to the rank of sergeant. He could claim no operational knowledge, and neither was he a member of Ahmed Timol's interrogation team. Because he was based in Pretoria, he knew virtually nothing about what was going on at John Vorster Square. Despite not being in the field, Rodrigues could still deny allegations that my uncle had been mistreated or tortured by testifying at the 1972 inquest that he appeared unharmed, and was drinking coffee with his interrogators, moments before his death.

He testified that he had been at John Vorster Square, and in the room, quite by chance, to deliver salary cheques and a sealed envelope to two of Timol's interrogators, Captain Johannes Hendrik 'Hans' Gloy and Captain Zacharia van Niekerk. Minutes after his arrival, another man, they called him 'Mr X', briefly entered the room to inform them that certain suspects said to be linked to the detainee had been identified and arrested. Rodrigues claimed that my uncle who, he said, bore no signs of having been tortured or assaulted, suddenly looked shocked. Moments later, the interrogators left the room, asking Rodrigues to guard him. He told the inquest that my uncle somehow out-manoeuvred him and jumped to his death from the tenth floor window of the room. The magistrate was so impressed by Rodrigues's evidence that he founds any suggestion that Ahmed Timol's death had been anything other than suicide.

But that was 1972, when the security establishment believed it could uphold the apartheid regime forever. In those days, the state could rely on its network of police, prosecutors, district surgeons, magistrates and judges not to rock the boat. When the inquest was reopened 45 years later, it was in a democratic South Africa with its transformed institutions and accountability. Once again, Rodrigues was shaping up as a critical witness, not least because the policemen who were said to have interrogated my uncle were dead, but the big difference, this time, was that Rodrigues would not be testifying in a controlled environment. His testimony in 2017 followed damning evidence from former political detainees about the systemic use of violence by the police; from forensic pathologists who said Ahmed Timol had been brutally assaulted; and from a trajectory expert who found that he couldn't have jumped as Rodrigues described. Their collective version of events totally contradicted the testimony which Rodrigues presented in 1972. I prayed that this elderly security policeman would recant; I did not think he had any option, and I believed that he would benefit in the long term from clearing his conscience and telling the truth.

Over the course of my investigation into my uncle's murder, I tracked down several members of his interrogation team. They were unwilling to speak to me, despite my heartfelt assurances that my intentions were not malicious, that I was purely interested in establishing the truth. One by one, they passed away – taking their secrets with them. All those years during my investigations, Rodrigues was nowhere to be found.

By the time the new inquest started in 2017, I was no longer a one-man band. The Foundation for Human Rights (FHR), led by the former TRC commissioner, Yasmin Sooka, had stepped in to help, adding considerable muscle to the final push to force the National Prosecuting Authority (NPA) to reconsider the matter. A lawyer specialising in restorative justice, Sooka brought with her a team that included a world-renowned police detective-turned private investigator, Frank Dutton; Advocate Howard Varney; Moray Hathorn, a partner in the prominent law firm, Webber Wentzel; and the Legal Resources Centre, with its legendary associate Advocate George Bizos SC. We also roped in the services of the media team of Benny Gool and Roger Friedman, who had long supported my quest for justice.

On 4 June 2017, Benny forwarded me an email he had received, titled 'Ahmed Timol case reopens'. It read: 'Just to let you know of the wareabouts [sic] of JA Roderigues [sic] (nickname JAN) ex seargent [sic] – he is still alive and well. Website of his own – books from the wild.' The email detailed a physical address for him, and its author added, 'Hope this help [sic] in getting closure on this.' I forwarded the information to Frank Dutton, who visited Rodrigues on 16 June 2017 and confirmed his identity. Later that month he was subpoenaed to testify before the reopened inquest.

Before he appeared in court, his police file had revealed an extraordinary fact. Despite what was, by all accounts, a rather indifferent career in the police, featuring just one promotion and regular bouts of sick leave, and despite the fact that he was a relatively anonymous administration clerk, he received a letter of commendation from no less than the national commissioner of police. This was only days before the apartheid inquest magistrate had returned his finding of suicide. The police commissioner only rarely wrote letters of commendation and, usually, only in circumstances of unusual courage or in recognition of a particular contribution to the cause.

The only reasonable inference one can draw was that Rodrigues was commended for the evidence he gave at the inquest, which mitigated embarrassment to the state and helped to cover up my uncle's murder. Under cross-examination at the reopened inquest, Rodrigues was asked about the letter. He said he had no idea why he had received it. He must have been lucky.

Testifying before Judge Billy Mothle in the second inquest, Rodrigues said that soon after the 1972 inquest, he had resigned from the police to take up a new career as a journalist. He briefly returned to the police to do a counter-insurgency course and then quit again – this time for good. He had the perfect qualifications to become a game ranger in the Kruger National Park. It was located along the border with Mozambique, which harboured many enemies of the apartheid state.

The former security policeman became 'Oom Jan' Rodrigues, a narrator of fireside bushveld tales and the author of wildlife and nature books. He had moved on with his life, while our family remained stuck in the past, not knowing the truth of what had happened to my uncle.

I am mature enough to know that context is important and that Rodrigues was a minor player in an insidious and dirty war against black emancipation; it would have been very difficult for him to resist whatever instructions he was given to cover up my uncle's murder. But that was then, and this is now. We've had more than two decades since the end of apartheid to recalibrate our positions on morality and justice.

I have no feelings of hatred or desire for revenge in my heart. But I believe that Rodrigues holds special redemptive powers, insofar as sharing his knowledge of events that day would bring closure to my family, help to unburden his conscience and open a window of hope for other families still searching for the truth about lost loved ones.

He was in a tricky position. If he recanted his 1972 evidence, took responsibility for his role and revealed details about the other participants, he ran the risk of being charged with perjury. I do not believe that the court or society would be totally unsympathetic to him but if he did not recant, and stuck to his previous version, he would run the risk of perjuring himself before the reopened inquest, and to potentially being charged for murder. I prayed then that he would take the opportunity to do the right thing. I still pray for it.

At the second inquest, Judge Mothle took great care to explain his quandary to Rodrigues. In order to accept that he was telling the truth, he would have to find that a pair of highly qualified forensic pathologists, a trajectory expert and the witnesses who testified about the torture of political detainees had misinformed the court. In the end, Judge Mothle recommended that Rodrigues be investigated for making contradictory statements while under oath and referred the judgment to the National Prosecuting Authority for further processes to be followed.

We now know that Ahmed Timol did not commit suicide, that he was murdered after being brutally assaulted. He had suffered ante mortem injuries to his head that most likely rendered him unconscious and had injuries to his foot that would have left him unable to walk – and more importantly, that from the distance in which he landed on the street below, he was either pushed from the tenth floor window or shoved off the roof. We do not know for sure what Rodrigues was doing in the interrogation room, whether he was indeed alone with Ahmed Timol, or in the room at all. We still do not know the real extent of his involvement.

As a nation we remain trapped by our past – economically, socially and psychologically. We began a process of accountability and justice, only to abandon it mid-stream after the TRC. What history can we teach our children if we ourselves do not know the truth?

By far the most contentious aspect of my investigation was my quest to establish the role of police informants in the investigation into Ahmed Timol's political activities and his arrest. I wanted to know whether he was simply unlucky to have been arrested at a random roadblock, as the police had claimed, or if it had been set up to camouflage the fact that he had been sold down the river by someone he knew or members of the community working for the police. While I have my suspicions, I probably will never have them confirmed.

Roadblocks were a common method adopted by apartheid security police to arrest activists. Nelson Mandela was captured at a roadblock, so was Bantu Stephen Biko, as were the Cradock Four.[1] Either the police were extraordinarily fortunate in their ability to catch big fish thus or there was nothing random about the roadblocks.

A 1990 newspaper report[2] alleged that a tip from a paid informant of the Central Intelligence Agency (CIA) led to the 1962 arrest of Mandela. Quoting a retired US intelligence officer who was stationed in South Africa at the time, the newspaper said a senior CIA official claimed credit for Mandela's capture within hours of his arrest on 5 August 1962. According to reports in the mid-1980s, the US official who delivered the information about Mandela to authorities in Durban was Donald Rickard, allegedly a CIA officer working as US consul there.

The claim also surfaced in a 1996 newspaper report[3] that a former US diplomat who was working as a spy for the CIA revealed that he was responsible for the tip that led to Mandela's arrest, beginning the leader's 27 years behind bars. The London *Sunday Times* reported comments made by Rickard to British film director John Irvin.[4]

Anyone remotely politically conscious in the apartheid era often heard rumours or themselves harboured suspicions that certain members of the community worked with the police. Occasionally, these suspicions would be confirmed. But mostly, they were left to ferment over the years. Several former operatives have confirmed that our communities and organisations were riddled with people who reported, directly or indirectly, to the security police. Some were paid for information; others had their university fees paid; some received a favour such as a passport; some compromised, sexually, criminally or financially. Yet others were tortured and assaulted and some were threatened. The state's pervasive and opportunistic endeavours to keep abreast of the operations of anti-apartheid activists led to extreme paranoia in communities and organisations.

My investigation into Ahmed Timol's murder revealed that the security police had an elaborate surveillance network with a local, national and international reach. Some comrades, who became politicians in post-apartheid South Africa, decided not to reveal any names to me. I understand that there is an argument to be made for deliberately damping down divisions of our past or, at least, to not inflame them. There is no doubt that revealing lists of names of people who – whether voluntarily or through police coercion – involved themselves in the unsavoury actions of the former regime would cause extreme anger and bitterness in the short term. There is also the risk of implicating innocent people. But one could also argue that the biggest beneficiaries of the decision not to unmask them are those who worked with the apartheid state. By retaining their masks, many would have been well placed to profit from South Africa's political transformation.

The Indian community in Roodepoort, Lappies as we called it, where the Timol family lived, is relatively small. As I went about interviewing people who knew my uncle in an effort to help put together pieces of the puzzle of events surrounding his arrest and death, it became clear to me that deep suspicions and resentments continue to swirl in the community. Some of those who have been regarded with suspicion took the decision to share their pain with me, elderly people with tears streaming down their faces unable to prove or disprove their innocence.

I have very consciously taken the decision to confront these issues, not to judge anyone but because this uncertainty is part of the fabric of our post-apartheid society. How do we process information that we do not know for certain is true? Would it be better to remain silent, until everyone involved is dead?

In the last paragraph of his autobiography, *Long Walk to Freedom*, Mandela famously reflects on how much work still lies ahead. 'I have walked that long road to freedom. I have tried not to falter; I have made missteps along the way. But I have discovered the secret that after climbing a great hill, one only finds that there are many more hills to climb,' he wrote. 'I have taken a moment here to rest, to steal a view of the glorious vista that surrounds me, to look back on the distance I have come. But I can rest only for a moment, for with freedom come responsibilities, and I dare not linger, for my long walk is not yet ended.'[5]

Twenty-four years ago, I began a journey of discovery that culminated in the reopening of the inquest into my uncle's death and the reversal of the apartheid magistrate's finding of suicide. But I, too, cannot linger, for many more hills lie ahead. Reopening the inquest broadcast a message of hope to many other families who had their loved ones brutally taken by security police, never to return. I believe that my uncle would be proud to know that the quest for justice in respect of his murder has laid the foundation for bringing closure to other families.

PART I
Ahmed Timol's Journey

I

Shaping my life

I have sketchy, but precious, memories of accompanying Uncle Ahmed to the Roodepoort Club where I would watch him swim. I am told he was an excellent swimmer. I remember also going with him to visit a family friend in Roodepoort, Amina Desai, whom I fondly called 'Mummy'. She had a white cat. Uncle Ahmed would drive me in Mummy's yellow Ford Anglia, the same car he was driving when he was detained at a police roadblock on the evening of 22 October 1971.

That evening I was visiting my maternal grandparents' apartment, No. 2 Choonara Flats, 76 Mare Street in Roodepoort. The adults sat around the kitchen table whispering to each other; suddenly, there was a loud knock on the door and a bunch of burly Afrikaner men entered the flat.

My family regularly made the 180-kilometre journey from their home in Standerton, Mpumalanga to Roodepoort to visit my maternal grandparents. But everything changed when my uncle was arrested. My last recollection of that horrendous evening was of my grandmother, Hawa Timol whom I called Ma, standing at the window while hundreds of people stood outside. My dad had told me that he hoisted me onto his shoulders at my uncle's funeral a week later, but I have no memory of this.

In May 1976, some five years after my uncle's death, my grandparents moved to Azaadville, an area west of Johannesburg set aside for people of Indian descent from the towns of Roodepoort,

Krugersdorp and Randfontein. My grandfather, Papa Haji Timol, would often take me to the Roodepoort *qabrastaan* (cemetery) to visit Uncle Ahmed's grave. Upon our return my grandmother would always ask me, 'Did you pray for your uncle?' And I would reply that I had.

Papa loved to hear me recite verses of the Quran and rewarded me with a few cents after each recital. He was a travelling salesman who worked across the entire Transvaal province, as it was then known, with his driver at the wheel of his green Peugeot station wagon. His eyesight was poor and he wore spectacles with thick lenses and he carried a magnifying glass for reading newspapers. Listening to the news on the wireless was a daily routine for Papa. After each individual news report, he would express a 'sigh' in acknowledgment. He would consistently rise in the middle of the night to perform the optional *Tahujjud*[6] prayers and his constant calling and praising of the Almighty in his sleep still echoes in my mind. He was a cool, calm and collected individual with a great temperament – and a walking stick always by his side.

I was in Roodepoort when Uncle Mohammad, Ahmed's younger brother, was released from police detention on 14 March 1972 after being held in solitary confinement for about 141 days. I remember phoning my father in Standerton from a neighbour's apartment to tell him the good news. Uncle Mohammad had been denied permission to leave detention to attend his brother's funeral despite the valiant efforts of the prominent anti-apartheid activist Fatima Meer, who pleaded with Prime Minister B.J. Vorster to intervene.

Uncle Mohammad was detained under Section 10 of the Internal Security Act and was held at the Modderbee Prison in Benoni. He was released after four months without being charged and was immediately served with a five-year house arrest order. His movements were restricted to the magisterial district of Krugersdorp, which included Azaadville. Largely confined to his home, he could only go out on weekdays between 6 am and 7 pm to attend to his job in Johannesburg. If he arrived home a minute after 7 pm, he risked immediate imprisonment. I recall how my grandmother would keep looking anxiously at the clock as 7 pm approached.

He was forbidden from entering his old hometown of Roodepoort where his childhood friends lived and was not allowed to visit his brother's grave. On Saturdays he was permitted to leave home between 8 am and noon, restricted to the Krugersdorp district, but he still discreetly met other activists at the bird park in Krugersdorp. He had to be in the house from noon on Saturday until Monday morning when he left for work. If a public holiday fell on a Monday he had to remain indoors till Tuesday. He was prohibited from being in the company of more than one person at a time in a public place. This restriction was not always technically possible and was not applied to his attending Friday prayers, or while travelling by kombi with other passengers to and from work, or during his lunch break.

He was also prevented from meeting any other restricted person and was not allowed any visitors at home. However, because he lived with his parents, there were loopholes. I recall regular visits by my mother's cousins, Iqbal, 'Baboo' and his brother, Farouk Dindar, with their families, to the Timol home in Azaadville. Such visits were not without risk as the residence was closely monitored by security police informants. My own family home in Standerton was occasionally visited by Security Branch officers from Middelburg wanting to know the reason for our blue Ford Granada being seen outside the Timol residence in Azaadville on specific dates.

This is how I first realised, from a young age, that there must be people in the community feeding certain information to the police. Who were they, and did they have no conscience? How could they cooperate and support the brutal and oppressive apartheid regime? One of the hardest parts of my investigation into Uncle Ahmed's murder has been how to deal with unproven allegations that he was possibly betrayed by someone he knew.

In January 1977, there were two weddings in the family, including that of my uncle Ismail, but his brother Uncle Mohammad was denied permission to attend either of the celebrations. He was forced to spend so much time alone. An image I have of Uncle Mohammad, from around that time, is of him sitting in a chair in the front garden with his radio, listening to the BBC, not necessarily to the political broadcasts. He was an ardent Leeds United supporter largely due to the presence of a South African in the team, Albert Johanneson,[7] who was the first black player to play in an FA Cup Final. He was in the team playing against Liverpool in 1965, when Leeds lost 2–1. Johanneson made 200 appearances for Leeds from 1961 to 1969 and a plaque to honour him was unveiled on 11 January 2019, at the Leeds United grounds of Elland Road.

During school holidays, my younger sister Amina and I spent more time than usual in Azaadville and would eagerly await the return from work of our immaculately dressed Uncle Mohammad. One of my mother's self-imposed routines during these visits was cleaning the cupboards of all the rooms in the house. I remember her finding enlarged pictures of the Bantu Stephen Biko[8] funeral under Uncle Mohammad's bed. There was also a yellow T-shirt with the image of Biko and his hands in chains.

I was playing in the sun, hitting a tennis ball against the wall on 1 January 1978, when my mother broke the news to me that Ma had called from Azaadville to say that Uncle Mohammad had left. Ma only noticed his absence when he did not come for breakfast. Upon inspecting his room in the back of the main house, she found his bed made up, neat and tidy. I was 11 years old and battled to come to terms with the loss of a second uncle – although this one went into exile and would later come home.

The Citizen newspaper reported on 7 January 1978[9] that mystery surrounded the flight to freedom of the banned chairman of the Johannesburg-based Human Rights Committee, Mohammad Timol. It said relatives had received a call from him from Swaziland. Government officials in Mbabane had expected him to have reported his presence as a political refugee to police or to immigration officials, and then to file an application for political asylum but he had not done so. The truth of his movements would only be determined many years later.

Without him there, the Timol residence in Azaadville was no longer the same during the school holidays. I filled the void with new activities like reading newspaper clippings about Uncle Ahmed and leafing through his photo album. I was overwhelmed to read letters published in newspapers from ordinary white South Africans condemning the actions of the security police and supporting the Timol family. They left an indelible impression on me and made me realise that I could not blame all whites for the heinous murder of my uncle. I began asking my grandmother what happened to this smartly dressed man in tie and jacket, stovepipe pants and cool sunglasses.

Whenever we drove on the highway through Johannesburg on our way from Standerton to Azaadville, we would pass the imposing blue and grey building called John Vorster Square police station. My mother would always remark that this was the place where her brother Ahmed had been thrown from the tenth floor. Silence would always follow her words. I would stare at this monstrous building trying to visualise my uncle falling to his death. As we drove along Main Reef Road, the Roodepoort *qabrastaan* could be seen in the distance. 'Pray for your Uncle Ahmed,' she would say. She would remind me over the years that he would always tell her to keep her heart clean. 'Allah does not like it when the heart is dirty', he would say to his sister. She would sometimes remember how popular he was and how he loved speaking at school functions.

My own political consciousness was slowly emerging in Standerton as I witnessed the routine raids by Administration Board officers – a white official in a van, accompanied by black colleagues on the hunt for African domestic workers without permission to work in an area designated as Indian. Standerton was typical of the racially divided towns of the time, spiritually, socially, economically and geographically. The white residential area was close to the business centre and municipal institutions. The absurdity of apartheid spatial planning meant that slightly further away was the coloured area, then the Indian area – and finally, the overwhelming majority of the people, Africans, in a township with only one entrance and exit.

I was in my early teens when my father, Ebrahim Cajee, insisted that I take on part-time work during the school holidays and on weekends. My first job was at Essop Bhai Pochee's shop in the Stanwest Indian

Shopping Complex. Later, I worked in the family business, mainly packing shelves and cool drink fridges. I felt an affinity with the workers and wondered how they managed to survive on their meagre salaries. My dad would often say that I should never run behind money. I found this difficult to comprehend at the time. Only in later years did I realise what he meant.

I read the daily English language newspapers, the *Rand Daily Mail* and *The Star*, which provided a measure of coverage of political events in the country. Listening to Capital Radio,[10] broadcasting from the so-called independent bantustan of Transkei, gave me an alternative source of news. I felt there was an uprising within the borders of South Africa and I was hungry for news of it; I wanted to be part of it.

Another incident that impacted me was witnessing the arbitrary arrests of Mohammad Bhabha,[11] and the brothers Haroon and Azhar Cajee at Standerton School in 1976 (who are not related to me). Many years later Haroon recalled:

> The previous evening the school principal's car was vandalised. The principal was convinced that we were somehow involved, as he had seen us amongst a group of people nearby where the incident occurred. At the time, the principal was a hated figure as he represented the apartheid establishment forcing people to sing the widely despised national anthem, as part of the school systems' wider collaboration with the white regime. The following day, the principal instructed the police to arrest the potential suspects who were all minors at the time, without due cause and notification of their parents and guardians. They were all beaten by the police and forced to sign confessions. At the trial, the case was dismissed as the principal could not recall the exact sequence of events during the alleged event and conceded that the damage could have occurred during normal operation of his vehicle.[12]

My teenage years were difficult and frustrating. I was deeply angry about apartheid but there were no avenues in Standerton for me

Shaping my life

to express my rage. My family was understandably jittery about discussing politics, as they were still grieving Uncle Ahmed's death and Uncle Mohammad's sudden departure into exile. My education suffered and I had no desire to continue attending school after failing my Standard 5 examinations. Why did I have to sit behind a desk? What possible benefits could be derived from this? I wanted to liberate the country, join the African National Congress' military wing, uMkhonto we Sizwe (MK), and avenge the murder of my uncle.

I was a member of an avid sporting family; we would have soccer training sessions at the local school led by my cousin, Rashid Ahmed Cajee, who was a teacher there. To build our stamina he would take us through our paces, including getting us to run up and down the school stairs. I never looked forward to that part of our training and preferred to work with the ball. The way I motivated myself to run up those stairs was to imagine that I was an MK soldier involved in skirmishes with the Afrikaners.

I was 15 when I participated in the school boycott at the Stanwest Secondary School around 1981. Pink Floyd's iconic song, 'Another brick in the wall' with that most inspiring line 'We don't need no education', was a favourite anthem of protesting students across the country. One of the boycotting students, Faizel Abrahams, was brutally gunned down near his home by the apartheid police in February 1983. Fondly known as 'Pele' due to his looks and love of football, he was of mixed Swazi, Mauritian-Indian and coloured ancestry. One awful Saturday evening, Faizel was accosted by the police, arrested for a misdemeanour and shot three times – twice from the front and once from the back, facing away from the police as he tried to run away. By all accounts, he was afforded no medical assistance and was left to die. Constable Piet Pelser, who shot Faizel, was overheard at the Standerton police station regaling the story like some hero returning from battle. This was another example of a brutal and rogue regime that disregarded the rule of law and a system that facilitated the murder of innocents with impunity, like that of my beloved uncle some years before.

It was illegal to possess certain political literature and the Internet and social media platforms had yet to be invented. During school holidays, I would read *The Hardy Boys* adventure books for teenage boys; never in my wildest dreams did I imagine that I would one day become a writer.

The apartheid government's initiative was to cosy up to Indian and coloured communities by establishing what it called the Tri-Cameral Parliament in 1984 to co-opt coloured and Indian politicians. It excluded any representation of African citizens and was rejected by the overwhelming majority of the country's people. In Standerton, the school principal attempted to convince me to support the Tri-Cameral Parliament. I rejected this proposal with the contempt it deserved, and informed him that the only solution for South Africa was to hold a general election on the basis of one-person, one-vote, to release political prisoners and to unban the liberation movements.

I began attending public meetings organised by the Transvaal Indian Congress (TIC) at the local civic centre and listened attentively to the likes of Dr Ram Saloojee and Azhar and Firoz Cachalia dismissing the Tri-Cameral Parliament as an apartheid government sham. I used the school debating platform to express my views on the political situation in the country. This prompted a teacher to inform my father, whom he advised to caution me on my utterances. My dad was visibly upset and threatened to send me to India. He said that the family had endured enough pain and suffering, and questioned the intention and motive behind my political outbursts.

But my dad supported me when I stood up for a fellow student who was being picked on by a teacher because he came from a poorer section of the community. From a young age, I refused to be influenced by the norms of society. My mates were not from affluent families and I openly socialised with friends from the coloured community. Despite supporting my stance against the bullying teacher, my dad instilled in me a duty to respect all my teachers. This included referring to them with the appropriate titles of 'Sir' or 'Mister' at all times, even after I finished school. I continue this practice even today.

I did, however, once contemplate petrol bombing the home of a local teacher who also worked as a police reservist. He would don the much-hated blue South African Police uniform and drive around the area in a police van. He took it upon himself to inform pupils about the situation in the local Sakhile township, condemning violent protest action by the community without acknowledging the political context in the country. I would watch from my bedroom window as large contingents of police, local reservists and army commandos made their way to the township.

I would listen to unrest reports broadcast by Capital Radio 604 and engage in my own analysis of events in townships across the country. I also closely followed the hunger strike of the Irish Republican Army's Bobby Sands, who lost his life on 5 May 1981 at the age of 27 after 66 days on the hunger strike against the withdrawal of political prisoner status for IRA prisoners in Northern Ireland.

Around 1986, I witnessed an incident in the Indian business complex that continues to haunt me. A mentally ill African man holding a knife was involved in a stand-off with the police. They could easily have overpowered and disarmed him, but a white policemen with a limp shot him in cold blood, in full view of the public. This incident increased my hatred towards the apartheid police.

In 1981 the family received the news that Uncle Mohammad was to be married in Zimbabwe that December. I was desperately keen to attend, but my father did not approve; nor did he want my mother to go. My mother's sister, Zubeida – 'Gorikala' – and her husband, 'Bhai' Chothia from Machadodorp, attended the wedding. I recall the final day of school when students were in typically high spirits ahead of the holidays. I did not share their joy. I was miserable and angry; there was an uprising in the country and I couldn't attend Uncle Mohammad's wedding. There was nothing to celebrate.

While I did not like school, I did like History and related the French and Russian revolutions to the political situation in our country. Learning about the First and Second World Wars convinced me how grossly wrong it was. When I listened to the debates on political ideologies, I was automatically drawn to the values of socialism and communism, and the principle of equality. There was no equality in South Africa. I was a black South African, but as a member of the

Indian community I was semi-privileged and could access many of the basic necessities and amenities that were denied to Africans.

I staggered along, completing my matric in 1985 – just about. My application to the teachers' training college in Laudium was unsuccessful as my school results were simply not good enough. In 1986 I found a job at a major motor vehicle plant in Standerton, but that did not last long. A family friend, Madan 'Charlie' Dayal, worked in the finance section at a big factory in Standerton and employed me in 1987. It was there that Charlie instilled in me a work ethic. I was too immature to appreciate these values then, but in later life I came to realise that Charlie was a mentor. What he taught me empowered me for life and, for that, I am eternally grateful. Throughout my life, I have been fortunate to have mentors and 'guardian angels' to guide me and open doors of opportunity.

II

A painful past

I was on my way home from work in December 1986, stopping over at the family business in the Indian complex in Standerton, when I heard the report on the radio. A number of African National Congress (ANC) members had been asked to leave Mozambique under the Nkomati Accord of 1984.[13] The names listed included those of Jacob Zuma, Sue Rabkin, Mohammad Timol, Bobby Pillay, Keith Mokoape and Indres Naidoo. I knew then that my uncle was considered a threat to the regime. Years later, in his book on South Africa's intelligence services, Kevin O'Brien noted that those named had all been targeted for 'collection and possible elimination'.[14]

Aunty Julie, a Mozambican citizen and Uncle Mohammad's wife, visited South Africa in 1987 with their young son Yusuf, my cousin. She told us that my uncle believed that they would be coming home in five years. I found this extremely odd as South Africa was in the throes of a bloody revolution following the call from the exiled ANC to make the country ungovernable. How could he consider returning home? It only emerged years later that the ANC had been holding secret talks with the apartheid regime to find an amicable solution to the political situation in the country.

In 1988, I attended the UEFA Euro 1988 Soccer Championship in Germany, arranged by my cousin, Abdul Hamid 'Bloms' Nanabhai. I had tickets for the group stages of the England group, the semi-finals and the finals. There were numerous skirmishes between British and German supporters, and I was caught in the centre of many running battles. I recall, most of all, the passion with which the supporters of all participating teams sang their national anthems. The thought crossed my mind about whether there would ever come a time when citizens of a free and democratic South Africa would sing our own national anthem with similar passion and commitment? During my schooldays, we had to sing the apartheid anthem *Die Stem*, which included the assurance that we should live and die for our country. Many of us refused to sing that song. How could we die for a country ruled by a racist minority which repressed the majority of its citizens?

Another eye-opener for me during that trip was the Nelson Mandela 70th birthday concert at London's Wembley Stadium, which was broadcast on German television. To see our icon celebrated in that way, filled me with hope and pride. The Netherlands beat the USSR in the final and upon receiving the FIFA Ballon d'Or[15] in 1987, the inspirational Dutch captain, Ruud Gullit dedicated the award to Nelson Mandela.

I quit my job in 1989 and followed my future wife, a single mother, to Johannesburg, and shortly thereafter I began working for a national supermarket chain, Pick n Pay, in Steeledale. I developed close friendships with many of the workers and shop stewards with whom I engaged in animated political discussions. Together, we heeded the calls to stay away from work as part of the campaign to exert pressure on the apartheid regime as the talks proceeded.

One afternoon, in the open plan office at work, I observed two burly Afrikaner men enter our supervisor's office. After they left, a short while later, I was called by the human resources manager to his office. He asked if I had noticed his visitors, saying they were members of the Security Branch of the South African Police – and that they were stationed at John Vorster Square police station in Johannesburg. They had received information that I was in possession of an arms cache at my residence. I was startled. It was simply not true. He warned me to be careful as this was a dangerous accusation. I suspect they received the tip-off from colleagues who were disturbed by my close association with African workers.

I did not feel it was appropriate for me to share this with my wife as it would have caused her unnecessary anxiety. The weeks that followed were highly stressful, with the sound of every passing motor vehicle filling me with dread that they were coming to arrest me. There were times that I was aware of being followed, but was comforted by the knowledge that I really had nothing to hide.

I have often wondered how my uncle had conducted himself, knowing that he was under surveillance and that his arrest was probably imminent. Was he frightened? Did he understand the peril he was in?

Ma visited Uncle Mohammad in Harare in 1989, almost 11 years after he had left the country. Papa had passed away in July 1981, but my uncle could not attend the funeral as he was in exile.

On 15 September 1989, Reverend Frank Chikane and Mama Winnie Mandela, two prominent anti-apartheid leaders, led a protest march to John Vorster Square police station. I was part of that procession which culminated in the handing over of a petition[16] deploring recent police violence, demanding freedom of expression and listing the conditions under which black leaders would agree to peace talks. Their demands included the release of political prisoners, lifting the state of emergency and legalising opposition parties.

This was the first time that I had a close-up view of this notorious building where my uncle was murdered. Police officers were hanging out of the building, and I visualised the window where it all happened. Little did I know, that 16 years later, I would return to this site with my first book about his life and death.

On 11 February 1990, Nelson Mandela was freed after 27 years in prison, 18 of which he was held on Robben Island. He addressed a crowd of approximately 50 000 people from the balcony of the Cape Town City Hall. Jubilant crowds celebrated throughout the country. I was amongst the throng of joyous supporters in the streets of Johannesburg.

When the ANC delegation arrived home from its headquarters in Lusaka, Zambia, to participate in the Groote Schuur Talks[17] in Cape Town from 2 to 4 May 1990, I was reunited with my uncle Mohammad after 12 years. The ANC and the apartheid government had reached an agreement on conditions for full-scale negotiations to end political conflict in South Africa, and he was part of the ANC delegation.

I met him at the Braamfontein Hotel and travelled in his convoy to a rally at the FNB Stadium in Soweto. There I met the leadership of the ANC and the South African Communist Party, including Joe Slovo. Uncle Mohammad collected the signatures of the entire ANC delegation that participated in the Groote Schuur Talks, which I am honoured to have in my possession. He later invited me and my sister, Amina, to visit his family in Lusaka in July 1990. Due to security concerns, he would not allow me to visit his office.

I became a card-carrying member of the Mayfair branch of the African National Congress immediately after it was unbanned in 1990. A moment I had yearned for for many years, it felt as if I was now, officially, an activist. It was here that I met other political activists such as Valli Moosa, Cass Coovadia, Gcina Malindi and David Robb.

On 16 February 1991, 32-year-old Bheki Mlangeni, who had been investigating activities of police assassination and hit squads arrived at his home in Jabulani, Soweto, and opened a parcel that had come by post. It contained a Walkman-type tape recorder and ear phones, including a tape marked 'Hit Squad Information'. He pressed the play button and the right headphone exploded, killing him instantly. I attended his funeral in Soweto with my friend and comrade, David Robb. We marched and toyi-toyied with the massive funeral procession, unintimidated by the large police contingent.

David recruited me to join the Alexandra Health Centre (AHC), an NGO in Alexandra township, in 1992. There, I witnessed unprecedented levels of violence in the war between the ANC and Inkatha, which resulted in the tragic loss of many innocent lives. I drove the clinic's kombi with my colleague Willie Lekoloane, collecting injured victims and rushing them to the clinic for treatment. We pushed maimed victims on trolleys to the casualty section and we were exposed to the sight of mutilated bodies. I assisted David to compile a list of injured victims, and we faxed these important details to the media. This was my contribution to helping keep the South African public informed on the levels of violence taking place in Alexandra township.

David Robb and Professor David Power, a paediatrician at AHC, further developed my work ethic and skills. Due to Professor Power's brilliant technical and analytical skills, the AHC had its own health information system by the early 1990s. Once again, I had been blessed to have been mentored by great people whose faith in me I will value till the end of my days.

It was also at the clinic that I met Stephanie Kemp,[18] a community physiotherapist and ANC activist. Many years later, I discovered that she was responsible for the compilation of cover letters – secret coded text messages used to convey messages from London that were sent to Uncle Ahmed upon his return from London to South Africa in February 1970 to help set up underground structures for the banned Communist Party of South Africa (SACP).

I continued visiting Ma in Azaadville, asking questions and trying to understand the circumstances of my uncle's death. One of the things that puzzled her was why there was no major public outcry after the death in detention of Suliman 'Babla' Saloojee.[19] He died in police detention on 9 September 1964 after falling from a window of the Johannesburg Security Branch police headquarters, the Grays, on the corner of Von Wielligh and Main Streets. The forerunner to John Vorster Square police station, Grays took its name from Grays Tea which had premises in the building. Saloojee was widely believed to have been brutally tortured and murdered but, like the inquest into my uncle's death, his enquiry accepted the police version that he had jumped to his death.

In 1995, the TRC[20] was established to help South Africa deal with its painful and divisive past. It convened a series of public hearings across the country, beginning in East London in April 1996, to hear evidence from victims of human rights violations. It granted amnesty from prosecution to qualifying perpetrators in exchange for them telling the truth, and recommended that the government should pay reparations to help the country to overcome its divisions from the apartheid era.

Ma was asked to testify but she was reluctant. I helped to convince her of the importance of relating her son's story to the commission and the country. Flanked by her sons, Mohammad and Haroon, she testified in Johannesburg on 30 April 1996:

> They hit my son tremendously. They arrested him on a Friday and they killed him and said that he committed suicide. I want to know who assaulted him and I want to know who lodged the complaint about my son. It took me quite a bit of difficulty to raise my children. It is 25 years now and that I will not forget what happened. I ask the Almighty that I will not forget what happened and that I need to know who lodged the complaint and what happened. I will not forget what happened, I need to know.[21]

Her poignant, dignified, emotive testimony – delivered in her mother tongue of Gujarati through an interpreter – remains etched in the hearts and minds of many South Africans. Listening to her anecdotes about my uncle, I could not contain my tears.

None of the security police officers involved in his arrest or detention had applied to the TRC for amnesty, none were subpoenaed to give evidence, and the commission's investigative unit lacked the capacity to unearth new evidence. Those involved in his case included, amongst others Sergeant Leonard Gysbert Kleyn, Constable Adam Alexander Cecil Thinnies, Constable Stephanus le Roux Fourie, Warrant Officer A.S. Verster, Warrant Officer Neville Els, Captain Carel Joseph Dirker, Colonel Greyling, Lieutenant Colonel Willem Petrus van Wyk, Captain Johannes Zacharia van Niekerk, Captain Johannes Hendrik 'Hans' Gloy, Captain Richard Bean, Brigadier Cecil William St. John Pattle and João Anastacio Rodrigues. As a final insult, the state did its best to ignore the commission's recommendations; there were no follow-up prosecutions and therefore no official consequences for those perpetrators who did not receive amnesty.

Our family continued with life as normal after Ma's testimony and the matter of my uncle's death was not pursued further. With no academic qualifications or professional experience, I began to research his life. Initially, I had no intention to publish my research. I was cognisant of resounding mumblings within the community on the role of informants in his capture and murder, and of cynics who doubted my ability and questioned my motives. But, ultimately, the overwhelming majority of family members supported the publishing of a biography and, critically, I also received the backing of the broader community.

Ma's health deteriorated rapidly after her testimony. Perhaps she sensed that her appearance would not deliver the Holy Grail: the truth that she craved. After a period of poor health, she passed away on 22 May 1997. It comforts me to know that she is back in the company of her beloved son, Ahmed, and husband, Haji Timol.

In February 1996, I started working for the National Intelligence Agency (NIA) in central Pretoria. This was one of the proudest moments of my life. I felt privileged to be able to serve my country and to honour the memory of thousands of dedicated fighters who had been martyred in order for us to obtain our freedom. My intention was to make my uncle proud, and to ensure that his death and that of all the others were not in vain. A few months later, the NIA offices moved to their newly constructed offices at the Musanda Complex in Delmas Road, Pretoria. I fitted into the community with relative ease; it was an advantage that my arrival followed the prickly integration of previously competing intelligence services in 1995 and I was therefore not regarded with suspicion by former members of either side.

It also helped that my colleagues were unaware of my relationship to Mohammad Timol who was by then a senior member of the South African Secret Service (SASS). I developed cordial relationships with officers from both the former liberation movements and apartheid services, the old National Intelligence Services.

On 29 March 1999, at a ceremony in Azaadville, Mogale City, President Nelson Mandela renamed the Azaadville Secondary School as Ahmed Timol Secondary School. He said:

> Few things in life are as painful as losing one's child. Anyone who doubted that had only to listen to the testimony of Ahmed Timol's mother as she told her story to the Truth and Reconciliation Commission. The memory of the suffering,

frail woman, like thousands of other mothers who appeared before the Truth Commission, still brings us as much pain as the inhumanity of her son's death. Like most of you, I did not know Timol personally. But all of us, I'm sure, wonder who he would be if he were alive today. Would he have been a father and a teacher himself and perhaps have taught at this very school? What we can say with certainty is that Timol was a brave young man who believed in freedom and justice, and who fought for non-racialism and democracy.[22]

In January 2001, I attended a meeting at the Union Buildings in Pretoria with Essop Pahad, who had been a close friend of Uncle Ahmed's. I showed him my draft manuscript and he said he would be willing to help me finish it. I worked with his wife, Meg, a former newspaper editor; former newspaper editor Tony Heard; author Ronald Suresh Roberts; and Professor Sifiso Ndlovu. They patiently guided and nurtured me until I was able to publish *Timol: Quest for Justice*.

The book was launched in January 2005, nearly four years after my initial meeting with Comrade Essop and 34 years after my uncle's brutal death. It depicted the migration of my maternal grandparents from India to South Africa; the family's move from Mpumalanga to Roodepoort; Uncle Ahmed becoming an educator and conscientising his students. I showed him as a sports administrator-turned activist, who received political training in the Soviet Union and who built underground structures for the banned South African Communist Party that led to his arrest, detention and death. The final word was the 1972 inquest ruling that nobody was responsible for his death.

I maintained a low profile after the book was launched, pleased with myself at having been able to record his life so many years after his brutal death. But I was also walking around with a bunch of proverbial pebbles in my shoe, the unanswered questions that the project had unearthed.

After the book was launched, my relationship with Mohammad Seedat, whom I knew as Uncle Tony, grew quickly, and we began discussing my irritation that the work was incomplete and that I intended to pursue the unfinished story. A seasoned intelligence operative who was responsible in 1981 for the opening of the ANC missions in the Federal Republic of Germany and in Austria, he cautioned me to have patience and convinced me that the timing must be right.

Uncle Tony shared his own experiences of living in exile and his association with comrades in London; he related personal anecdotes of exile politics and the amalgamation of the intelligence agencies in 1995 which had led to the formation of the National Intelligence Agency (NIA) and the South African Secret Service (SASS). I was devastated when he suddenly passed away in March 2007.

In October 2009 on the 39th anniversary of Ahmed Timol's death I announced my intention to produce a second book. I appealed for the reopening of the 1972 inquest, emphasising the importance of getting those policemen responsible for Timol's detention, torture and death to come clean and make full disclosures. I also wanted the informers I believed to be responsible for selling him out to be exposed.

My father was concerned about my safety and told me that nobody would be willing to speak about the informants and that I would be killed. I responded calmly, 'We pray five times daily to our Creator; it is only Him, Allah, that has appointed our time on Earth and we will only depart and return to Him upon His call.' The matter was not brought up again, although I observed his uneasiness as I continued to pursue it.

An intelligence operative, who had served the apartheid regime in both counter intelligence and domestic security, confirmed by reaffirming in 2010 that certain chapters in my 2005 book were incomplete. The names of Ahmed Timol, and other Indian activists, he said, were frequently mentioned in reports that were evaluated by a dedicated Indian desk.[23] These reports were archived and filed in 'Organisations' and 'Persons' files, respectively.

As a Muslim, I am frequently reminded by western media of the *jihad* committed by Muslim freedom fighters globally. There are different forms of *jihad*, an inner spiritual struggle as well as an outer physical struggle. The outer struggle, which can include violence and the sacrifice of life, is the form that is prevalent in global Muslim struggles and media narratives. The inner struggle, relating to one speaking the truth, is the struggle I have embarked on. This form of *jihad* is hardly spoken about, but forms an integral part in the life of any Muslim.

Some comrades warned me, after the 2005 book was published, not to pursue the matter any further. The Ahmed Timol story was told and it was now over. It was going to create problems and make many people uncomfortable. I noted their warnings but continued unearthing new evidence. My spiritual beliefs made me more resolute, and the following verses from the Holy Quraan (Surah Al-Imran, 160) made my quest easy to understand: 'If Allah helps you, none can overcome you: If He forsakes you, who is there, after that, that can help you? In Allah, then, let believers put their trust.'

After much encouragement from my friend Sello Kgoshi Mathabatha, in 2015 I enrolled at the Wits School of Governance for a diploma in Management Studies. I was admitted into this management programme because I was already performing senior management duties in my work. I had overcome the paranoia and anxiety of undertaking further education. The course provided me with the skills necessary to constructively contribute to the rapidly evolving South African contemporary political discourse – besides completing the task of writing a second book.

It is 26 years since South Africa's transition to democracy, 49 years after my uncle's murder, and there are still many unanswered questions. I have been blessed with new friends and relationships along the way with people who have unequivocally supported me on my journey to uncover the elusive truth of my uncle's murder. I am truly sad that there are those from both the liberation movement as well as the apartheid regime who are uncomfortable and uneasy about my raising the unanswered questions. They ask: What is the need to pursue this matter? Where lies the benefit? Philosopher George Santayana, the Spanish-born American author of the late 19 and early 20 centuries, might have had them in mind when he said, 'Those who cannot remember the past are condemned to repeat it.'[24]

III

Getting involved

By the time he had completed his second year as a teacher at the Roodepoort Indian High School at the end of 1966, Uncle Ahmed had travelled only in a small corner of South Africa. His horizons were about to be broadened immeasurably. He left South Africa on 25 December 1966 to perform the hajj in Saudi Arabia. At the time, few Muslims embarked on the pilgrimage to Mecca at such a tender age. He was just 24 years old.

Uncle Ahmed was in Saudi Arabia for the final days of the fasting month and Eid on 21 March 1967 (09 Thul Hajj 1386). During the hajj, my uncle met Dr Yusuf Dadoo, known as 'Doc' or 'Mota', an anti-apartheid leader with impeccable credentials, who chaired both the South African Communist Party (SACP) and the South African Indian Congress. Molvi Cachalia, another senior South African anti-apartheid activist, was also present during the hajj that year. After completing the hajj, Molvi went on to India where he established the ANC office in 1967 with Alfred Nzo, who was later to become democratic South Africa's first foreign minister. The Indian office was the inaugural mission of its kind in Asia.

I was privileged to perform hajj in 2014, which I experienced as a truly humbling journey and a reminder that all of humanity is equal, irrespective of race, colour and wealth. I assume that my uncle would have experienced it as spiritual affirmation of his mission.

After completing the hajj, Uncle Ahmed went on to Egypt where he met medical student Sadique Jinna. Then, in April 1967, he arrived in London and stayed at the flat of Essop and Aziz Pahad in North End House, West Kensington. Essop and his brother Aziz had gone into exile in 1964 after being banned for five years. The Pahad brothers were old friends of Uncle Ahmed's and were overjoyed to have him live with them. It is not known if my uncle intended to settle permanently in the English capital.

Other South African exiles in the United Kingdom at the time included Joe Slovo, Jack Hodgson, Dr Yusuf Dadoo, Robert Resha and Tennyson Makiwane. Around the middle of 1966, the SACP formed a committee to deal with the situation in South Africa. It comprised Dadoo as chairperson, Slovo as secretary and Hodgson as founding member. In an interview with Howard Barrell in 1990, MK and communist leader Ronnie Kasrils described his arrival in London in late 1965, and said it was Dadoo, Slovo and Hodgson who had interviewed him and recruited him to the party.[25]

To make a living, Uncle Ahmed taught at an immigrant school in Slough, approximately 34 kilometres from London. He was also an active member of the National Union of Teachers and attended evening classes in fulfilment of the requirements to write A-Levels, a prerequisite for acceptance to study at a British university or polytechnic. I learned that he was not studying in order to enter university, but to broaden his mind.

Meg Pahad recalled that he was an impressive teacher:

> Ahmed was a teacher who was respected throughout the community for his dedication to his work and for the tremendous effort and sacrifices he made for his students and friends in every aspect of their lives. Those that had the opportunity of meeting Ahmed for the first time or of renewing old acquaintances were impressed by his dedication and his abhorrence of injustice, whether it was in the UK or in South Africa.
>
> Wherever Ahmed taught, he would work closely with particular pupils who needed coaching. He would do extra work with them, and go to the trouble of finding them additional material to read. He believed in treating his pupils as individuals

and responded to their individual needs.[26]

During his stay in London my uncle experienced freedom for the first time. After the confines of South Africa, he had an opportunity to properly express himself freely. In an autobiography he wrote in 1969 upon entering Lenin University in the Soviet Union, he described his stay in London:

> My experience in England was invaluable because of the following reasons: Firstly, the myth of the Welfare State and classless society was exposed. Secondly, the opportunity of observing how bourgeois parliamentary democracy operates, in the present crisis stage of Monopoly Capitalism in Britain, in the interest of vast monopolies and against interests of both normal and menial workers who are being deliberately deprived of their 'limited' parliamentary rights; thirdly the peddling of abstract political concepts masked in hypocrisy and deceit like freedom of speech, justice, democracy, equality and so forth.
>
> I joined the Communist Party of South Africa[27] after I had discovered – by reading a few Marxist works and journals in England – that I was always a communist at heart. I also fully realised that sincerity alone is not enough; one must either understand the social forces which move society onwards, or become the blind tools of forces which one cannot understand and therefore cannot control or bend to our will.[28]

Early in London, Uncle Ahmed met Ruth Longoni, who worked for the *Labour Monthly*, a journal edited by Rajani Palme Dutt, a founder member of both the journal and the Communist Party of Great Britain. Ruth remembered their meeting:

> I met Ahmed around Easter in 1967 at an Aldermaston march organised by the Campaign for Nuclear Disarmament. It was the day before the march reached London, and Ahmed was busy talking to people on the march about their reasons for

being there. Ahmed was very interested in people and very enthusiastic about this sort of demonstration. About a week after that I got a phone call from Ahmed asking whether we could meet up.[29]

Uncle Ahmed visited Ruth at Arkley in Hertfordshire – a hamlet outside High Barnet – which was where she was living at the time. She realised that they had a great deal in common, despite coming from different backgrounds. Emotionally they were on the same wavelength and Ruth was a member of the Communist Party of Great Britain.

Uncle Ahmed shared with her his experiences of living in South Africa and spoke about his deep affection for his mother. He described her as a kind, simple and loving woman. He also talked to Ruth about the daily humiliations suffered by Indian South Africans.

> I think Ahmed also was aware of the particular experience of Indian South Africans. He knew about the whole history of indentured labour of the Indian community. He also knew that, humiliating and horrible as the experiences of Indians in South Africa were, it was infinitely worse, he felt, to be [a] black South African. He had tremendous feelings of compassion and anger at the treatment of black South Africans. He was a man of tremendous compassion and he empathised a great deal with the oppressed people and wanted to change their situation. He couldn't tolerate that level of suffering and injustice.

The internationalist and anti-imperialist contexts of the Vietnam War were very influential in shaping both Uncle Ahmed's and Ruth's thinking at the time. She moved from pacifism to supporting the armed struggle in Vietnam and felt that both she and Uncle Ahmed believed that a similar sort of struggle would take place in South Africa. He told Ruth that he felt compelled to return to South Africa. Watching the terrible images coming out of Vietnam, he wanted to contribute to avoiding bloodshed at home. According to her, he could not envisage staying in England, happily married with children, while seeing similarly disturbing images from South Africa. She understood his dilemma and it is clear they were in love.

After my first book was published, Uncle Mohammad pursuaded me to launch it in London and a date was set for December 2008 at South Africa House on Trafalgar Square. A day before the launch, my cousin Yusuf Timol and I lugged the heavy package of books around in the chill of a British winter.

I met Ruth for the first time on that trip after we had been communicating by email for a number of years. We had had an opportunity to meet previously at the launch of a television documentary about my uncle's death, titled *Indians Can't Fly*,[30] but Ruth could not face looking at the gruesome images of him and turned down the invitation. The security police had jokingly coined the term 'Indians can't fly' after Uncle Ahmed's death.

Author Gillian Slovo, the daughter of Joe Slovo and Ruth First, and political activist Advocate Tembeka Ngcukaitobi SC spoke at the London launch. Ngcukaitobi recalled that when Ahmed Timol was killed, he was not yet born, nevertheless, the powerful message of his death reverberated from Johannesburg to the formerly independent Republic of Transkei, where he was raised in the 1980s, through the moving song, '*Bambulel'u Timol inkokheli yethu* – They have killed Timol, our leader'.

Amina 'Mummy' Desai and her family were also there. I had last seen her when she left South Africa in 2004 as her health was failing and she wanted to be with her children abroad. She was frail, and it was painful seeing her in this condition. She passed away in June 2009 at her daughter Zarina's home in Dublin, Ireland.

In the years before she left South Africa, Mummy and I had engaged in numerous deep conversations about past and current South African politics. I enjoyed her company and felt that we had a special bond. My uncle had spent much time at her house after his return from London, and it was her car he was driving on the night of his arrest. She was detained and kept in solitary confinement for several months after his death and she was charged under the Terrorism Act for furthering the aims of the ANC and the SACP by conspiring with Uncle Ahmed. She was sentenced in November 1972 to five years in prison and on her release in 1978 the government immediately banned her for five years. She was the longest serving Indian woman political prisoner. In 2013, she was posthumously awarded South Africa's Order of Luthuli for her fight against apartheid.

Direct contact between the Communist Party of the Soviet Union and the ANC leadership was established on 5 April 1963. That moment was described by O.R. Tambo[31] as an historic day in the history of the South African people. It resulted in many cadres being given opportunities to receive political and military training in the Soviet Union, among them Thabo Mbeki, Ann Nicholson and Ahmed Timol, who went there in 1969.

According to Vladimir Shubin, the Deputy Director of the Institute for African Studies at the Russian Academy of Sciences and author of *A View from Moscow*, the International Lenin School in Moscow of the 1930s, which was attended by South African freedom fighter, Moses Kotane, among others, was resurrected in the early 1960s, 'to meet an increasing number of requests from foreign communist parties and later from Liberation Movements'.[32]

Describing the setting, a former interpreter, instructor and chair of social psychology at the insitition, Alexandra Rodionova (Comrade Shura) said:

> The building is monumental, Stalinist, neoclassical ... looming on the west side of Leningradsky Prospekt (number 49) opposite the Aeroport metro stop on the road to St Petersburg and Sheremetyevo. The façade, ochre plaster and sandstone, looks out over a square and is inlaid with a recruiting motif: two open books flanking the hammer and sickle. A sign of the times: after 1991, when it was taken back from the CPSU, it was first given to Gorbachev for his foundation, which now occupied a

small part of it. The rest is used by the new Finance Academy, Government of Russian Federation, where students specialise in banking and law.[33]

When I visited London in 2008, my cousin Yusuf Timol and I went to visit Dr Dadoo's *qabr* (grave) at Highgate Cemetery, a few metres from the grave of Karl Marx. The inscription reads: 'Yusuf Dadoo, Fighter for National Liberation, Socialism and World Peace.'

My maternal grandfather had studied at the prestigious Aligarh Muslim University (AMU), southeast of Delhi, and matriculated in 1927. He forged bonds at AMU with colleagues he would count among his closest friends in the decades to come. Among them was Dadoo, who was also from the village of Kholvad, 15 kilometres from Surat in Gujarat on the banks of the Tapi River.

One of Dadoo's many patients was my uncle, Ahmed, who suffered from bronchitis. This contact was a turning point in his life and ensured the steady growth of his commitment to non-racialism. This friendship provided Uncle Ahmed with opportunities to engage with his political thinking as well as that of his family and comrades. It was Dadoo and the South African Communist Party leadership in London that decided that Uncle Ahmed, Thabo Mbeki and Ann Nicholson should undergo political training in the Soviet Union. They enrolled for political studies from February until October 1969.

An art student, Ann had been an accused in the 1964 trial, *State versus Abram Fischer and Thirteen Others*.[34] She was sentenced to two years' imprisonment and after serving her sentence she went into exile in London.

All training recruits upon entering Lenin University were expected to write a short autobiography. Thabo Mbeki, alias Jack Fortune, wrote:

> In 1962, after attending classes on Marxism & Leninism and the programme of the SA Communist Party (SACP), I joined the Party. In September 1962, on instructions of the ANC and with the agreement of the SACP, I left South Africa to study in

England. This was at the University of Sussex, Brighton, where I studied for four years till 1966, September, when I completed my MA Degree in Economics.

Except for the period May 1967–August 1967 I have worked in the London office of the ANC full-time and part-time since September 1966 and up to the time I left, February 1969. During the time I was in England I participated in the normal activities of the SACP and was put on to its Editorial Board (*The African Communist*) in 1967. During this time also, I have represented the ANC student and youth sections in various countries, events and international organisations.[35]

Mbeki converted his course to a one-year programme, ending in December 1969. The trio received training in disciplines that included conducting underground work, developing structures and counter intelligence techniques. Uncle Ahmed also received extensive training in secret communications.

Interviewed later by Wolfie Kodesh, Ann remembered: 'Timol was such a sweet person; really nice ... he wasn't an ambitious person. To my mind, he would be a leader, because I think all teachers are leaders.'[36]

After completing his political training and returning to London in 1970, Uncle Ahmed received additional training lasting four weeks at Jack Hodgson's flat. Hodgson,[37] a miner at an early age, participated in the white miners' strike of 1938 in South Africa, which led him to join the then legal Communist Party of South Africa. In 1940, he enlisted in the South African army to fight racism and was deployed in North Africa. In 1953, he became one of the founding members and the first national secretary of the white anti-apartheid grouping, the Congress of Democrats. He was served with a banning order in November 1953, restricting him from attending public gatherings and effectively blocking his affiliation to approximately 20 organisations. In 1956, Hodgson was arrested and charged in the Treason Trial with 156 other activists, and by the end of the trial in March 1961, none of them had been convicted. After the 1960 Sharpeville Massacre and the State of Emergency that followed, Jack fled the country to Swaziland. He returned five months later.

Hodgson became a founding member of the MK, and a member of its Johannesburg High Command. His military experience and knowledge of explosives, gleaned from his mining days, enabled him to develop the bombs and timing devices used in the sabotage campaign and to train MK cadres ahead of its launch on 16 December 1961.

The introduction in 1963 of the 90-day detention laws and the fact that he had been placed under 24-hour house arrest led Jack and his wife Rica to illegally cross into Botswana, then Bechuanaland. They were deported to London after refusing to give an undertaking that they would not become involved in politics.

In 1964, Hodgson travelled to Moscow where he received specialist training in secret work. Upon his return to London, he established a workshop where he produced fake passports, letter bombs and suitcases with false bottoms used to smuggle covert material to South Africa.

My uncle and Jack worked very closely together and had many political discussions. Uncle Ahmed had to convince him of his readiness to be sent back to South Africa to set up an underground network. Before sending him back, Jack had to be sure that he possessed the necessary skills and discipline for an underground mission.

One can only imagine his state of mind on leaving London to return home. He was leaving Ruth, with whom he was in love, and a close circle of friends, including Essop and Aziz Pahad, and he was giving up the freedom of life in London. Awaiting him was segregation, discrimination, fascism – and danger.

His brother Haroon recalls that Uncle Ahmed's return from London in February 1970 was totally unanticipated at home. Ma was in the kitchen cooking *kurma* (fried lamb) normally prepared after the celebration of Baqri Eid (day of festivities at end of the annual pilgrimage), when animals are slaughtered, when she heard a knock on the apartment door and was surprised to see her son Ahmed standing there. 'You are the reason for me coming to South Africa. Nobody could have stopped me from coming home,'[38] he told her.

The Timol household had changed in the four years of his absence. Aunty Zubeida – 'Gorikala' had married Rashid Ahmed Chotia 'Bhai' and they had moved to Machadodorp in Mpumalanga; my mother had married my father Ebrahim Cajee and they were living in Standerton; Uncle Ismail was studying at the Aligarh Muslim University in India; Uncle Mohammad was studying textile engineering at Leicester Polytechnical College in England; and Uncle Haroon, the youngest, was working. My cousin, Fatima Chothia, Gorikala's daughter, was enrolled at the Roodepoort Indian High School and living at the Timol flat.

Uncle Ahmed began teaching at the Roodepoort Indian High School on 10 April 1970, the same school he taught at before leaving for the hajj. He also registered to study for a BA degree, by correspondence, with the University of South Africa. At the same time, he was fervently setting up underground structures for the banned ANC and the SACP. He was effectively living a double life.

My uncle was to establish small underground cells which would disseminate political literature as a signal to the masses and the apartheid regime that the freedom struggle was still alive within the country.

Abdus-Samad Abdul Kader,[39] aged 27, took up a post as a senior Islamic teacher at the Roodepoort madrasa in 1963. Newly married, he and his wife, Shareefah, had moved into a house next to the Roodepoort Indian High School where he befriended Ahmed and Yusuf 'Jo Jo' Saloojee. They had a common interest in politics.

Abdul Kader recalled that one day:

Ahmed approached me to take part in some activities to enlighten the pupils at schools and elsewhere. My role was to cyclostyle literature prepared on stencils by Ahmed, Jo Jo and Hilmi Desai. This was the practice in schools those days preceding the advent of computers. We did this late at night, and when Ahmed and others would leave, Shareefah would assist me in cleaning and wiping all traces of the illegal printing in and around the machine before dawn.

When the school authorities found these 'illegal' pamphlets calling on the masses to oppose apartheid, Security Branch policemen rushed to the school and other places they suspected might be involved in their creation. They frequently visited the residence of Abdul Kader, whom they suspected knew more than he let on. He denied any involvement and always insisted that he was merely preparing Islamic sheets for his pupils.

They could never definitively link the pamphlets to Kader's machine. Shareefah said she was:

> Initially very scared by the visits of the burly security officials, especially with my naiveté as a young bride of not knowing exactly what my husband was involved in. However, I soon realised that this was an important part of the work that had to be done to free all fellow South Africans. Hence, I went about my task of ensuring all traces were removed with renewed vigour.

Ronnie Kasrils, a former MK and SACP leader, who served in the post-apartheid government, provides some detail of the secret communication systems set up for underground propaganda operations in his book, *Armed and Dangerous*.

> The originals would have arrived at various 'safe' addresses in London or quiet villages in the home counties. The originals would be an apparently innocuous letter to someone's friend or relative. On the reverse side of the page would be a hidden text written in invisible ink. The form of address indicated what invisible ink had been used, and consequently, what developer was required to bring out the hidden message. 'My dear Aunt Agatha' would indicate one type, 'Dearest Aunt Agatha' another. We used a variety of chemicals, usually dissolved in alcohol or distilled water. The writer would use a clean pen to write out the secret text. Steam from a kettle would be applied to the paper to iron out any indentation marks left by the pen.

After the paper had dried, the innocent text would be written or typed in.[40]

One of the comrades involved in these clandestine activities in London was my friend and former colleague at Alexandra Health Centre, Stephanie Kemp. Born in 1941 in the Karoo, Stephanie studied physiotherapy at the University of Cape Town (UCT) in the 1960s and was a volunteer for the Defence and Aid Fund in Cape Town. She was later recruited to the SACP and the Armed Resistance Movement (ARM). Detained in 1964, she was the first white woman to report being assaulted in detention. During her trial, she pleaded guilty to belonging to an unlawful organisation, the ARM, and was sentenced to five years in prison, three of which were suspended. She was released after more than a year-and-a-half in prison due to the intervention of her father who had petitioned B.J. Vorster, the then Minister of Police Justice and Prisons, for her early release.

Stephanie arrived in London in 1966 and was re-integrated into the structures of the Communist Party and drawn into the clandestine activities of people such as Dadoo, Essop Pahad, Reg September and Slovo. There was a lot of work to be done reviving and re-developing political activity in South Africa and Stephanie was assigned to the Operational Committee led by Dadoo. Her task was to assist comrades such as Ahmed to conduct underground work in South Africa.

She had discovered that many British citizens, appalled by the actions of the apartheid regime, were more than willing to assist, including Stephanie Seagal, the sister in-law of the exiled activist Kader Asmal. Stephanie Kemp would approach sympathetic people and ask them to put together an innocent 'cover' letter with details about the weather and such things, to be sent to someone back home in South Africa. The contents of these letters would not generate much interest from potential prying eyes. She would then insert encrypted secret messages that she got from the SACP centre and post the letters to South Africa. Typewriters were rented, and Stephanie took care to use a variety of envelopes and stamps. As an extra security precaution, she wore gloves.

Stephanie had also worked as a paediatric physiotherapist in London. She returned to South Africa in 1990, after the organisations were unbanned and Nelson Mandela was released from prison. When I met her at the clinic in Alexandra, I was completely oblivious of her role in underground operations and her connection to my uncle.

I found copies of some of my uncle's communications to London after I retrieved a partial set of the 1972 inquest records[41] from the law firm, Cachalia and Loonat, in the late 1990s. They were one of very few firms to represent victims of state repression and had some experience defending Indian clients challenging the Group Areas Act and other apartheid laws. The records were very useful as they complemented what I had learned while reading newspaper cuttings over the years.

In a conversation in London between Essop Pahad and Uncle Ahmed before he returned to South Africa, great emphasis was placed on the likelihood that he would come under surveillance and would need to lay low for a considerable period.[42] When he was back home, Uncle Ahmed did not heed this advice; eager to make a difference, he immediately began conducting his underground activities. This can only be attributed to his enthusiasm to build the underground structures as he was instructed to do.

In less than two months after his return, Uncle Ahmed had already produced his first report and sent it back to his handlers. He had compiled a mailing list of 8 000 names, predominantly African, which he identified as needing political literature in the form of a monthly student letter. He further requested material of a religious nature to assist with the discontent of the Muslim community about the Group Areas Act. There was also need for an Indian newspaper, he said.[43]

Another report to London, dated 12 May 1970,[44] provided details on the political situation in the country. Correspondence from London, dated a week later,[45] provided him with formulas to decode messages for his operations. This posed a huge security risk if this mail was intercepted by the Security Police. Uncle Ahmed once wrote to London[46] providing details of available production equipment including duplicating machines used by the apolitical Mrs Cajee of

Cajee's Commercial College and Mr Boorany of Dress Centre. He had used these machines for school work without any suspicion.

The correspondence also revealed that he was under enormous pressure.[47] In one, he reported: 'I must confess my inefficiency and lack of discipline in not maintaining regular contract [sic]. There is also no reason or justification to blame this inadequacy on the petty family problems besetting me at the moment.' He remained resolute in fulfilling his revolutionary duties and added:

> Despite these difficulties, presented by life in our close communal societies, we are surviving and managing to do out [sic] little bit. Not much has been done, yet there is so much to be done. In order to accomplish our revolutionary tasks it is of primary importance to improve my style and tempo of work, to fulfil our duties with the devotion and absolute dedication which are basic requisites for achieving our noble historic ideals.

Uncle Ahmed was also under pressure from London to deliver. He was informed about London's intention to circulate a cyclostyled party newspaper to coincide with the 50th anniversary of the South African Communist Party on 30 July 1971. London 'urgently requires Ahmed to obtain tape recorders, reference books, tax receipts and travel documents. If by hook or by crook you should lay your hands on any of these (and we know this is a tall order) please insert them in a "present" of the sort we send you.'[48]

How did all of this impact on his ability to conduct his operations? He was clearly vigilant about his personal security and that of his underground operations. London had requested more details of an earlier matter he reported, suggesting that he had been visited by a suspicious character.

He wrote:

> I can safely state that I am not under any S.B. [Security Branch] observation. My mail is not tampered with. When I arrived back, I was however visited by a local Indian connected with the

S.B. The call I was told at the time of the visit was of a routine nature. Such checks are observed on all persons coming from abroad. However, another incident was a bit more intriguing. Some six weeks after my arrival two persons visited 'Quarter Khota's' shop in Jhb wanting to see me and asking for my phone no or address in Rdpt [Roodepoort]. They claimed that they were told to contact me by my friends in London (which friends – they did not mention to Quarter) and that they were on their way back to London after spending their holidays in Durban. However, they never came to see me and that was the last that I heard of them.[49]

In further correspondence to London, Uncle Ahmed stated that the enemy was well aware of any new form of organised activity by 'non-whites'.[50] He spoke of a social club of 25 members of youth living in the West Rand, Krugersdorp, which was regularly raided by the Security Branch and that some members had been interrogated. It is unknown if any of the members had broken down during the interrogation and provided information on Uncle Ahmed or whether this was what had brought him under the security police's radar.

Uncle Ahmed appears to have committed a number of security breaches according to this set of correspondence from London: 'If you wish to write to Ruth Longoni, please do not discuss any form of politics. She has been given similar advice'; 'In this letter as well as previous one you signed your real name. Please avoid and sign Stephen'; 'Please also do not mention the names of Thabo and Jenny in the open text.'[51]

Indres Naidoo, who worked as a lecturer in the Pharmacy Department at the University College for Indians on Salisbury Island in Durban, was concerned about Uncle Ahmed being too lax about security. He recalled, 'I told Ahmed that I was worried about the way he was operating. Uncle Ahmed was too relaxed. He had written a letter to me and posted it through the normal post. This was not safe. One knew how good the cops were. Friends were regularly detained for other activities and you had to be vigilant. Ahmed agreed.'[52]

London, however, also saluted him for his sterling work:

Dear Stephen. The Central Committee sends its heartfelt congratulations to you on the progress you are making in the difficults [sic] mission which you have accepted. Your letter was indeed inspiring in its dedication to our work and the steps you have taken to implement the tasks. We are confident that you will go about them with all the necessary care and that you will ensure all necessary security.[53]

In another correspondence,[54] he is told to keep up the good work and his fine revolutionary ardour. He was reminded that 1971 was a crucial year for the party and they were confident that he would continue to make his invaluable contribution to the revolution. The message ends with greetings of Amandla (Power)!

There are some critical pieces of evidence in the series of correspondence between Uncle Ahmed and London that sheds light on the line of questioning during Uncle Ahmed's interrogation. This relates to the planting of bucket bombs. Correspondence sent by Ahmed to London reads: 'We have selected several suitable places on the Reef where future "bombs" could be placed. These are points where masses of our people congregate daily, as [sic] station entrances, busstops, lunch-time meeting places, pass offices, specific routes taken by workers to and from work.'[55]

In correspondence to London,[56] Uncle Ahmed sent his congratulations on 'last week's publicity campaign'. He added that the impact was tremendous and the distribution had generated great excitement and discussion amongst all the sections of the population group. Is this evidence that he was aware of the simultaneous activities of another underground cell operating within the country?

PART II
Capture

IV

Taken

Uncle Ahmed spent Thursday evening, 21 October 1971, at home. He was visited by his cousin Dr Farouk Dindar, who brought along his three-year-old daughter, Nazneen. It was a conscious decision to bring her along, Farouk recalled, so that it would appear to any spies in the community that he was paying a social visit to his Aunt Hawa. Among the matters he and Ahmed discussed were the developments in Sudan, where President Gaafar Nimeiry had recently quelled a communist-led coup.

According to Farouk,[57] Uncle Ahmed looked well that evening. He noticed no bruises on his body and saw that he walked without difficulty. These observations are important because they contradict the state's subsequent 'evidence' that bruises and wounds on Ahmed's body were incurred before his arrest and not at the hands of security police.

The next day, Uncle Ahmed went to work at school as usual. Yacoob Adam,[58] a fellow teacher at the Roodepoort Indian High School, said they were close and that Ahmed usually took him home for lunch after Friday prayers, enticing him with the words, 'Ma has cooked'. We do not know whether they shared lunch that day but what Yakoob did remember was him saying that Friday, the day of his arrest, that he believed that Suliman 'Babla' Saloojee did not commit suicide, but that he had been murdered.

Yunus Cajee, a student in Uncle Ahmed's last class, the Standard Eight Geography class, is still haunted by his teacher's parting words.

He told the class: 'I will live for 500 years and I will become more famous than the President of the World.'[59]

Papa last saw his son on the day of his arrest. It was the second day of the holy month of Ramadan (Second Ramadan 1391), and Papa was returning home around 6.45 pm from *Magrib* (obligatory) prayers. Uncle Ahmed was on his way out and he told Papa that he would return shortly, without indicating where he was going.[60] He went to Mummy Desai's house on 12 Harold Street, a few minutes' walk from the Timol apartment, to borrow the Anglia. This was not unusual as he often drove Mummy, who could not drive, and she never questioned his movements when he took the car out on his own.

She lived alone in her home, opposite the mosque, as her children were all abroad. Zarina, the eldest, was a doctor in Ireland. Bahiya, 15 months younger than Uncle Ahmed, was studying at Salisbury Island, Durban. Hilmi was studying in Sweden; his father, S.M. Desai, had sent him at the age of 15 to Lawrence College in Rawalpindi, Pakistan, a secondary school which had been set up for the children of men in the British Army. The youngest child, Adella, 16, had been sent to London to complete her schooling.

When Zarina left South Africa in the late 1960s, she left her Anglia behind and Mummy's driver taught Uncle Ahmed to drive. After her husband's death in February 1969, Mummy continued to run his shoe agency and Uncle Ahmed would drive her to Johannesburg on Saturdays to post the shoe agency letters, which had to be done before 11 am. Then he would drop Mummy off at her cousin's place, returning to collect her again around 6 pm.

As he reversed the Anglia from Mummy's driveway, his friend, Salim Essop, was waiting in the street. He lived close by at 12 Small Street. A former pupil of Ahmed's, Salim was then studying medicine at the University of the Witwatersrand where he was also a member of the university bursary committee. They had reconnected when Uncle Ahmed returned from London in February 1970. As the Timol house was on Salim's route to the station, from which he took the train to university, they bumped into each other on a few occasions and soon a friendship developed.

'I saw Ahmed come out from Mrs Desai's house without any boxes or anything. Ahmed did not put anything in the boot of the car,' Salim said.[61] He jumped into the car and they were off on their normal Friday evening routine, to socialise with friends.

Mummy Desai had earlier asked Uncle Ahmed to deliver a parcel to a dressmaker in Newclare that evening. According to the dressmaker,[62] he arrived at around 8.30 pm and she was later visited by security police who wanted to know what was in the parcel. From this we can deduce that Uncle Ahmed was under surveillance on the evening of his arrest. But why did the police not arrest him? Why did they say that they had snared him at a random roadblock? Who or what were they trying to hide?

Friday evening was prime social time for Uncle Ahmed and Salim Essop. They dropped in on a number of friends, like Rashida Mangera, a third-year medical student at the University of the Witwatersrand, who was spending her 21st birthday ill in bed at her Fordsburg home. They also visited an individual in central Johannesburg, who has asked that his identity be withheld. Salim chose to wait in the car. According to the man, Uncle Ahmed initially asked to leave a parcel at his home but later changed his mind. He told him that he and Salim were on their way to visit another friend.

That fateful night Uncle Ahmed and Salim also visited 10 Bernadette Flats, in Newclare in Coronationville, the family home of Irene[63] and Jane Kruger, who worked for South African Associated Newspapers (SAAN). Their social circle included journalists David Barritt, Alan Kwela, Mike McCann and Peter Magubane, who all worked in the same building.

The sisters do not remember exactly when they first met Uncle Ahmed and Salim but Jane recalled an early interaction: 'Mike McCann and his colleagues once invited us to a party. Ahmed and Salim were also present. As the party proceeded, it turned out to be a forum for vibrant political discussion. Due to our friendship, Ahmed and Salim had access to journalists working at SAAN.'[64]

According to Irene, they frequently visited the Pearl Restaurant in Fordsburg on Friday evenings and other entertainment venues such as Shakespeare House, The Blue Danube and various jazz clubs. These clubs had mixed audiences of black, Indian, coloured and white revellers, which was against the law forbidding racially mixed gatherings. Although it was illegal for people classified Indian, coloured or white to visit Soweto, they also visited the Pelican Club on Friday evenings to listen to jazz.

They knew that they could always be arrested, but made a point of deliberately breaking the law as a form of protest against the iniquitous system. They read banned books, such as James Baldwin's *Go Tell It on the Mountain*, and listened to illicit music. The Kruger sisters' apartment was something of a social hub. Friends and colleagues would come round to listen to jazz and talk politics. It was a safe and relatively permissive environment in comparison to Uncle Ahmed's and Salim's conservative family homes.

Irene assisted Salim with the recruitment of African students for the University of Witwatersrand Bursary Committee. She also helped him with typing as she had a typewriter at home. The committee offered 10 bursaries annually to academically disadvantaged and deserving African, coloured and Indian students. Trustees included the well-known academics John Blacking and John Dugard.

According to Irene, Ahmed also had his typing done by a Mrs Cajee at Commercial College. It is evident that my uncle had taken her into his confidence. She was aware that he had visited the Soviet Union and was involved in distributing pamphlets. In her view, Uncle Ahmed saw his role as constructively contributing to the conscientisation and mobilisation of the masses. Irene describes their relationship as one of siblings. Her husband, Joe Summers, who worked far away and could only return home on weekends, was a friend of Uncle Ahmed's and Salim's. They had a standing commitment to look after Irene while Joe was out of town for work purposes.

The week of 22 October 1971 had been a difficult one. There was a planning meeting at the home of Naseem 'Naz' Pahad, the younger brother of Essop and Aziz, to plan protest action in support of the Anglican priest, Father Bernard Wrankmore, who was fasting on the slopes of Lion's Head in Cape Town to demand that the government hold an inquest[65] into the cause of the death in detention of Imam Abdullah Haron. Imam Haron was killed on 27 September 1969, at Cape Town's Maitland Square police station, four months after being arrested. The police had claimed that he had fallen down the stairs. Banners and pamphlets were made, but somehow the police got wind of the protestors' plans. Irene said she had a premonition the whole week that something rotten was going to happen.

That Friday evening, Uncle Ahmed and Salim did not stay long at Irene's and they planned to get together the next day. Irene was surprised to hear a knock on her door about 20 minutes after they had left. Uncle Ahmed was standing at the ground floor window; he wanted Irene to accompany them to a party at his friend Dawood's place in Vrededorp. She declined; Joe was on his way, and she was heavily pregnant.

Uncle Ahmed was wearing the ring with a black onyx stone with red streaks that he got when he was on hajj. Whenever he asked Irene for a favour, she said she would only oblige if he gave her the ring. It was a standing joke. He could not part with the ring as it was from his hajj trip. However, that evening he removed the ring from his finger and gave it to her, telling her never to part with it. She clearly remembers the hair on his finger standing up after he had removed his ring. She immediately put it on a necklace around her neck. His parting words were: 'Look after yourself, and don't worry when the baby is born, I will be there.'

Irene then asked Uncle Ahmed and Salim not to take the 'stuff' in the boot of the car to the party in Vrededorp. It included the banners in support of Father Wrankmore, long-playing records and bursary application forms for Wits University. The material was unloaded from the boot of the Anglia and stored under the bed in the lounge at Irene's apartment. She insists that there was nothing in the boot of the Anglia when they left.

A few minutes later, Joe arrived home. What was happening, he asked? He had just seen the yellow Anglia at the top of Fuel Road, at a police roadblock. The couple quickly got rid of the materials under the bed, taking some to a neighbour and burning the rest. They also got rid of their typewriter and the record player.

At approximately 2 am on Saturday morning, 23 October 1971, Irene and Joe had an unexpected visitor, Foxy, a policeman who was stationed at Newlands Police Station. He was delivering a message from Uncle Ahmed to Irene to 'destroy everything', including his black notebook. The message from Foxy, who was considered a trustworthy friend, confirmed Irene's fears that Uncle Ahmed and Salim had been detained and were in serious trouble. She remains convinced to this day that someone betrayed their plans to demonstrate in support of Father Wrankmore, and that this is what directly led to their arrest.

Ahmed's and Salim's arrest was part of a nationwide crackdown in October 1971, described as the most extensive since Rivonia.[66] *The Sunday Express* reported that at least 17 people were to appear in the Supreme Court under the Suppression of the Communism and Terrorism Acts. The state was to argue that they were actively engaging in attempts to undermine law and order and in aiding and abetting subversion.

In his response to the raids on 24 October 1971 on the homes of teachers, students and churchmen and the detention of at least 48 individuals, General van den Bergh said in an interview with the *Rand Daily Mail:* 'According to information in my possession the present actions and arrests being carried out by the police are definitely more than justified and critics will be swallowing their words.'[67]

After my uncle's murder, security policeman Sergeant Seth Sons, regularly collected Jane Kruger for questioning at John Vorster Square. There, the police would remind her of what had transpired on the tenth floor with Uncle Ahmed, and warned her to tell them the truth or she could meet the same fate. What they wanted were the names in Ahmed's black book. She did not tell them since she had it destroyed.

According to a former police officer interviewed during the research for this book, seasoned policemen usually carried 'a little insurance' with them when reporting for roadblock duty. Regular uniformed policeman would, for instance, stash an Okapi pen knife, long a favourite of South African gangsters, in their patrol vehicles, in case it was needed to plant on an individual to justify them having to shoot a suspect. Members of the feared Brixton Murder and Robbery Squad carried stolen firearms in the boots of their vehicles. South African Narcotics Bureau officials carried 'a spare bag' of marijuana in case the people they apprehended were shot at – perhaps with fatal consequences – and were then found to be 'clean'. Security Branch members carried a few pieces of banned literature, which they could use to explain the arrest and detention of 'political suspects' – and as an excuse to visit their homes or work places without having to meet the requirement for a search warrant.

According to the police, on Friday 22 October 1971 they set up a roadblock on Fuel Road in Coronationville at about 10.40 pm. Quite by chance, about 30 minutes later, the yellow Ford Anglia bearing Ahmed and Salim – and banned literature in the trunk – drove straight into the trap.

An analysis of police statements at the 1972 inquest indicates that the policemen running the roadblock were stationed at Newlands police station. There were two constables, a sergeant and a warrant officer present. These are not senior ranks; there were no officers there that evening, and no members of the Security Branch. Nor is there any evidence that the police deployed what are referred to as 'stopper groups' – ahead of, and behind, the roadblock – to stop fleeing suspects from escaping. The deployment of stopper groups at roadblocks is standard practice across the world.

Sergeant Leonard Gysbert Kleyn[68] was a sergeant in the South African Police stationed at Newlands. On Friday 22 October 1971, he reported for special duty at 3.45 pm under the supervision of the station commander, Major J.M. Kloppers. Kleyn's statement to the 1972 Timol inquest provided no further detail on the nature of the special duty.

According to him, at approximately 10.40 pm he and his colleagues proceeded to Fuel Road in Coronationville, where they set up a roadblock. At approximately 11.10 pm, they stopped a Ford Anglia motor vehicle, with the registration number, TU 22315, travelling from east to west. He motioned for the vehicle to come to a standstill;

the driver obliged, and as Kleyn walked over he observed that that there were two Indian men in the vehicle.

According to Kleyn's evidence, he approached the driver of the vehicle and enquired where they were going. He answered, 'We are going to a party in Vrededorp'. Kleyn asked him, 'This time of the night?' He also asked, 'Are you people still going to work tomorrow?' an odd question to ask, as Saturday was not a working day.

Kleyn said he requested the driver to open the boot of the car. Both men disembarked and proceeded to the back of the vehicle. Other members of the police who were part of the roadblock also approached the boot. They were Constable S. Le R. Fourie, Res/A/Off. A.S. Verster and Constable A.A.C. Thinnies.

The driver opened the boot and Kleyn said he observed shoe boxes on the right-hand side of the boot as well as articles wrapped in newspapers on the left. He said he asked the driver: 'What are these?' to which the driver replied, 'They are books.' Kleyn said he told the driver that to him it looked like shoe boxes. But the driver repeated: 'It is books.'

According to Kleyn, he opened the newspapers lying to the left of the shoe boxes and noticed that there were pamphlets of a banned organisation. Constable Thinnies took one of the pamphlets and handed it over to Major Kloppers. The boot was then closed, and the two Indians climbed back into the vehicle accompanied by Constable Thinnies. Kleyn, himself, drove the vehicle to Newlands police station.

Kleyn then telephoned the security police. He had by now determined that the driver of the Anglia was Mohammad Salim Essop, a third-year medical student at the University of the Witwatersrand, and his passenger was Ahmed Timol, a teacher at the Roodepoort Indian High School. Kleyn observed that the two Indians were talking to each other in an Indian language and proceeded to lock Timol in a cell. Salim was left to sit on a bench as they all awaited the arrival of the security police.

Warrant Officer Els of the security police arrived at Newlands where Kleyn gave him a report. He opened the boot of the Anglia, showing him the documents. Els took the documents and telephoned his fellow officers, Captain Dirker and Colonel Greyling, both of the security police, who arrived shortly thereafter. They then took possession of the Anglia, the documents and the two Indian detainees. Kleyn accompanied Captain Dirker and Timol to the security police offices at John Vorster Square, where Kleyn guarded Timol until 5.40 am the following morning.

At around 3 am on Saturday 23 October 1971, three white men arrived at the Timol flat in Roodepoort. They wanted to know from Papa where his son was. Proceeding to Ahmed's room, they found that he was not there. The room was searched and a typewriter and certain documents removed, with a receipt provided for the confiscated material. Papa was told that his son was under arrest at John Vorster Square, but they provided no other information. After they searched the flat, they told Papa to accompany them to John Vorster Square, resulting in him missing the obligatory morning prayer at 4.15 am.

The construction of a new building to replace Johannesburg's Marshall Square police station began at 1 Commissioner Street in 1964. Designed by the firm Harris, Fels, Janks and Nussabaum, the building was intended to facilitate the growing requirements of the Security Branch for space for detention and interrogation.[69] In *The History of the South African Police: 1913–1988*[70] written from a police perspective, it is said that Prime Minister Balthazar John Vorster officially opened the new complex, named John Vorster Square in his honour, on 23 August 1968. This was the first time that the South African Police had honoured the prime minister in this way. The impressive new building was the new home of Divisional Headquarters of the South African Police, and featured a number of other offices, special facilities and features.

John Vorster Square was regarded as a new concept in police buildings, which housed a large concentration of administrative and executive functions under one roof. In an article published by the

Sunday Express on 15 January 1967, under the headline, 'R2m HQ for Police'[71], it was reported that the building contained a lecture theatre with tiered seats, a cinema projector and sound equipment, large fully equipped photographic laboratories and a spacious fingerprint laboratory. 'The offices to be occupied by the Security Branch represent the last word in security,' the article continued. Access to the ninth floor of the building was solely by two special lifts from the basement. Passengers emerging from the lift were faced by a bulletproof glass cage housing a policeman, who would check their identity and verify their visit before allowing them to pass through an electrically operated door.

The lift generally did not go the tenth floor, the top level, with prisoners having to walk up a final flight of stairs to reach it. It was here that an undetermined number of detainees were tortured.[72] Special steel grilles protected all the entrances to the Security Branch offices. The facility contained special soundproof rooms with folding steel grilles across the windows. Access to the soundproof rooms was through a thick, steel, bank-vault door. The police had their own darkrooms, and direct-line telephones connected to the Security Branch headquarters in Pretoria and other centres.

Security Branch officers continued visiting the Timol residence while Uncle Ahmed was in their custody. That Saturday, the first full day of his imprisonment, Ma argued with them, insisting that she wanted to see her son. 'No, you cannot see him,' they replied. Papa and Ma were interrogated during the day, and later in the evening. Questions were posed about Uncle Ahmed's friends and their whereabouts. The flat was ransacked but they found nothing.

On Sunday, 24 October 1971, the Security Branch did not visit the Timol residence. Ma asked her nephew, Ahmed's cousin, Iqbal 'Baboo' Dindar, and his wife Jameela, to take food to her son. Jameela arranged a food basket and, without fear, she and Baboo proceeded to John Vorster Square. Ma was concerned that Ahmed had not eaten for two days and that he would not have eaten the food provided by the police as it was not halaal.

Baboo recalled: 'It was raining heavily and it was very cold that day. At about 2 pm Jameela and I made our way to John Vorster Square police station. An African policeman at John Vorster Square greeted us and we enquired as to where the Security Branch offices were. He told us that they were on the tenth floor and we proceeded to be greeted by a hefty policeman.'[73]

This is the conversation that took place between Baboo and the policeman:

> Policeman: 'Ja, wat soek jy? (What do you want?)'
> Baboo: 'Ons wil net vir Ahmed Timol sien asseblief. Ons het kos vir hom gebring. Hy is seker honger. (We just want to see Ahmed Timol. We have brought him some food, as he must be hungry.)'
> Policeman: 'Nee, jy sal hom nooit sien nie. Dit is hel koud. Daardie donder soek iets om te dra want hy kry baie koud. Gee jou trui hier. (No, you will never see him. It is very cold. That man is feeling cold and needs something to wear. Give your jersey here.)'

Baboo continued, 'I handed over the jersey that I was wearing to the policeman. We had gone over to deliver food to Ahmed and ended up leaving a jersey for him. The policeman then escorted Jameela and me back to the lift and pressed the button for us to go down. Jameela and I informed Ma that we had left the food basket for Ahmed. Ma felt a bit relieved, as she knew that Ahmed was alive, as he had asked for a jersey. A few weeks after Ahmed's death, Ahmed's clothes were returned. The jersey that I had given to the policeman was also returned. However, it was returned full of blood.'

V

'Detainee dies in police custody'

The regular visits by security policemen to the Timol residence continued, at times more than once a day, seeking answers about Ahmed. On Monday, 25 October 1971, Papa's driver was interrogated; he was so traumatised that Ma sent him home. The flat was again ransacked, and Ma again pleaded to see her son.

On Tuesday, 26 October 1971 when Ma repeated her routine plea to see her son, she was told that she would not see him again. She told the policemen that he should go home and ask his wife what it means for a mother to rear a child and not be able to see him. Papa overheard the conversation in Afrikaans between Ma and the officer, Warrant Officer Carel Petrus Janse van Rensburg.[74]

The officer told Ma: 'Jou seun moet pak kry,' ('Your son must get a hiding.')

Ma asked: 'Why are you going to give my son a hiding?

The man replied: 'Because you did not give him a hiding that is why we will give him a hiding.'

Ma responded: 'I never hit my children. Why will you hit my children?'

The visits had been so frequent that Ma and Papa could not provide exact details on the total number. But they never brought Uncle Ahmed with them, a clear indication to Papa and Ma that he was in serious danger. According to the police, my uncle committed suicide on Wednesday, 27 October 1971. That morning, the security police raided all the dustbins in the apartment block. They climbed up on the roof, and the landlord was asked to open the storeroom after the *Zohar*, the obligatory midday prayers. The domestic workers from all the apartments were interrogated, intimidated and forced to say that Uncle Ahmed had asked them to distribute papers in the townships.

On the police version of events, on the day he died, Uncle Ahmed, who was in perfect health and in a friendly state of mind and had suffered no torture or assault, was interrogated by Captains Gloy and Van Niekerk from 8 am to 3.30 pm. At 3.30 pm, a Sergeant J. Rodrigues entered the room with coffee for the interrogators and Timol. At 3.45 pm, another security policeman 'Mr X' entered the room and claimed to have named some 'white' people who were part of their investigation. The policeman said that Uncle Ahmed looked shocked on hearing the names. At 3.48 pm Gloy and Van Niekerk left the room, telling Rodrigues to watch Timol while they did some research on the white people who had been mentioned. According to Rodrigues, Timol requested to go the toilet, but as they both stood up (on opposite sides of the table), he rushed to the window and dived out.

Ma recalled:

After the early evening prayers (obligatory *magrib* prayers, also after *iftaar*,[75]), they came back again ... they told me that my son had jumped from the tenth floor of John Vorster Square and that he had died ... I told them that I do not believe that my son had committed suicide ... and that they did not look after him, and they told me he had jumped.

Papa was at the mosque when he was called to the flat (approximately 7 pm) and told by Ma that their son was dead.

A headline in *The Rand Daily Mail* the following day reported: 'Teacher plunges from tenth floor – DETAINEE DIES IN POLICE CUSTODY.'

On Friday, 29 October 1971, Papa identified his son's body at the government mortuary in Hillbrow. The body was released for burial and placed in a hearse driven by Mohammed Khan. Papa followed the hearse in a car to the mosque in Newtown where he performed *ghusal*, the washing and preparing the body for burial according to Muslim rites. Salim Gabba, who was present during the *ghusa*l, recalled in an interview with me in 2003 that there were signs of torture on Uncle Ahmed's body.[76] After the Friday prayers in Newtown, the body was placed in a coffin and driven by Khan to the Timol flat in Roodepoort.

The Roodepoort community waited for the arrival of Ahmed Timol's body from Newtown. At the Roodepoort mosque, at Friday prayers, the owner of a local business A.G. Ally stood up and requested all the local businessmen to close their shops in tribute to his close friend, Haji Timol. At the flat, women read from the Quran and prayed around his shrouded body (as is the norm according to Muslim burial rites). Family and friends insisted that Ma must not see his body but they could not stop her. It was her beloved son.

The surrounding balconies on Mare Street strained as people piled onto them. Photographs taken from an adjacent balcony by Saeed Gabru provide an aerial view of the street, and the large crowds outside the home.

The front-page headline of *The Star* newspaper read, 'Death of Detainee: Reaction Mounts'.[77] The story was accompanied by a photograph of Ma, with the caption, 'A distraught Mrs Hawa Timol, mother of Mr. Ahmed Timol, the security police detainee who died yesterday, recounts the details of her son's arrest.'

Mourners narrated their experiences in the 2015 SABC documentary, *Indians Can't Fly*.[78] Mohammed Dindar, a family friend who was in the funeral procession, said:

> I don't think the community of Roodepoort will ever experience a funeral of that stature ever again; the cosmopolitan crowd, the mood of the people was extraordinary. We were always suppressed by the apartheid regime and this was an unreal experience. What was nice is that we were walking with a totally mixed crowd. Typically, the authorities were looking on, but for once we were untouchable. The mood was sombre, yet there was a lot of anger

amongst the people considering what happened to late Ahmed.

Yusuf 'Chichi' Cajee recalled:

Ahmed was a very good family friend of my parents, specifically my mum, the late Amina Cajee, who was arrested in the morning after Ahmed was arrested. My memory as a nine-year-old at that time is that of the Security Branch coming to our apartment, approximately three, four o'clock in the morning, banging on the door. My brother and I were sleeping when they took our mum away with them. I couldn't understand what was happening. They just kept saying they were taking Mummy for politics. I would never forget that Friday; school broke out early and there were thousands of people outside the Timol's residence. We lived around the corner from them. Even in our street, where we lived, there were thousands of people just lined up all over. As a nine-year-old, I also walked from the house to the cemetery. The prayer area at the Roodepoort *qabrastaan* was too small to handle the large crowds. A decision was taken to perform the prayers in an open field adjacent to the cemetery. The other thing I will never forget is that immediately after burying Ahmed Timol, as the last people were leaving the cemetery, the Almighty just showered his blessings on the funeral by sending out a storm.

Dr Haroon Dindar, Ahmed's cousin from Breyten, remembered battling through the crowds to get to the Timol apartment:

I came to the flat after Friday prayers (*jumma*). It was impossible to get into the flat due to the large crowds that had assembled in the streets. It was the biggest funeral which I had ever witnessed. It was a very peaceful procession. We followed the hearse on the way from the flat to the cemetery. There was no chanting or calling of any political slogans. The Security Branch was everywhere and everybody was quiet. There was no talking. It was a very dignified funeral. As we walked from the house to the cemetery, it was evident that everybody was deeply hurt. Mourners included Ahmed's family members, friends, students, associates and individuals who did not know him. We all realised what had been done to Ahmed. It was a very sombre, the most peaceful and dignified funeral procession that I had ever attended, and one that I, and many others, will never forget. The normal practice at the *qabrastaan* is that mourners assemble in rows that are made for performing the final *Janazah* prayers. Due to the large crowds, it was impossible to arrange into rows. Mourners remained standing in their positions and performed the final prayer.

The imam of the Roodepoort mosque, Molvi Osman Poothawala, was scheduled to lead the prayers. But Papa led the congregation in the final prayer before my uncle was laid to rest.

The next day, *The Saturday Star* reported that the funeral had been attended by several thousand Muslims from all parts of the Transvaal. 'Many schoolchildren, including Ahmed's[79] pupils from the Roodepoort Indian High School, were present. Several white university students also mingled with the crowd. Residents of Roodepoort say it was one of the biggest funerals ever seen on the West Rand.'[80]

Images of the procession surfaced in all the newspapers. The entire community was convulsed by Uncle Ahmed's fate. A newspaper carried a photograph of Papa and my uncle Haroon with the caption: 'An old man weeps for his son – a young man for his brother.'[81] The same newspaper reported the funeral as a mere inconvenience to the white citizenry of Roodepoort:

Impatient motorists leaned on their hooters as a seemingly endless stream of white-capped Indians held up traffic for more than a dozen blocks at a time in Roodepoort. Schoolgirls pressing handkerchiefs to their faces, T-shirted whites engaged in serious talk with immaculately dressed Muslims – they all formed part of the 1 500 mourners following the hearse of Ahmed Timol. After a 3 km trek, the green velvet bier with its golden tassles was lifted from the hearse outside the Roodepoort Muslim cemetery. Shoulder-high, hand by hand, it was passed through the crowd. When the congregation broke into mass prayer, loud sobbing rose from the ranks of children whom Mr Timol had taught up to last week.[82]

A neighbour, Ebrahim Choonara, also remembered a heavy storm in Roodepoort the day after the funeral. The downpour was so heavy that the ceilings caved in at his flat. Choonara recalls some members of the community questioning Uncle Ahmed's activities and wanting to know what he had achieved. How was his death going to assist them? Ebrahim's wife Choti reminded them that Uncle Ahmed could have left the country, but had been prepared to sacrifice his life for the oppressed people of this country and, in the long term, they would reap the benefits of his ultimate sacrifice. Ebrahim and Choti's hearts cried for Ma and the rest of the grieving family. What must she as a mother go be going through? Allah must grant Ahmed paradise, they said.

Baboo, Uncle Ahmed's cousin, and a regular visitor to the Timol home, helped Papa to place bricks around his *qabr*. Baboo was working at Shamrock, producing bricks, at the time. He and Papa loaded his small car with bricks and within a few hours had neatly placed the bricks around the *qabr*. They remain in place even today.

Whenever I visit the Roodepoort *qabrastaan*, I silently visualise the burial with large crowds bidding him farewell. I think of those who were there, who did not know my uncle personally, but were profoundly moved by his gruesome death. I think of the Security Branch officers watching the procession from a distance, taking photographs. I think of Papa delivering the final prayers over the body of his beloved, broken son.

The Johannesburg community had buried Babla Saloojee in 1964, the fourth detainee to have died in police detention. Uncle Ahmed had attended his funeral not knowing that seven years later, he would become the 22nd detainee to die in police detention. Most people in the community were terrified and fearful of the security apparatus of the apartheid regime. Involvement in politics was very risky and could lead to detention, torture and ultimately death.

There were clear signs that showed torture marks on Uncle Ahmed's body. Salim Gabba recalled:

> We found out that *ghusal* (ritual preparation for burial) was to be given at the Newtown Mosque. I remember Yusuf 'Tara' Seedat holding Ahmed's head. They said that he had died from a fall. It was clear that his neck was broken as his head was just falling back. I saw clearly that Ahmed's fingernails were taken out and his elbows were burnt.[83]

Uncle Ismail,[84] who was studying in India at the time, was unaware that his brother had even been detained. On Friday, 29 October 1971, at approximately 5:40 pm, he was having *iftaar* in his room, listening to the BBC. The 6 pm news bulletin announced his brother's death. Ismail calculated that as India was approximately three and a half hours ahead of South Africa, his elder brother's funeral would have just taken place. He was also totally unaware that his younger brother Mohammad was in police custody. Uncle Ismail immediately sent a letter to his parents in South Africa enquiring about the tragic loss of his brother.

Uncle Mohammad had been detained in Durban on the Monday, 25 October along with Yakoob Varachia. 'I was detained at Himalaya Heights, where I had been staying with some students from the Transvaal. I was arrested by Lieutenant Nayager and 10 other officers. At the time of my arrest I was not aware that Ahmed had also been arrested a few days earlier,' he said. The *Sunday Times* had carried a small article on Ahmed's arrest but Mohammad had not seen it. Papa and Ma were unaware of where he was staying in Durban, and were, therefore, unable to warn him.

Uncle Mohammad recollected the details of his ordeal at the Security Branch headquarters in Fisher Street in Durban:

The officer in command was Colonel Steenkamp. There I was subjected to interrogation by Lieutenant Nayager, Sergeant Andy Taylor and an officer Botha. The interrogation began around nine in the morning and continued until 11 that night. I was assaulted and made to stand for long periods of time on a brick with two telephone directories raised in the air. The so-called 'golden chair' torture position was also used. During the interrogation I realised that Ahmed had been arrested. The security police wanted to know of my activities in the UK as well as my contacts in South Africa.

At 11 pm that night, I was taken to the Berea police station and locked up in a cell. In the cell I had a little time to reflect on the situation. I was very confused. During my stay in the UK as well as during my training, I had read numerous books on resistance movements and operations during World War 2. I had also read books on interrogation and torture methods, especially those practised by the South African security police. This information helped me to cope during this ordeal.

On the morning of 26 October 1971, I was taken back to the Fisher Street headquarters, and the interrogation resumed with different officers in charge. It went on until late at night. The same methods were utilised again. I was taken back to the cells afterwards.

On 27 October the same procedure was followed once again. However, at approximately 7 pm the interrogation took a completely different turn. I was asked whether I wanted anything to eat and the tone of the situation changed completely. The security police officers were anxiously hurrying to and fro. The interrogation session was terminated and I was taken back to my cell at the Berea police station. I realised later the reason why the situation changed completely, the sudden stop of the interrogation, as the news broke that Ahmed had died in security police custody – and the public outcry. Therefore, the Durban SB may have received instruction [sic] to moderate the method of interrogation as they did not want another death in detention – or, like Salim Essop, critical at hospital due to torture during interrogation.[85]

On Thursday, 28 October, two different security policemen came to fetch me. The previous evening they had given me some paper on which to write a statement. When they came to fetch me they said that I would have to stay in the cell until I had completed my statement. To me it was a breather. It was the first day since my arrest that I was on my own during the day.

In the evening at 7 pm, two security policemen came to see me and informed me that they had received a message from Pretoria that Ahmed had died. My first reaction was to ask how he had died. They told me that they did not have any further information. After they had left, the uniformed policeman on duty, who came to give me food, conveyed his condolences. I was confused as to whether this was a tactic to break me or whether Ahmed had really died. The death of Babla Saloojee several years earlier while in detention came to mind.

That night was extremely difficult from an emotional and psychological point of view. I had to remain strong under all circumstances. I was still not certain that Ahmed had indeed been killed.

On 29 October they fetched me and took me to their Fisher Street headquarters. While they drove I saw a newspaper billboard which said, 'Death plunge, Vorster speaks'. I wondered why Vorster would comment on a death plunge. I was suspicious and related this billboard to Ahmed's death. In the lift at the Fisher Street headquarters an Indian security policeman conveyed his condolences to me. These incidents confirmed that something terrible had indeed happened to Ahmed. It was only after my release on 14 March 1972, that I got to know all the facts surrounding Ahmed's detention, death and funeral.[86]

Uncle Ahmed was detained and murdered in the month of Ramadan. Later that month, Papa sat in *ittikaaf*, the state of seclusion in the last 10 days of Ramadan, but the torment by the security police did not cease. Even as she mourned her son, they continued to visit Ma, pestering her and her family. Not satisfied with killing Uncle Ahmed, the Security Branch members now wanted to enlist Uncle Mohammad to work for them as an informer.

My mother would walk from the apartment to the mosque followed by Security Branch policemen in their car. She refused to sit in the car with them. She would shout out to Papa to come out, as they wanted him to sign papers agreeing that Mohammad would work with them. Papa responded that he would think about it, though obviously they could never seriously consider their son working for the same people who had murdered his elder brother. The police showed utter contempt for Islam and the holy month of Ramadan.

The Security Branch's harassment of the Timol family was relentless. They would visit the flat and search all the dustbins, and they would deliberately work on Ma's nerves by asking the silliest of questions. They showed no remorse or sympathy towards the family. Ma leaned on her neighbour, Choti Choonara, for support. The family and community were literally terrorised. There were constant rumours that the police were going to raid again, and it was well known that there were informers in the community.

Roodepoort resident Arvind Naik recalled the environment in the Indian area of Roodepoort, which we called Lappies:

> The community of Lappies was generally very conservative in their outlook. Ahmed was part of a minority of individuals within the community that were progressive and forward thinking. He and Jo Jo Saloojee, the late ambassador, were outspoken in their condemnation of the Muslim community for not allowing access to non-Muslims to the Roodepoort Club. Ahmed Timol made everybody who was in contact with him aware of the injustices of apartheid.
>
> There was a clear distinction between teachers at the Roodepoort Indian High School who supported the Republic Day celebrations and those who were opposed to it. Timol

always came across as a caring person. I was aware that Timol was approaching teachers and pupils as possible recruits for his covert activities. Ahmed's younger brother, Haroon, and I were close friends. We shared a common interest in sports.[87]

Arvind remembered how, after the arrest of Ahmed and Salim, Lappies was gripped with fear and suspicion.

After we received the news of the death of Ahmed Timol, I had stolen a can of paint from our house and painted the school walls with 'Our Hero is Dead'. There are very few people that know that I was responsible for this. The security police were ever-present in Lappies for several days after the arrest of Timol and Essop. This definitely heightened fear amongst the community. Normal conversations became whispers. Mistrust and suspicion was the order of the day. The atmosphere in Lappies was never the same again. Tension set in and people were wary of even talking to each other. Individuals that were speaking to each other for years suddenly began avoiding each other. It went further. Suspicion created hatred amongst certain families for others. As the Naik family, we had also taken unnecessary abuse from certain families. This occurred even though we had family members that were arrested and detained for up to six months. My brother Dinesh, known as Dan, and cousin Dr K.C. Naik, known as Kanti, were also arrested. Dan was an upholsterer who frequented the townships. It emerged during the Case of the Four that Timol had tasked Dan to obtain reference documents. Due to their mere association with Timol, individuals within the community were identified as 'suspects' by the security police.

Over time, certain wounds would heal. However, sadly, the bitterness remains, but support for the Timol family was overwhelming. Many South Africans, irrespective of their race, religion or political affiliation, demanded a public enquiry.

On 28 October 1971 about 200 students from the Transvaal College of Education for Indians in Fordsburg held a silent sit-in before noon to mourn Uncle Ahmed's death. They staged a spontaneous walkout of lectures shortly after 10 am. About 200 of the 250 students at the college, most wearing black armbands, sat down in the grounds of the college. Pupils at the Nirvana High School in Lenasia staged a similar protest. Many of them were Uncle Ahmed's former pupils from Roodepoort Indian High School.

At mass meetings held at the Johannesburg College of Education and the University of the Witwatersrand Medical School, students and academics called for a commission of inquiry into his death. A Presbyterian minister, the Reverend Ian Thompson, told the meeting that no reasonable person could any longer doubt that violence was being inflicted on detainees.

At the University of the Witwatersrand Medical School, 87 third-year students signed a statement sent to *The Star* newspaper protesting against the detention of their colleague, Salim Essop. Five hundred lecturers and staff at the Durban and Pietermaritzburg campuses of the University of Natal passed a resolution calling on the Minister of Justice, P.C. Pelser, 'to bring those detained to trial by conventional processes of justice, and to respond to widespread public demand for the appointment of a judicial commission to inquire into the treatment of prisoners held under detention laws'.[88]

At a meeting attended by more than 1 500 people in the Great Hall of the University of the Witwatersrand, poet and journalist Don Mattera said, 'It is because of the laws of this country that my brothers on Robben Island beat against the battered breast of liberty.'[89] Another speaker at the meeting called for the scrapping of the Terrorism Act. The only long-term solution to the critical situation on South Africa's borders, which was supposed to be the rationale for the Act, was to create 'such conditions of life in South Africa that all men, black, brown and white, would be proud to live here in freedom', he said. The vice-chancellor of the university, Dr G.R. Bozzoli, and the university's Academic Staff Association also protested against the detention of five of the university's students.

There was also an outcry in the United Kingdom.[90] The National Union of Students (NUS) of the United Kingdom sent a telegram to the Timol family. 'We extend our deepest sympathy on the death of Ahmed, victim of a brutal regime. Representing half a million students we honour him and continue the struggle against South African repression'.[91] The annual conference of NUS had sent a telegram to Vorster condemning the detention and death of Ahmed Timol, as well as the detention of other South African students and calling for the release of all political prisoners.

The North London Association of the National Union of Teachers (NUT), of which Ahmed was a member while he was in England, passed this resolution:

> This North London Association of the National Union of Teachers deplores the death of Mr Ahmed Timol, formerly a member of the NUT, and demands that the South African government make an official public inquiry into the circumstances of his death. It also demands the release of other political detainees in South Africa. Furthermore it recommends that the National Executive of the NUT instructs its members to uphold the academic boycott of South Africa.[92]

Resolutions condemning Ahmed Timol's death were also discussed at meetings of the Westminster, Hackney and Wandsworth NUT associations. The Anti-Apartheid Movement asked individual supporters and sympathetic organisations to send letters and telegrams to Vorster deploring his death and calling for the release of other detainees.

Faith communities rallied around, too. More than 3 000 people packed the Juma mosque in Durban to offer a special prayer for my uncle. The Reverend Bernard Wrankmore, who had just ended his 64-day protest fast over Imam Haron, said:

> I am deeply shocked that another life has been lost and naturally hope that the matter will be thoroughly investigated. But

there is nothing more that I can do actively anymore as God has removed me from the scene and has now taken over ... It is now up to the public, the newspapers, the churches and all the people who asked that I come off the hill ... they should do something themselves to show their mettle.[93]

The chief rabbi of the United Progressive Jewish Congregation in Johannesburg, Dr A.S. Super, said that many rabbis had addressed their congregations on the subject of the detainees at that evening's services. An appeal was made to all faith communities from the Johannesburg Muslim community to attend a prayer meeting in Johannesburg commemorating Uncle Ahmed's death in detention. 'The hour-long meeting will begin at 2 pm at the Indian Sports Ground in Vrededorp, near the corner of Krause and 17th Streets,' said Mrs M. Coovadia. 'We especially appeal to other members of the community to come along – they will be most welcome.' She said that although Muslim men and women did not normally pray together they would do so at the event because of the special nature of the occasion.

In Cape Town, Cardinal Owen McCann, the Catholic archbishop of Cape Town, called for an immediate public inquiry into Uncle Ahmed's death. He announced that there would be a night vigil prayer at St Mary's Cathedral in Cape Town. The Christian Institute called on all South Africans to observe a day of prayer, penitence and denial to show their concern over detention and Ahmed's death.

A special call was made to the people of Pretoria to observe a day of penitence and prayer, after a meeting by representatives in Pretoria. The Anglican dean of Pretoria, the Very Reverend Mark Nye, said the meeting had been 'very deeply concerned' at Ahmed Timol's death and the illness in detention of Salim Essop.

Speaking at a prayer meeting in Johannesburg attended by 1 200 people, Miley Richards, a leader of the Coloured Labour Party, said, 'We are all being challenged. It is time for us to stand up and be counted. Are we just going to sit down and pray? God will not answer my prayers if I don't take positive action.'

In Durban, a packed meeting of all races called for a national day of mourning to be observed on 10 November. Large numbers of black-owned shops closed that day and students and schoolchildren stayed away from school. The anger of the people was summed up by Mr I. Bhagwandeen, an executive member of the Natal Indian Congress, who told the Durban meeting, 'If we have to pay the final penalty that Ahmed Timol paid, let us pay it.'[94]

Political organisations also responded to Uncle Ahmed's death. The Indian Congress issued a statement saying that it abhors 'beyond belief the death of Ahmed Timol', and it called on bantustan heads, the Coloured Labour Party, and the white opposition Federal Party, who were cooperating with the government, to display in tangible terms their opposition to the government in power.[95]

Even the conservative South African Indian Council sent a telegram to Vorster asking for a judicial inquiry. It reported that there was 'a tremendous amount of unrest' in the Indian community over my uncle's death.[96]

Mike Mitchell, the United Party Shadow Minister of Justice, told the *Sunday Times* that ordinary South Africans strongly suspected that detainees were being tortured in dark little rooms, and feared that the methods of the Gestapo were being used by the security police.

International organisations also entered the fray. Amnesty International called on the Minister of Justice to order an 'impartial' inquiry into Uncle Ahmed's death. Such an inquiry would respond also to the broader issue of police interrogation and the torture of detainees. It encouraged the global community to approach South African foreign missions to make known their abhorrence of the system of detention without trial, and to demand the release of those still being held. The organisation sent a cable to the secretary-general of the United Nations urging an investigation.

At the United Nations, India proposed that the General Assembly issue a statement deploring the deaths of Asians and others while in detention in South Africa, and to declare those responsible as 'criminals'. The Soviet Union and Guinea co-sponsored a draft Convention on the Suppression and Punishment of the Crime of

Apartheid. The UN Special Committee on Apartheid was given the task of preparing a report on all known cases of 'maltreatment and torture of prisoners' in South Africa.[97]

In London, the ANC issued a statement calling for South Africa's expulsion from the United Nations. It read: 'These brave patriots who are challenging the fascists' regime inside South Africa are in dire need of the support and protection of every self-respecting human being throughout the world.'[98] The external mission of the ANC called on all its supporters and sympathisers around the world to urge their governments to support South Africa's immediate expulsion from the United Nations Organisation and all its agencies, and the adoption of mandatory sanctions against South Africa.

The ANC urged its supporters to contribute towards its fund to maintain and strengthen its underground machinery and fighting forces; to encourage their organisations such as trade unions, student unions, political parties and churches to send messages of protest to the government of South Africa; to support its call to boycott and isolate white South Africa in every field; and to demand the release of all political prisoners.

'We, for our part, pledge to avenge the death of Timol and all the others who have been murdered in order to maintain white supremacy in our Motherland. We shall not allow these murderers to get away with their crimes and shall redouble our efforts to prosecute our struggle inside South Africa. Vorster and his gang will be destroyed!' the organisation said.[99]

The outpouring of anger and grief was overwhelming, and was also mirrored in the letters of ordinary white South Africans to their local newspapers. The extensive media coverage of the whole terrible story, from the day after Uncle Ahmed's murder through to the inquest that followed, enabled me – as a youngster then, and later, as a researcher – to significantly broaden my understanding of the events that unfolded.

The first inquest into my uncle's death concluded on 22 June 1972 with Magistrate J.J.L. de Villiers affirming the police story that he had been well treated but that he had committed suicide. He found nobody responsible. His findings contrasted starkly with evidence that was beginning to emerge in a trial that had started in the last phase of the inquest, the so-called Case of the Four in which Mohammed Salim Essop – who was arrested with Ahmed – Amina Desai, Yusuf 'Moe' Essack and Indres Moodley were charged with conspiring with the South African Communist Party. It was from this trial that evidence of torture in John Vorster Square began to emerge.

Meanwhile, family members, relatives, neighbours, friends, students from the Roodepoort Indian High School and Uncle Ahmed's comrades converged at the Timol apartment on Mare Street on 31 October 1972 to commemorate the first anniversary of his death. Despite ongoing intimidation and harassment by the security police, there was a sizeable turnout to publicly demonstrate support for the Timol family and for justice.

One of the speakers was Helen Joseph, the renowned anti-apartheid activist and close ally of Nelson Mandela and other leaders of the Congress Movement. In 1956, she was one of the 156 people arrested on a charge of high treason. In 1957, she was banned, and in 1962 she became the first person in South Africa to be placed under house arrest. After she was diagnosed with cancer in 1971, her banning orders were lifted, but they were reimposed in 1980 for another two years.[100]

VI

Re-awakening

After the public outcry about Ahmed Timol's death in detention, a new initiative was brewing to establish structures to preserve his legacy and to mobilise forces against the apartheid regime.

It was at the event to mark the first anniversary of his death that his brother Mohammad met several well-known political families opposed to the apartheid system, including the Naidoo family from Rockey Street, Doornfontein; Sheila Weinberg, the daughter of Eli and Violet Weinberg; and Caroline Clark, a journalist from the *Sunday Times*. Those meetings led to lifelong comradely friendships – and organised political resistance.

In April 1973 Indres Naidoo, Reggie Vandeyar and Shirish Nanabhai were released from Robben Island after serving 10 years for sabotage. Uncle Mohammad increased his visits to the Naidoo residence in Doornfontein where he met other politically inclined families and activists, and participated in intense discussions. During one such conversation, the idea emerged to establish the Ahmed Timol Memorial Committee.

Just before the second anniversary of his murder, the Ahmed Timol Memorial Committee was established. Its founding members were Prema Naidoo, Murtie Naidoo, Jeanette Curtis and Rookaya Saloojee, the widow of Suliman 'Babla' Saloojee. Sheila Weinberg was the secretary and Uncle Mohammad was the chairperson. The committee's primary objectives were to commemorate the second anniversary of Uncle Ahmed's death and all other deaths in detention, and to campaign for the release of political prisoners.

Indres Naidoo, who was banned at the time, played an influential behind-the-scenes role for the committee, as did his brothers Prema and Murthi. Helen Joseph, who was listed and could not legally be a member, was also quietly active.

An open-air rally was organised to mark the second anniversary of my uncle's death and was scheduled to be held at the Queen's Park grounds in Vrededorp on 21 October 1973. But three days before, the state imposed a ban on all public meetings where any government principle or policy would be attacked, criticised or discussed, 'or which is held in protest against or in support of or in commemoration of anything'. That was about as comprehensive as it could get. Work quickly began to persuade the University of the Witwatersrand to host an indoor 'private' meeting on campus to sidestep the ban.

Brigadier G.L. Prinsloo issued a stern warning that his men would be watching the event and would take action if the law was contravened. Jeanette Curtis was contacted by a member of the police and warned that if an offence was committed at the meeting, he would arrest 'every Bantu there' as well as the organisers.

The university's Great Hall was packed and the meeting took place without any incident. Speakers included Helen Joseph and Rookaya Saloojee. Committee members sat on the stage, each with a placard bearing the name of a detainee who had died in security police custody. Congress Movement veterans present included a former Treason Trialist, Reverend Douglas Thompson, who spoke about the Muslims who had died in detention, and led the gathering in a non-denominational prayer.

There was local and international condemnation of the regime and mass mobilisation across many sectors of the community. This was a time of a re-awakening of the political consciousness. My uncle was murdered at a pivotal moment in South Africa's history, when the apartheid regime believed it had crushed all opposition. Instead, it became a catalyst to intensify the struggle. In his book, *The New Radicals*,[101] Glenn Moss writes about how Uncle Ahmed's death had deepened his own political consciousness and involvement and had drawn him into the wider political struggle.

The work of the Ahmed Timol Memorial Committee was widely embraced and played a pivotal role in keeping the struggle alive in the build up to the Student Uprising of June 1976 in Soweto, and beyond.

Tokyo Sexwale was a student at Orlando West High School in Soweto in 1971 when he read in the *Rand Daily Mail* about the death of Ahmed Timol. He recalled one of his frequent visits to Winnie Mandela at her home near the school:

Around 1973, Winnie informed me that there was a memorial committee set up after the death of Ahmed Timol and that I was to represent her at this forum. They needed representation from Soweto on this committee. Mohammad Timol and Sheila Weinberg were prominent in this committee.

I attended a meeting where I witnessed for the first time, white comrades, who were also attending this meeting. For us who came from the Black Consciousness Movement, this was strange and quite odd. We were always aware of white comrades, such as Joe Slovo and Ronnie Kasrils, amongst others, but it was new for me to attend a meeting with white comrades. My interaction with Mohammad and Sheila had granted me an opportunity for the first time to know more about the ANC apart from what Winnie was teaching us.

I became involved in the Ahmed Timol Memorial Committee only for the planned gathering to be banned in October 1973. The meeting proceeded at the Wits Great Hall. This was my first interaction where I was involved in the preparatory work for arranging an event of this nature.

During my later years, I also went to the Soviet Union for training. It was here when I held discussions with the Soviet officers when they discussed training the Indian comrade who died in detention. I immediately made the link to Comrade Timol and my involvement with Mohammad and the Ahmed Timol Memorial Committee.[102]

Another Soweto activist, Karel Maseko, said many township residents followed the story of Ahmed's murder and inquest:

> Timol's death was very significant for us in the townships as we were now convinced that the fight against the enemy and the apartheid regime was not only fought in the townships, but also by Indian comrades. This led to my political consciousness. I was part of the generation of the Soweto 1976 uprisings who went into exile. It was here where I met Comrade Farouk, Mohammad Timol, and we worked closely together in fighting the racist apartheid regime from exile until we returned to South Africa for the Groote Schuur Talks between the apartheid government and unbanned ANC in 1990.[103]

South Africa's Minister of Foreign Affairs, Pik Botha, who served as the country's ambassador to the United Nations, stunned the world with his first speech to the Security Council in September 1974 by contending that the South African government did not condone discrimination.

The Johannesburg-based *Financial Mail* commented, 'sadly, however, his words will be immortalised not because of noble sentiments or shining truth, but because they will surely rank among the most breath-taking falsifications ever presented to the world today. He must be kidding. Not only does the SA government condone racism, it systematically practices and enforces it.'[104]

Inspired by the successes of the Ahmed Timol Memorial Committee, and with the encouragement of Indres Naidoo and other seasoned activists, it was decided to change the committee's name to the Human Rights Committee to continue the task of keeping alive the spirit of the ANC. Formally renamed in September 1974, the Human Rights Committee aligned itself to the set of internationally recognised principles and values embodied in the United Nations' Declaration of Human Rights, from which it drew its name.[105]

Among its first public activities – after it commemorated the third anniversary of Ahmed's death – was to call a public meeting on 8

December 1974, the closest Sunday to United Nations Human Rights Day on 10 December, to challenge Pik Botha's so-called diplomatic offensive. The meeting took place at the Gandhi Hall in Johannesburg. Prominent activists, including Lillian Ngoyi, addressed an audience of about 500 people.

The Committee further announced its establishment through a public letter that it would produce publications – for distribution to homes locally and internationally – and that it would convene meetings on issues of importance and engage in protest action against the state. It developed its own publication called *Human Rights* and the first edition juxtaposed the harsh realities of life in apartheid South Africa against various articles of the UN Charter on Human Rights. The second edition documented cases of deaths in detention and issues relating to political detainees.

Thanks to the generosity of various donors, the Human Rights Committee arranged a Christmas party for the children of political prisoners, detainees and exiles. Music, food, presents and entertainment were provided to over 100 children at the party on 29 December 1974.

Early the next year, Vorster pressurised his Rhodesian counterpart, Ian Smith to release a number of important political prisoners and leaders of the oppressed black majority. By doing so, he attempted to cast himself as a peacemaker, which was ludicrous considering the situation in South Africa.

Around this time, the imprisoned Afrikaner anti-apartheid lawyer and communist Bram Fischer[106] was diagnosed with terminal cancer. The Human Rights Committee called a public meeting for Sunday, 23 February 1975 to call for his release from prison, but the meeting was banned. Despite the prohibition, about 150 people turned up and it was decided to postpone it until after the ban expired on Tuesday morning. Once again, it was banned. The committee was forced to cancel the event altogether. Bram Fischer passed away on 8 May 1975 and a memorial meeting was held on 20 May at the Gandhi Hall in Johannesburg. Helen Joseph and Barney Ngakane paid moving tributes to Fischer, and the meeting ended with the singing of the

Congress anthem, *Nkosi Sikelele iAfrika* (God Bless Africa).

The committee's *HRC Bulletin* said in April 1975 that it's role would be:

> To protest the lack of freedom in society; protest the violation of human rights by the Government that is not even prepared to sign the UN Declaration; to promote consciousness among the people of South Africa and overseas of the injustices of the present regime; and to join the increasingly popular movement to bring about full rights for all the people of the country.[107]

Around this time, Aboobaker 'Baker' Ismail, whose MK name was Rashid, contacted Uncle Mohammad, who remembered having been informed by a comrade in Durban that Rashid would make contact.[108] Mohammad had been told that Rashid was a good comrade and that he should be included as a member of the Human Rights Committee. Mohammad met him at his brother's music shop on Commissioner Street and then introduced him to the Naidoo family and other members of the Human Rights Committee, after which he was incorporated into its activities.

Baker attended the lunchtime Bram Fischer memorial meeting and as he was unemployed then, when the other committee members had to rush back to their jobs, he assisted the caretaker of the Gandhi Hall to lock up. As he was walking back to his brother's shop, Baker was intercepted by members of the Security Branch and taken to John Vorster Square where he was interrogated, assaulted, intimidated and warned not to associate with the members of the Human Rights Committee.

He left South Africa after the 1976 Soweto Uprising and went to Belgium to study medicine, but then arranged with the ANC to undergo military training instead. Baker was sent to the German Democratic Republic (GDR) for a six-month infantry course and became one of 10 students selected for specialised training in military engineering, explosives and sabotage. Mzwai Piliso, MK's chief of staff, was on the lookout for instructors for the training camps in

Angola, and Baker was deployed to one at Funda in Angola. Uncle Mohammad was also training at Funda in 1978, and was pleasantly surprised to meet Baker there. They joked about having a Human Rights Committee reunion in the bush.

The Human Rights Committee congratulated the people of Mozambique on attaining their independence from Portugal on 25 June 1975 and commemorated the 20th anniversary of the Congress of the People of South Africa, when the Freedom Charter was adopted on 26 June 1955.[109] The second edition of the *HRC Bulletin* reproduced the text of the banned Freedom Charter. This initiative was very well received by the public, with many people choosing to display it in their homes.[110] The state responded with Government Notice 1494 of 1 August 1975, declaring the *HRC Bulletin* of June 26 undesirable. It was considered prejudicial to the safety of the state.

The UN had designated 1975 as its International Women's Year, and in August that year, the *HRC Bulletin* No 3 was published to commemorate the 19th anniversary of the 9 August 1956 march of over 20 000 women of all races to the government offices at the Union Buildings in Pretoria.[111] It also paid tribute to the heroism of women in the struggle against apartheid. Predictably, this edition was also declared undesirable.

On 11 October 1975, which had been declared as the UN day of solidarity with South African political prisoners, the Human Rights Committee held a poster demonstration on Jan Smuts Avenue in Johannesburg. The acting chairman of the special UN Committee Against Apartheid, Vladimir Martynenko, had written to the Human Rights Committee saying that the ongoing detentions, 'belie the protestations of the South African regime that it seeks peace and intends to move away from racial discrimination'.[112]

In December that year, the Human Rights Committee commemorated UN Human Rights Day in Johannesburg at an event with speakers including Uncle Mohammad, Sheila Suttner, the mother of political prisoner Raymond Suttner, and Sampson Ndou, a former trialist under the Terrorism Act. The meeting was chaired by another former ANC veteran and detainee, Elliot Shabangu.

Despite the authorities exerting pressure on the printing company to turn down the job, the *HRC Bulletin* No 4 was published. An alternative printer had been found, and a number of copies were air-freighted to Durban and East London for distribution at Human Rights Day events in those cities. Durban duly received its copies, but at East London Airport, the packages were seized by zealous officials who termed them 'potentially dangerous'. By the time the publication was officially declared undesirable on 23 January 1976, distribution had long been completed.

When the next issue of the bulletin was published, the government did not only declare possession of it as unlawful, the Publications Control Board banned all future Human Rights Committee publications. One of the likely offending passages was:

> There are many forms of dummy institutions that the Vorster regime has created in order to sow disunity and confusion in the people's minds. We are referring to the homeland governments, the Coloured Representative Council, the South African Indian Council, the Urban Bantu Councils, advisory boards and management committees ... Because Vorster is permitted to suppress any movement that represents people in South Africa, none of the homeland governments and none of the political parties operating within the apartheid system can claim to be the true voice of the people. They have all divided themselves into racial, tribal and political camps to please their masters in Pretoria. Therefore, they cannot claim to be using the system for the liberation of the people. Therefore, they are Pretoria's instruments of oppression.[113]

The HRC had invited a television crew from New Zealand, which was in South Africa to produce a documentary, to attend a public protest meeting on 22 May 1976 to commemorate the signing of the Charter of the Organisation of African Unity. Uncle Mohammad chaired the meeting under the watchful eyes and ears of the many Security Branch policemen present. The Anglican dean of Johannesburg, who was shortly to be appointed bishop of Maseru, Desmond Tutu delivered a militant speech in which he pledged his support for an economic, cultural and sports boycott of South Africa. He added: 'They always say that we, blacks, will suffer most... But I say, aren't we suffering now without hope of change?'

Three weeks later, the apartheid regime and its security services were shaken to the core by the June 16 Soweto Uprising, which quickly spread across the country. By the end of August, at least 575 people were dead, many shot by the police. Hundreds were arrested and scores left the country for military training.

That year proved particularly challenging to the Committee. Sheila Weinberg, was served with a five-year banning order, preventing her from participating in its work. Uncle Mohammad, was detained for four months and banned on his release in December. He was put under house arrest and confined to the magisterial district of Krugersdorp. It became increasingly difficult for him to continue his underground activities and he was eventually permitted by the ANC to leave the country. On New Year's Day in 1978, he was smuggled into Swaziland by the ANC, and eventually to Mozambique to join the external mission of the ANC.

Toine Eggenhuisen, a Dutch citizen, priest and active member of the Human Rights Committee was deported to Holland and prohibited from returning to South Africa.

Fifteen years after Uncle Ahmed's murder, an M.K. Gandhi Unit was established in December 1986, in tribute to Mohandas Karamchand Gandhi, the world renowned Indian political leader responsible for India's independence in 1947. The foundation of Gandhi's philosophy and struggle, developed during his period in South Africa as a young lawyer and activist, was passivism, or passive resistance. At the time, and in the context of political struggles of the day, his approach clearly had its merits. But the political landscape in South Africa had dramatically changed, and the only language the apartheid regime seemed to speak and understand was the language of violence.

The ANC agreed to a proposal that the Gandhi Unit be renamed the Ahmed Timol Unit in honour of the young, resilient and energetic fighter for peace. The Ahmed Timol Unit was led by Prakash Napier as the commander and Jameel Chand as its political commissar. In 1987, Yusuf Akhalwaya was recruited to the unit. In 1988 Prakash and Jameel received training in Angola and in the following year Prakash went to the Soviet Union for additional specialised military training.

The Ahmed Timol Unit continued its sabotage campaign while the apartheid regime and the ANC were beginning talks about talks, which ultimately led to full political negotiations. According to the TRC's Final Report:

> Eight of the 33 limpet mine sabotage operations carried out by the Ahmed Timol MK unit were on the homes of persons associated with local or parliamentary government structures such as the President's Council and the Management Committees. The limpet mines were timed so that they would explode outside houses between midnight and 04h00. No injuries or deaths resulted.[114]

In his successful application for amnesty from prosecution, Jameel Chand said:

> The unit always carried out the attacks between 11 pm and 4 am. We would also monitor the scene of the intended action. The limpet would be placed in a location that would not cause injury or death. If [the] explosion did not take place within the time it was scheduled to have we would contact the police and inform them of the device. We would also do dummy runs and evaluate afterwards.[115]

Yusuf, 23, and Prakash, 22, were tragically killed in the line of duty on 11 December 1989 around 11:15 pm when the unit planned two attacks in the Johannesburg CBD. These actions were planned after very careful consideration of all the relevant factors. The first attack was at the Hillbrow police barracks as this was an obvious high value enemy target and the second was at Park Station in support of a railway workers' strike.

On the night of the operation, the unit proceeded to the police barracks first and waited for the ideal moment to successfully place the limpet. Once this was achieved, the unit proceeded to Park Station to carry out the second attack of the night, as was initially planned.

After carrying out a final reconnaissance exercise at Park Station, they proceeded to carry out the attack. Prakash was carrying the limpet with Yusuf walking ahead of him and Jameel was in the rear acting as a look-out, just in case someone approached the target area while they were still carrying out the operation. Jameel could then alert his comrades and they could take cover until the area was clear to proceed again. As he stood guard at the rear, Yusuf and Prakash proceeded to plant the limpet when it exploded. Jameel fell to the ground and by the time he had come back to his senses, the force of the explosion had set off alarm sirens. Security guards from the station were already running to the scene.

Jameel left the country a few days later, first to Botswana then to Zambia. He eventually went to the Soviet Union for advanced military training before returning to South Africa to establish another MK unit, picking up the fallen spear.

My uncle's death gave impetus to people from all walks of life to vent their anger against the apartheid state. There was local and international condemnation of the regime, and mass mobilisation across many sectors of the community.

The work of the Ahmed Timol Memorial Committee and the Human Rights Committee was widely embraced and played a pivotal role in keeping the struggle alive – in the build-up to June 1976 in Soweto, and beyond.

PART III

My Investigation

VII

Gathering intelligence

Just a mention of the name Ahmed Timol within his community elicits a sense of uneasiness and awkwardness – a glance over the shoulder, a sigh and a general reluctance to speak. This still happens, decades into a democratic South Africa in which one would imagine fear and paranoia have become a distant memory. Unfortunately, some people are simply too afraid to openly discuss the circumstances that led to his arrest, detention and death.

Many families who lost loved ones in the fight against the apartheid regime have said that they were not aware of any investigations by the liberation movement into these deaths. I have found no evidence in either the ANC or the SACP archives of any such probes. To compound matters further, democratic South Africa has not declassified the apartheid-era records which could shed light onto these deaths. In fact, there appears to have been a deliberate attempt not to adhere to the Promotion of Access to Information Act (PAIA), which was designed to promote transparency and accountability of the government towards its citizens.[116]

With limited resources, no access to official archives and a general reluctance of some comrades to openly share information, I have conducted my own investigation into what led to my uncles's arrest. And I have reached my own conclusions.

Uncle Ahmed's underground work was conducted in a climate in which all forms of opposition to the apartheid regime had been crushed: liberation movements were banned, leaders imprisoned and others forced into exile. The majority of citizens lived in fear of the state and its security structures. It was in such an atmosphere that apartheid intelligence services relied on informants to supply them with information about activists and their activities to enable them to maintain this control.[117]

South Africa began using spies to collect intelligence about communism, subversion or sabotage after the establishment of the security police in 1947, known as the Security Branch of the police force. In June 1963, the Republic Intelligence, commonly known in the industry as RI, was set up as a separate wing of the South African Police. Five years later, the government created a Central Intelligence Service, which Vorster had instructed General Hendrik van den Bergh to build.

In April 1969, Vorster told Parliament that South Africa had three independent security bodies: Military Intelligence, headed by General R.C. Hiemstra; the Security Branch of the police, run by Brigadier 'Tiny' Venter; and the newly formed Bureau of State Security (BOSS) with General Hendrik van den Bergh at its helm. State President Jim Fouche had approved of the establishment of BOSS with effect from 1 May 1969.[118]

South Africa's Deputy Minister of Finance introduced the Security Services Special Account Bill establishing a special account for BOSS, which was not subjected to normal Treasury control. It operated as an autonomous department; the size of its staff secret, although it was later described as comprising six divisions dealing with: subversion, counter espionage, political and economic intelligence, military intelligence, administration and national evaluation, and research and special studies.[119]

BOSS was to gather intelligence, both from within South Africa and from foreign territories, on all groups and individuals thought to be present or potential enemies or subversives, based on their published work, public speeches, newspaper reports or other sources.[120]

The sharing of intelligence and potential threats it posed to operatives was known. One of the London Recruits, Ken Keable wrote: I kept absolutely nothing by way of a souvenir of my exploit[s], or any physical evidence, as I didn't feel safe from the possibility of investigation even at home. This was because Ronnie had told me that the ANC believed that the British Secret Service shared information with the CIA and with BOSS, South Africa's Bureau of State Security, in order to protect the apartheid regime.'[121]

It was well known that there were informers in our community. We know that BOSS's 'Division N' controlled the activities of 14 regional offices in South Africa, largely staffed by ex-policemen, whose duties were to handle informers, intercept mail, tap telephones, bug premises and tail suspects.

A former member of the South African Police with 30 years' experience, that included serving in the Security Branch, then as a senior collector/researcher for the National Intelligence Service (NIS) and also in counter intelligence and counter espionage operations, shed some light on practical operational matters leading to identifying and recruiting of potential sources or informants during his years of service.[122]

It was critical for the security police to collect intelligence in advance, so that decisive action could be taken to accomplish the end result that benefited and protected the state. The security police would target specific individuals involved in community spaces like churches and town halls to become informants as they had easy access to these premises where political rallies were often held. This allowed the security police to be informed on proposed meetings and logistical matters.

Another area of surveillance was printing companies responsible for printing banned political literature for banned political organisations. Their telephones were tapped and often recruited as paid or unpaid sources.

Field operatives would continuously monitor the conduct of informants. If they were active in generating intelligence, they were recruited to be sources. The file of a potential source was scrutinised, phone calls monitored and surveillance conducted. Individuals in senior positions in organisations were identified and their 'skeletons' highlighted. This was critical as when an approach was made to a potential source, and if there was refusal to cooperate, the 'skeletons' would be used against them. They had a choice – either cooperate – or get exposed. Sources were registered and paid for their services in accordance to their access to the targets and value of information provided.

―∽―

Another source of information available to the police were gangsters. It is now relatively common knowledge that they worked in cahoots with gangsters and drug dealers.[123]

One of the stories that did the rounds was that Uncle Ahmed's activities were betrayed to the police by a marijuana smuggler who sought to use the information as a bargaining chip to avoid being charged.

What is known with more certainty is that some of the major underworld organisations operating in Johannesburg maintained close relationships with the police. One of the most feared Johannesburg criminal mobs of the early 1950s was known as the Sheriff Khan Organisation. It was led by Sheriff Khan who controlled much of the illegal gambling industry in and around the city. Sheriff Khan's power was considerably enhanced when he joined forces with the bulk of the Durban and Y gangs that had been engaged in open warfare on the streets of Johannesburg.

In addition to drug dealing and extortion, the organisation excelled at breaking into shops and warehouses carried out after meticulous planning masterminded by Sheriff Khan himself. They had their own vans to transport stolen goods to their own warehouse.

A second notorious criminal organisation called the Msomi gang operated from Alexandra from the mid-1950s. It was more township-based but both gangs shared close contacts with the police. Most of the members of the Msomi gang had acted as informers for the police prior to their arrests.[124] After committing their crimes in Alexandra, for example, gang members would typically approach detectives with information that tended to lead to an address of a member of the rival Spoiler gang.

When Sheriff Khan was caught in Fordsburg by the Pretoria police, while in the process of robbing a warehouse, there was a flying squad car in attendance to ensure that no one disturbed his work.[125] Throughout his reign of more than three decades as an organised crime leader, Sheriff Khan frequently appeared in court on charges such as extortion, bribery and murder, but he and his gang members were usually acquitted. Witnesses suffered unexpected memory lapses or inexplicably disappeared.

According to a former Roodepoort resident, members of the community could never understand how known gangsters could openly carry firearms – and use them with seeming impunity. There is empirical evidence demonstrating the link between the security police and informants. To what extent did local gangsters share intelligence with security police on Uncle Ahmed's activities?

In its analysis of the arrests, the International Defence and Aid Fund reminds us that BOSS's visible activities are only the tip of the iceberg. It believed the entire operation was executed and possibly masterminded by the security police themselves. In these types of operations, it is BOSS's role to collate information on all forms of activities designed as subversive.[126]

In his submission to the TRC on 10 November 1997, Lord Hughes, the former chair of the Anti-Apartheid Movement (AAM), confirmed that London served as a major central hub in Europe for anti-apartheid campaigns.[127] He reported repeated attempts to plant informers within the anti-apartheid groups and how BOSS agents had tried to bribe and coerce South Africans in Britain to inform on people regarded as enemies of the state.

The TRC reported that the South African Defence Force (SADF) actively propagated its views on counter insurgency through courses and lectures to groups from both the security and non-security sections of the public service in the 1970s. America's Central Intelligence Agency (CIA) considered South Africa to be a local ally against the

Soviet Union and they cooperated in countering what they saw as the spread of communism.[128]

I wanted to know more about the sharing of intelligence with foreign intelligence agencies and how it might have contributed to my uncle's arrest, as well as to what extent informants were used. By then, the South African security police had successfully conducted a number of intelligence-driven investigations: the Rivonia trialists were prosecuted in 1963/64 and Bram Fischer in 1966. Intelligence agent Gerard Ludi[129] had infiltrated the SACP and operated in its inner circles. He was only exposed when he testified for the state at Bram Fischer's trial.

The sentencing of uMkhonto weSizwe's High Command at the Rivonia Trial and the Little Rivonia Trial, which in a matter of months, convicted another group of freedom fighters for sabotage, had a devastating impact on the leadership of the banned ANC and the SACP. It forced liberation movements, including the Pan Africanist Congress (PAC) – whose leadership had also been decimated by imprisonment and bannings – to review their strategies. The ANC focused on developing its external infrastructure, including securing military facilities for the training of existing and prospective combatants. Initially, training for the fledgling guerilla army was provided by countries such as Algeria, which provided Mandela with some of his military training in 1962 in Morocco, Tanzania and the former Soviet Union. These training opportunities expanded considerably over the years to include virtually all the members of the so-called Eastern Bloc.

After the banning of political organisations in 1960 and the beginning of the armed struggle to end apartheid, the security police began beefing up it's operations to counter the threat posed by trained fighters infiltrating into the country. To this end, in 1962 for instance, three fully equipped mobile security police units each boasting 32 motor vehicles, a mobile workshop, a mobile radio station, five water-carts with trailers, and ten trailers to carry supplies were created and allocated to different regions around the country.[130]

Radio communication was considerably enhanced by the

installation of direct contact between divisional headquarters and the police head office in Pretoria. Towards the end of 1962, nine of the country's divisional headquarters had been equipped with sophisticated radio sets, representing a major step towards more effective police communication.

In March 1965, a central radio headquarters was established, on a hill close to the police head office in Pretoria. This put the Commissioner of Police and his staff in radio contact with remote corners of South Africa and the neighbouring South West Africa, allowing Pretoria to maintain law and order and protect the lives and property of white South Africans.

A year before Timol's arrest, Police Commissioner General J.P. Gous issued a special standing order[131] reminding members of the police force of their responsibility to contribute to the collection of information on enemies of the state. National security was not only the responsibility of a selected unit, but that of all police members.

The security police had also become frustrated by the lack of progress in their efforts to identify the perpetrators of a series of pamphlet bombs and other activities in South Africa which were designed to 'pierce the wall of silence' in South Africa,[132] according to Ronnie Kasrils. What police did not know was that the campaign was carried out by a group of British sympathisers from different backgrounds called the London Recruits.[133]

Kasrils, who was pivotal in the formation of the operation, on meeting the sister of one of his contacts who had been on holiday in the United Kingdom, persuaded her to take a suitcase full of leaflets back to South Africa. To commemorate the Communist Party's 45th anniversary in 1966, a pamphlet featuring Bram Fischer amongst others, was produced and distributed in this way in South Africa.

The London Recruits was led by Dadoo, Slovo and Hodgson. Ronnie Press, a South African teacher living in Bristol assisted Hodgson. Kasrils focused on recruitment and was later joined by Aziz Pahad as an additional full-time worker. Rica Hodgson and Stephanie Kemp handled the secret communications. Kasrils's wife, Eleanor, helped to identify safe houses and addresses and provided general back-up. Dadoo and Slovo communicated this work to ANC President Oliver Tambo and the ANC leadership in Zambia.

In May 1967, the recruitment of operatives began in London with the assistance of the Communist Party of Great Britain. One August day, at approximately 3 pm South African time, the London Recruits' first successful operation was conducted in South Africa, with leaflets distributed and banners unfurled in Johannesburg, Port Elizabeth and Cape Town. Early the next year, leaflets were smuggled to South Africa and posted to addresses identified in London by a seaman who worked on the Union Castle Line, which was then plying the route between the UK and South Africa. Soon thereafter, in April, Ken Keable, travelled to Johannesburg to post more material.

The mysterious distribution of banned ANC and communist propaganda baffled the security police who had been confident that, after the nationwide crackdown on political activists, political opposition had been neutralised. The activities of the London Recruits showed the majority of South Africans that the ANC and the SACP were alive and kicking within the country.

According to a former intelligence operative, who has asked to remain anonymous, the leaflet bombs were investigated by the security police countrywide, with the main investigation conducted from John Vorster Square under the leadership of Major Johan Coetzee. While Timol was not part of the London Recruits' operations in South Africa, my source tells me he became a suspect for the leaflet bombs, which might have led to his arrest. He and his colleagues had spent many hours searching for the Ford Anglia believed to be involved in the bucket bombs campaign across the country.

While the only information they initially had was that a white Anglia had been spotted near one of the 'crime scenes', every Ford Anglia had to be identified and ruled out. Thousands were traced and their movements monitored. It was a massive operation, but it paid dividends as potential suspects were identified and placed under surveillance.

The Ford Anglia Uncle Ahmed and Salim were driving on the night of their arrest was light yellow with a cream-coloured roof, and belonged to Amina Desai. The interrogation notes of Captain Gloy[134] record that Uncle Ahmed never lent the car to anyone else and that he had driven the Anglia to Durban in January 1971.

The information about the scale of the leaflet-bomb investigation and the nationwide search for the Anglia is pivotal to the truth of this story. It could have led to the Security Branch focusing its attention on Uncle Ahmed and identifying him as a target.

In a 1992 interview with the *Vrye Weekblad*[135] newspaper, John Horak, a journalist who confessed to having been an apartheid spy for 27 years, shared important operational details of the dirty operational tricks of the South African security police. These included the interception of mail, and a spin-off special project to steal trade union cheques. The cheques were intercepted, mostly at the Jeppe Street Post Office in Johannesburg, paid into false bank accounts – and the money was used to fund further operations to disrupt and sow division in union ranks. This project was run by the security police intelligence division operating out of De Villiers Building in Pretoria. After quitting journalism to work for the security police full-time, one of Horak's first functions at Jeppe Street Post Office was to oversee and evaluate the interception of letters from members of the public. He explained how it worked: 'There is a special staff at this post office handling this and they work from a place they call "The Hole". At one time I had about a thousand pieces of mail coming through to me every week,' he said.

Sophisticated equipment was used to open and close letters and parcels. There were very few letters coming from outside the country or addressed to someone outside the country that were not scanned, Horak said.

Security police and Military Intelligence personnel were specifically deployed to the post office to conduct this operation. They ran a parallel process, scanning the mail they were officially sanctioned to scan and relied on silently recruited and paid post office staff to clandestinely intercept whatever else was of interest.

Horak recalled instances of dishonest policemen stealing money and other items from the mail, including the theft of a large amount of money from overseas that was being sent to church leader Dr Beyers Naudé. He added that the 'finest selection of pornography' in South Africa was to be found at John Vorster Square – all stolen from the post. Piles of post vanished weekly, Horak said. 'It all ends up in the same building in Pretoria. There is a five-storey building with one large floor full of books and documents – and every book and document was stolen.'

If, in the course of intercepting letters, Horak could detect when an individual would be travelling abroad, or arriving in South Africa, he would proceed to Jan Smuts Airport and go through the person's baggage. 'When you book in your baggage at Jan Smuts it goes down a conveyor belt,' he said of the airport renamed O.R. Tambo International Airport, 'It is here where we have people trained in locksmithing and all sorts of things. They go through your things, or take something from it, and then send it off to the plane.' Horak advised travellers to, 'always go through the check-in point as late as possible, they must almost call your name, because if you check in an hour before the time you have a 100 percent chance of every item being searched. The later you check in, the less time they have.'

In his book, *Inside Boss*,[136] apartheid spy Gordon Winter wrote that one of Pretoria's best-kept secrets was that BOSS had people working at the main post office in London. Among them was Pieter Swanepoel, 'Oom Swanie', who headed BOSS's White Suspect Division. Winter's handler Piet Schoeman once showed him a letter posted in London by activist Dennis Brutus to Rica Hodgson or Sonia Bunting at a central London address. The letter contained a list of names and the full addresses of 103 delegates from all over the world who had attended a congress of left-wing leaders of student unions. Schoeman told Winter how his agents managed to get the letters to him, under the noses of vigilant British post office security men on the lookout for theft by dishonest postal workers. Postal sorters, working for South African intelligence, slipped letters under their armpits or into their underpants, taking them to the lavatory and then they were passed on to a contact waiting outside. The contact would meet Piet Schoeman in a nearby pub where the handover took place under or over the wall of two adjoining toilet cubicles. Schoeman then dashed back to the embassy in a taxi, where he carefully opened the letters and copied their contents – before returning the originals by the same procedure within an hour.

All mail entering South Africa was processed at Jan Smuts Airport, where BOSS had its own secret postal sorting set-up. BOSS called it the 'watching post', or WP for short. There were also watching posts in Cape Town, Durban and Port Elizabeth to monitor mail arriving by sea.

In Operation Buttonhole, the nickname for countrywide mail interception, BOSS personnel deployed to the watching post were helped by hand-picked postal sorters. They scrutinised a vast range of post every day, including mail to and from the landlocked states of Lesotho and Swaziland. The sorters claimed to be able to recognise a copy of the illicit *Playboy* magazine from its weight alone – even if it was disguised in a thick wrapper.

The watching post had noticeboards on the walls bearing the names and addresses of well-known suspects both in South Africa and in other countries. They were listed in alphabetical order and regularly updated. The sorters knew the identities of important suspects, the type of envelopes they used, the postal franking codes used by large firms, and the addresses of most liberal organisations, leftist magazines, youth or student movements and church bodies. They were even able to recognise the handwriting of well-known political exiles overseas, the suspicion of which might have contributed to the ANC and SACP instructing their members to type the addresses on envelopes sent to South Africa.

Testifying at the Truth and Reconciliation Commission, Security Branch officer Paul Erasmus confirmed the police's capacity to intercept mail at post offices and said his overall function was to monitor individuals or organisations perceived to be enemies of the state.[137] While Erasmus was a field operative for the better part of his career, in his last few months with the police, he was assigned to Head of Technical Services for the Southern Cape where he focused on the monitoring of post, telephonic communications, fax transmissions, the planting of bugs and other related technical matters. Describing his work to the commission, he said:

> This was a system instituted by the apartheid regime to monitor the citizens of the country. Literally all incoming mail into the Republic of South Africa, as well as outgoing mail was intercepted at Jeppe Street Post Office by Security Branch staff which worked 24 hours a day and around the clock and who intercepted post at random or on specific requirements. It also related to, in every single post office in the Republic of South Africa, an appointed person who worked for the post office would perform the same function, maybe not on the scale as grand as Jeppe Street Post Office, but certainly all post was monitored inside and outside the Republic.[138]

The Star newspaper of 13 April 2005,[139] in a report on the opening of a revamped national immigration centre in Cape Town, quoted President Thabo Mbeki stating that immigration officials should respect the culture of human rights, in line with the country's constitution and international standards set by the United Nations High Commissioner for Refugees. Mbeki said that the country's immigration environment in the past had been set back by a lack of co-operation between immigration officers and other security agencies such as the police and intelligence services.

Mbeki recalled the story of the late ANC exile Johnny Makhathini, who was hospitalised in London after surviving a car accident in Algeria in the 1980s. Makhathini had entered England using a false passport to evade the attention of South African security agents. The immigration officers processed Makhathini without blinking an eye. 'But as he left the counter, one immigration official politely said, "Welcome to London, Mr Makhathini",' Mbeki recalled. 'That was a good, polite, efficient and coherent working of an immigration system, and co-operation helps to face the great variety of challenges posed by the massive movement of people,' he said.

President Mbeki was illustrating to immigrant officials the level of

Gathering intelligence

co-ordination between immigration officials and security agencies in London. This sharing of intelligence led to the immigration officer being aware of the fraudulent passport. Makhathini was not detained, but subtly reminded that officials were aware of his fraudulent passport.

There is overwhelming evidence confirming the capacity of the security police to intercept mail. To what extent was Uncle Ahmed's mail intercepted? Did this contribute in bringing him under the security police's radar?

Another method of monitoring suspects was through their passport applications. In the 1970s, the applications of anyone regarded as even mildly out of kilter with the apartheid state was scrutinised by BOSS and the security police working in conjunction with the Department of the Interior.

My uncle's police file could not be found at the National Archives in Pretoria but a dossier held by the Department of Justice provided details of his correspondence about his passport application and other documentation. I was only given access to it after I made an official application in terms of the Promotion of Access to Information Act.

The file notes his home address and his travel plans. He first applied to the Department of Indian Affairs for a passport on 18 December 1964 and said he planned to visit the United Kingdom, Norway, Sweden, Germany and Belgium. Despite the fact that he was already known for his anti-apartheid views, he was issued a passport on 20 January 1965. This was not altogether unusual. The activist Ahmed 'Quarter' Khota, who was detained in the mid-60s, was issued a passport without a problem, and my uncle Mohammad was issued a passport after being convicted under the Suppression of Communism Act.

Uncle Ahmed's first passport was valid until 19 January 1968. He applied for its renewal from London and said that he intended visiting the United States of America and Canada before returning to South

Africa. It is not known what passport he used or the route he used to travel to the Soviet Union in 1969.

He applied again from South Africa in 1971 for another renewal and the document was signed by a Mr Renier Els at the Roodepoort police station. It is highly likely that, if they were not already doing so, the Security Branch began profiling him then. Correspondence between the Department of Indian Affairs and the Department of Internal Affairs about this application is in the file but a police report dated 19 August 1971 is missing.

Another copy of his passport application dated 10 September 1971 is in his file, but this time with a certified mail stamp and, mysteriously scrawled in the top left corner, the name and address of an 'Abramjee' of '1205 Hector Street, Lady Selborne'. Who was Abramjee, and why was the name appearing on Uncle Ahmed's passport application?

Uncle Ahmed had also registered to do a BA with the University of South Africa and made enquiries on 2 March 1971 about a 'Special Course in Russian'. Was this information shared with the security police? It would have made them more interested in him as a potential subversive.

New information provided by Cassim Timol,[140] a businessman in the Eastern Cape, who is not related to the Timol family in Roodepoort, shows that Uncle Ahmed was indeed on the police's radar. A few months before my uncle's arrest, Cassim Timol was visited by two security police officers. 'The short officer sternly wanted to know if I knew Ahmed Timol. I responded, "no",' Cassim said. 'In passing, the taller one remarked that I was the one and his colleague responded, "no".' Only much later did Cassim establish who Ahmed Timol was.

Roodepoort was a bigoted area, reactionary and structured along strict racial lines. There were regular clashes between Indian and Afrikaner residents. Police buzzed about like lethal flies, and paranoia reigned supreme, with some community members considered untrustworthy and suspected of being informers.

'Apartheid was at its most extreme and Ahmed was of the view that the environment would only get me into trouble. The prospects of studying in South Africa were also limited, and he encouraged me to leave the country and accompany him to the UK,' Uncle Mohammad recalled.

In September 1968, 19-year-old Uncle Mohammad arrived in England, with a scholarship from the Roodepoort Muslim Society, to study textile engineering at Leicester Polytechnical College. It was a remarkable experience for him, the first time he had travelled further than 200 kilometres from Roodepoort. Witnessing white people in England sweeping the airport floors and collecting garbage was a huge eye-opener, as was the non-racial society, the freedom to frequent whatever neighbourhood he wished – not to mention the magnificent architecture, museums and monuments.

As a cash-strapped student in Leicester, it was too expensive for him to regularly travel the 241 kilometres to visit his brother Ahmed in London. On one of his visits to Uncle Mohammad in Leicester, Uncle Ahmed informed his brother that he planned to travel to the Soviet Union. His immediate reaction was, 'This is dangerous'. He felt it was 'asking for trouble' because the South African apartheid government's view on communism was well known. But Uncle Mohammad kept his thoughts to himself and supported his brother's mission.

It is clear from the notes[141] taken during Uncle Ahmed's interrogation that the security police had indeed showed an interest in him at that time. One of his interrogators, Captain Gloy, noted Uncle Ahmed as having said, 'My brother Mohamed Timol was also in London at the Pahads. I informed them in secret coded letters that he was to stay there. HQ had decided to send him later. Mohamed [sic] Timol (my brother) went abroad during 1968 to England.' Gloy's notes continue, 'I never introduced him to my mutual friends. My brother is to my knowledge not a member of the Communist Party. I did not introduce him to Hodgson or Stephanie. (Sticks to statement that Stephanie is Stephanie Kemp). He is well known to the Pahads. My brother arrived back in the RSA during September after he completed his studies. He then worked for an engineering firm in Leicester. Dadoo, my brother is known to him.'

Upon his return to England from the Soviet Union at the end of September 1969, Uncle Ahmed told Uncle Mohammad that he would be returning to South Africa. Again, Mohammad sensed danger but did not express his concern to Uncle Ahmed, who admitted that if he remained in London he would marry Ruth Longoni. He felt, however, that was the first born child, he had a responsibility to support his parents. Uncle Mohammad believed that Uncle Ahmed felt it was his calling to conduct underground activities for the banned SA Communist Party. Uncle Mohammad did not enquire further about the extent of his brother's political activities or what they might entail.

Uncle Mohammad was also not aware of the underground work his elder brother conducted after he returned to South Africa in April 1970, or that he remained in contact with his handlers in London. After completing his studies, Uncle Mohammad worked for a short period in Leicester, but he too felt a need to return to South Africa to contribute to the country's liberation. His decision was put to Essop Pahad and Dr Dadoo, who gave him their approval.[142] By the time he returned home on 1 October 1971, three years after having left, he had been trained in security and underground work, and in the publication and dissemination of leaflets. Like Uncle Ahmed, he had learned from the legendary World War II veteran, Jack Hodgson, about how to handle explosives and detonate leaflet bombs.

It appears from a security file[143] on Uncle Mohammad at the National Archives that the Security Branch was relatively uninformed about his special training in England. The first entry relates to his arrest with seven other school pupils on 26 May 1966. They were charged with the intention to damage property related to the painting of anti-Republic Day slogans on the walls of the Roodepoort Indian High School the previous day. He was convicted on 13 July 1966 and sentenced to a fine of R20 and three years' imprisonment suspended on condition that he was not, in that period, convicted of damage to property.

Also in the file are references to a number of statements from Uncle Mohammad's friends in London, confirming that he was strongly opposed to the apartheid regime. The police knew he had been in contact with Dadoo, and Aziz and Essop Pahad, and that he had read books about the politics of America, Russia and Algeria. One of the documents in the file, a statement from a 'friend', reads: 'Sometimes

Mohammad Timol would also bring some ANC books like *Sechaba* to our house on his return from London, and leave some at the house. During our discussions at our house, Timol took the same direction as Essop Pahad for instance, referring to us as being selfish; we just wanted to make money.'

Uncle Mohammad had his final briefing session with Dr Dadoo in London towards the end of September 1971. He was informed that somebody would make contact with him and was given passwords to identify this person when he made contact. He was concerned to learn from Uncle Ahmed's handlers that they had not heard from him for some time.

Uncle Ahmed was at the airport in Johannesburg to meet him late at night on 1 October 1971. Uncle Mohammad conveyed to him Dadoo's message and then sent London a coded postcard to confirm that his brother had received the message. The brothers held no other political discussions as Ahmed drove them home to Roodepoort in the yellow Anglia. They shared a bedroom that night and in the morning, Uncle Ahmed left for work at the Roodepoort Indian High School.

Ma reprimanded Uncle Mohammad for his long hair and sent him to the local barber shop. She added, 'The security police were here asking for you. It was the same police that came looking for you when you were in London. They want you to report to the security offices in Roodepoort.' It had been less than nine hours since Uncle Mohammad's return and it seemed that he was already in trouble.

When Uncle Ahmed got home from school that afternoon, Uncle Mohammad told him of the police request and Uncle Ahmed said he should indeed go to the police station. As he entered the Roodepoort security police offices, a policeman in the corridor commented, 'Mohammad, you back'. 'Yes, I got back yesterday and you wanted to see me,' he responded. 'No, I did not want to see you, but your brother Ahmed. How is England and were you involved with the ANC? Behave yourself,' the security policeman said. Uncle Mohammad told Uncle Ahmed that the security police had claimed to have confused them and were actually looking for him. When he heard about this, Uncle Ahmed said it must be in relation to his passport applications made in September 1971.

This was, however, not standard police procedure in dealing with a passport application. Why were the same policemen, who had come looking for Uncle Mohammad when he was abroad, as conveyed by Ma, also looking into Uncle Ahmed's passport application? This gave him the sense that the security police were playing mind games; another clear sign of danger.

Uncle Ahmed reported to the Roodepoort security police offices the following day, and told Uncle Mohammad that it was nothing serious, that it related to his passport. Uncle Mohammad said that his brother had seemed calm and there was no further political discussion between the brothers.

Uncle Mohammad visited relatives in Breyten and was away for two weeks. On the evening of Sunday, 17 October 1971, he said that Uncle Ahmed's demeanour had changed. He appeared anxious. He took Uncle Mohammad to task for having had a political discussion with 'someone', and said that they were both under security police surveillance. He suggested that his younger brother leave Roodepoort for Durban the following day, which he did. They were never to see each other again.

Uncle Mohammad had asked his brother to establish the source of the information that they were being monitored before he left for Durban. He was to put two and two together only much later, when he was detained and kept in solidarity confinement in Durban. He recalled a visit to Harold Street in Roodepoort on 14 October 1971, to a friend who was on crutches, recovering from a motor vehicle accident. Uncle Mohammad and the friend sat and chatted outside the house. Uncle Mohammad noticed a short, stout African man wearing a checked jacket, standing near a house across the road. He did not pay much attention to him then. But when he was thinking about it in detention, he realised the African man was actually a security policeman who he had previously seen at the security police offices in Roodepoort when he was arrested in June 1966. They must have been monitoring his movements.[144]

VIII

Interrogation

The Truth and Reconciliation Commission confirmed that in 1968, a group of South African policemen received training in France on interrogation and counter-interrogation techniques. Those who attended this course included T.J. 'Rooi Rus' Swanepoel, Major J.J. 'Blackie' de Swardt, Roelf van Rensberg and Dries Verwey and Johannes Hendrik 'Hans' Gloy, one of my uncle's interrogators. This training and the practical experience of using it on suspects in Rhodesia had equipped the security police interrogators with new techniques to extract information from political detainees. What they learned and practised, and passed on to their colleagues in South Africa, I believe, laid the seeds for my uncle's murder.

Just days after Uncle Ahmed was murdered, a senior police interrogator, Colonel Theuns Swanepoel, denied that the South African Police tortured detainees. A newspaper report, quoted him as saying, 'When you torture a person, he will hate you and will do anything in his power not to give information … When you know a person has information you want, you must gain his confidence. We want the co-operation of the detainee because then he tells us everything we want to know.'[145]

I have analysed the documents from the first inquest, the full set of which is not available,[146] in order to understand what happened in the four-and-a-half days of Uncle Ahmed's detention. The first one was his own statement[147] that was made under duress and the other comprises a collection of notes taken by Gloy.[148] While under interrogation, Uncle Ahmed was forced to make a confession confirming his membership of the SA Communist Party. It reads in part, 'I joined the Party because of my stay in London at my relatives place – Mr. Essop Pahad. At two meetings of the ANC-youth branch which I attended in 1968 (around March and June) the slogan *Amandla Ngawethu* was shouted – this slogan in essence is transformed to that of an oath.'

He also mentioned the names of Central Committee members, Joe Slovo, Jack and Rica Hodgson, 'Yusuf' Pahad and Yusuf Dadoo. He had likely referred to Comrade Essop as Yusuf to mislead his interrogators and to protect Essop's identity. Essop's middle name is Yusuf. Uncle Ahmed also said he had received training at the Hodgsons' flat in the presence of Yusuf Pahad. I have no doubt that this information would have incurred the wrath and anger of the security police, and that they would have regarded him as a significant catch.

It is important to note that at no stage in the 1972 inquest was any reference made to his political training in the Soviet Union. It would certainly have been highlighted at the inquest were the security police aware of it. This was clearly not information that the police had and, therefore, not a secret that Ahmed needed to reveal.

According to the statement made to the 1972 inquest by Captain Carel Joseph Dirker,[149] a member of the security police stationed in Johannesburg, the day after Timol's arrest he received various documents from Warrant Officer Neville Els including:

- A six-page document dated 19 May 1970 addressed to 'Dear Ahmed from Stephanie', with writing on the back in red ink;
- A letter marked 'll';
- A letter under the heading, A/J/4/17/8/70 marked '21';
- A letter printed under the heading, New Series: A/J/1/10/11/70, marked '22';
- A letter dated 28 December 1970 to Timol from Stephanie marked '26';
- Eight pages of second-hand or used stencils, with copies of a short novel;
- Various pages from the official mouthpiece of the SACP titled,

No 1 *Inkululeko Freedom,* July 1971, that was distributed in South Africa from 25 July 1971;
- Various pages of the document, *Sons and Daughters of Africa,* published by the African National Congress and distributed in November 1970;
- A number of white envelopes containing various pages of the document, *The ANC Says to Vorster and His Gang, Your Days are Coming to an End*, published by the African National Congress and distributed in August 1970.

On the same day, 23 October 1971, Captain L.E. Roux gave Els a typewriter, a passport and 12 index cards that had evidently been discovered in a police raid on the Timol family home after Uncle Ahmed's arrest. Els told the inquest he was the security policeman on duty on the night of the arrest, and was called to the Newlands police station after documents were found in the Anglia. He said he was the policeman put in charge of investigating the distribution of the Communist Party's publication *Inkululeko* in July 1971. Is it purely a coincidence that Els was on duty the night of the arrest? Was he aware that the arrest was going to be taking place?

Inkululeko was distributed across the country, including in Johannesburg, Port Elizabeth, Cape Town, Bloemfontein, Kimberley and Durban. Els also happened to be investigating the distribution of the pamphlet, *The ANC Says to Vorster and His Gang, Your Days are Coming to an End*, which was widely circulated in August 1970. And he was investigating the distribution of the pamphlet, *Sons and Daughters of Africa*. The police had recorded 18 cases of these pamphlets having been distributed by bucket or leaflet bombs. Els was not aware that the bucket bombs were set off by operatives from the London Recruits.

Security policeman Colonel Willem van Wyk told the inquest that it was clear that Timol was a communist because of the statement he made during interrogation and that he was in continuous contact with the Central Committee of the Communist Party in England. He said Uncle Ahmed was in charge of what Van Wyk called the 'Main Unit' in South Africa, and was therefore of inestimable value to the security police.

It had been decided to detain him in the offices of the security police, on the ninth and tenth floors at John Vorster Square police station, rather than in the holding cells with other detainees. In the past, Van Wyk said, communists had managed to escape from custody or smuggle out information in inexplicable ways. Sergeant Frederik Bouwer conceded that there were cells available at John Vorster Square, but not on the tenth floor. He did not see anything wrong with the fact that my uncle was kept in an office. The aim was not to exhaust him, he said, and maintained that he was held in an office to prevent him from coming into contact with other prisoners.

While there is no full record of Uncle Ahmed's interrogation, we do know from surviving notes that he was asked what he knew about James April, an activist from Cape Town who had joined uMkhonto weSizwe and had undergone military training in Czechoslovakia in June 1964. April was one of the survivors of the Wankie Campaign, in the then-Rhodesia, who had returned to South Africa to conduct underground activities. He appeared in the Pietermaritzburg Supreme Court in May 1971 charged with four counts under the Terrorism Act, relating to him entering the country illegally and being in possession of materials to establish a system of secret communications. He was said to have carried out these activities between December 1970 and February 1971.[150]

Uncle Ahmed's response to these questions was recorded as:

> The secret coded documents is [sic] the same that was found in possession of James Edward April. I don't know April personally. I only read in the newspapers about the above-mentioned person in Durban. I was already back in the R.S.A. My arrest and the arrest of James April will have a shattering effect on the CC (Central Committee of the Communist Party, in London). I have never met April in Fordsburg. Did not know that he was here with the same instructions. The one will not know about the formation of another cell – Security reasons.

James April was in communication with activists from the London Recruits and was carrying out his mission at more or less the same time as Uncle Ahmed, but they never met. It emerged during April's trial that he might have been sold out by informers.

It appears from the following piece of correspondence, from London to my uncle, that his awareness of April's trial might have influenced him to resist his brother Mohammad being sent back to South Africa. The note written in May 1971 reads, '5/5/71: Urgently require information as to why you consider your brother should not return to SA. Mota considers it desirable he should do so in the new future. Reply immediately.'[151] This seems to have been the final communication between the parties. There was no other correspondence between May 1971 and Uncle Ahmed's arrest on 22 October 1971. Uncle Mohammad said that towards the end of September 1971, Dadoo had told him, 'Inform Ahmed that they had not received any letter from him or heard from him for some time and that they were concerned.' This, in some ways, is further confirmation of Uncle Ahmed's last set of correspondence with London. Secondly, Uncle Ahmed's desire for his younger brother, not to return to South Africa can only have meant that he was aware of the danger here.

This appears to be confirmed by an incident in September 1971 when he visited his cousin Mohammad Hanief 'M.H.' Desai and his wife Fatima in Azaadville. M.H. recalls, 'Ahmed came to the door and asked to spend a few days at our home. Fatima obliged and Ahmed moved into the spare bedroom with his typewriter in a cardboard box and a set of files and papers.'[152] Uncle Ahmed had parked Amina Desai's car a few streets away, in somebody's garage, and walked to M.H.'s home. M.H. added, 'Fatima and I never asked Ahmed any questions and we left him for two full nights in our home. We would go to work and return in the evening and leave Ahmed in the house. Ahmed made himself comfortable and would come to the kitchen, have his meals and return to the room.' Ahmed informed MH that it was not safe for him to remain in the house and then left. In a month, my uncle was dead.

Hassen Jooma was a friend Uncle Ahmed had met at the Johannesburg Training Institute for Indian Teachers in 1961. In his correspondence to London dated 24 April 1970,[153] Ahmed wrote that Jooma was, 'my college colleague honest democrat – V. good material for further to [sic] develop'.

It is worth noting that in the early 1990s, before the TRC was established, Jooma wrote to President F.W. de Klerk asking for his help in securing his early discharge from the Education Department. In this letter, he detailed the torture he underwent at John Vorster Square after his arrest on 24 October 1971 ostensibly for being in possession of pamphlets extolling the virtues of Ramadan.

He was taken to an office at John Vorster Square, the floor of which was 'littered' with tufts of long black curly hair. And there was blood on the floor. 'I was convinced that this was from the body of my friend and fellow student Ahmed Timol. Such a sight sent shivers up my spine and I pleaded with the officer not to assault me in any way,' he wrote.

Jooma was forced to sweep the floor and wipe it clean of the blood and hair. 'I was told not to whisper to anyone on what I had witnessed,' he wrote. 'Fearing [for] my life I had, [sic] to date, not told anybody outside my immediate family.' After cleaning up the mess, he was taken to another office, he told De Klerk, where a circle was made on the floor with chalk and he was told that he would not be allowed to sit down until he started 'singing'. 'They told me that Timol was in the next room and he was "singing" all about me. I couldn't believe this because there was nothing to be told! I was not and I am not a communist. I was then, and still am, a practising Muslim. I therefore support the kind of socialism which Islam preaches.'

Jooma said he was made to stand for about 36 hours. The more he pleaded his innocence, the more he was beaten and psychologically brutalised. He told the police all he knew; that he and Uncle Ahmed had been friends at teacher training college where he was elected chairman of the Student Representatives Council affiliated to NUSAS, with Uncle Ahmed the vice-chair. After their graduation in 1963, they met briefly at Uncle Ahmed's home after his return from

London. Jooma sensed that Uncle Ahmed was a communist and on a mission but declined to participate as he was a Gandhian pacifist.

On the morning of Tuesday, 26 October 1971, while Jooma was under interrogation: 'I heard a loud scream followed by a groaning sound and a thud. I knew then that that was the voice of my friend. I instinctively knew that he was being viciously assaulted. Mr President, it is my unshaken belief that Ahmed Timol did not commit suicide but that he was murdered by the security police,' he wrote.

He was not interrogated again. A week later, he was presented before General Johan Coetzee, and Messrs Smit and Loggenberg when he was told that Timol had committed suicide, and that since there was no case against him he was free to go. Jooma passed away in January 2006, 11 years before the second inquest at which he could have given this evidence.

Gloy's notes on his interrogation of my uncle reveals his courage under what must have been the most extreme circumstances. He clearly did not implicate his comrades despite the torture and assault he had endured. One can only imagine how this must have enraged the police.

Uncle Ahmed conducted his underground activities from the residence of Amina Desai. She was one of many individuals detained at John Vorster Square under Section 6 of the Terrorism Act of 1967 shortly after Uncle Ahmed and Salim Essop were arrested. The interrogation notes show:

> Amina Desai is my Aunty. She lives at 12 Harold Street, Roodepoort. Bahiya is my Auntie's daughter. My aunty Mrs Desai stays all by herself at 12 Harold Street Roodepoort. I at a time stayed with her at this address. She was unaware of the chemicals that were stored by me in her pantry. My aunty never asked me about the chemicals. I was in Durban January 1971. Myself, Bahiya Desai, Omar Vawda in my aunt's Anglia, T.U.

22315. I stayed at Isipingo beach at Bahiya's place. Stayed for two weeks.[154]

The chemicals he was referring to were used to decode the encrypted messages from his handlers in London.

In his correspondence[155] with London, Uncle Ahmed made reference to Bahiya. 'Have spoken to following persons who are interested – (1) Ruwaida Desai - B.A. Grad. Salisbury 1st. Lives in Rdpt. Marriage in June, settling in Durban. Politically very sound. Miss. Desai who could be recruited to our movement.' The correspondence continued:

> It will be okay to send literature to the undermentioned persons. Their addresses have been obtained indirectly thereby eliminating the possibility of them to suspect that I may have had a hand in them obtaining the literature. All of them are potential recruits. (g) MR. OMAR VAWDA,[156] 6 Ravine Road, Isipingo Beach, DURBAN. (BSc Graduate, worker).

Gloy's notes continue:

> Bahiya Vawda Desai had never shown any desire to work as a member of the Party and I dismissed her right from the onset. At present she is abroad with her husband (Omar Vawda) who is on a scientific course sent by the firm: J.P. Coats of Isipingo - the course lasts for three months. They should be returning to South Africa by January.
>
> I must point out that my Aunty was at no time approached by me to become a member of the Party or to do any political work for me. It was I who abused her privileges which she bestowed upon me, such as the use of her car and using her house without her knowledge for the efforts I made to further the growth of the Communist Party. She was unaware of the chemicals that were stored by me in her pantry. My aunty never asked me about the chemicals. I have prepared the experiments

in the kitchen of her house. Mrs. Desai had one African woman servant by the name of MARY. She left about 1½ months ago. She became pregnant. She had no husband. She stayed at the back yard. There is no other servant's yard. I did not explode my experiments. I have never bought any plastic buckets for explosions. I paid cash for the chemicals which I bought at from a chemist.

His insistence on Mummy's innocence didn't help her in the end; she received a five-year prison sentence for allowing him to use her residence for his underground activities. She told me many times she believed that the state used her to broadcast a clear message that anyone associating with anti-apartheid activities would be severely punished.

The Security Branch had been publicly humiliated by the Minister of Justice over its inability to identify the perpetrators of the bucket-bombs that had been dispersing leaflets with some success since 1968. They were under severe pressure to get to the bottom of the bucket bomb missions and the perpetrators. But Uncle Ahmed could not give his interrogators any information about them as he was not involved in that aspect of the operation.

His correspondence on 10 November 1970 with London, which must have aroused the interest of his security police tormentors to interrogate him as a possible suspect of these bucket-bomb operations, related to the following:

We have selected several suitable places on the Reef where future 'bombs' could be placed. These are points where masses of our people congregate daily, as [sic] station entrances, busstops, lunch-time meeting places, pass offices, specific routes taken by workers to and from work. (7) Will it be possible for you to send details/diagram of timing method used in pamphlet distribution.[157]

Gloy's notes record the following response from my uncle, clearly in relation to questioning about the leaflet bombs:

> I am not responsible for the bucket bombs. As the leader of my main unit I am the only person who had received pamphlets from abroad. I didn't supply any other person in R.S.A. with pamphlets I received from abroad. I didn't have any one else to help me with the distribution of the pamphlets. I cannot explain where the pamphlets in the bucket bombs came from. When I distributed pamphlets and Inkululeko I did it on my own. I had no contacts with Durban, P.E and Cape Town. Salim Essop also had no contacts as I would have known of it. I am the main leader and I am the only person responsible for the posting of the pamphlets. Salim assisted me to post pamphlets at Jeppe Street Post Office on the one occasion that is on 13/8/1970.[158]

Members of the underground operated on a need-to-know basis, Uncle Ahmed told his interrogators. He was unaware of who led other cells and had no contact with them. From the police's notes it is clear that Ahmed reiterated this point several times to his interrogators but it seems they did not believe him.

Retired policeman Hennie Heymans, interviewed for the television documentary *Indians Can't Fly*,[159] said Magistrate de Villiers's inquest finding that Uncle Ahmed was 'was caught coincidentally' was quite correct. 'This was not by informants. It was pure luck that police arrested him. Yes, we did have informants, we had informants all over,' he said.

Former police commissioner Johan van der Merwe and police officer Christo Davidson, in interviews[160] with Padraig O'Malley, also endorsed De Villiers's judgment. Van der Merwe said: 'Timol, for instance, he really jumped. There is no doubt about that. Timol, he jumped himself; he was not forced out of the building. There is no doubt about that because Timol actually was in possession of such valuable information there was no way – he jumped. Timol jumped.'

Davidson described Ahmed as 'more an ideological type of person than a sort of physical freedom fighter type of person'. It would have been in the police's interest to keep him alive, he said.

> A man like that was of more value alive because of the information he can give than dead, because if he's dead, there's a lot of knowledge in his head that's gone. You can't get it out but if he's alive and he co-operates you can work with him and you can gain a lot from that, from an investigation point of view.[161]

He argued that it would have been counter-productive for the apartheid security forces to get rid of ideological people as they wanted to understand their strategies. Davidson's distinction of 'the ideological type' is supported by a speech reported in *Rapport* newspaper on 9 July 1972 in which security police Major General P.J. 'Tiny' Venter, made it clear that the police were very concerned about the work of 'ideological terrorists'. He warned, at a conference arranged by Sabra, the Department of Education and Rapportryers, that 'sensitivity training' developed in Russia was being used to undermine the South African political and social order through, 'a sort of terrorism of the brain'. Such training reduced 'race inhibitions' and led people to question established norms, authority, and official race divisions. He added that South Africa's fight on her borders would be of no avail if ideological terrorists were allowed to brainwash the country's youth from within.[162]

Magistrate De Villiers said in his judgment, at the first inquest, that it was obvious to Uncle Ahmed's captors that 'a valuable source of information for the Security Police was in their hands'. He quoted from the testimony of Colonel Willem van Wyk:

> He repeatedly said that he was aware of the fact that he would go to prison for at least 20 to 25 years. He was not willing to get others into trouble. The deceased allegedly also told Van Wyk that he, the deceased, did not know why he kept the documents and that he, the deceased, had instructions to destroy them and this was the reason why many people and their families would suffer from his incorrect behaviour.[163]

The security police's insinuation that Uncle Ahmed had been reckless served two purposes, Magistrate de Villiers said. Firstly, that the police could claim that all the evidence they had was due to him being careless and neglectful, without having to reveal the hidden hands of informants and surveillance operations; and secondly, it questioned Uncle Ahmed's character, judgement and training, and by implication, the integrity of the struggle.

Certain comrades, who were active at the time, have since remarked that Uncle Ahmed was indeed reckless. He had been instructed to lay low on returning to South Africa in 1970, but was arrested with incriminating materials in the boot of his car, his arrest triggering the arrest of many others.

The overwhelming majority of people I have interviewed said it was difficult to describe to those who were not active in the underground how fraught with danger this kind of work was in South Africa at the time. One said:

> It is only comrades who were involved in operations who understand the circumstances under which we operated. It is inappropriate and disrespectful to question Comrade Timol's decision-making. This comrade, and many of us, put our lives on the line by returning to the country to conduct underground activities. We were risking our lives and we are questioned on our decision-making.

By the time the soldiers with rifles arrived, the masses on the ground had been politicised by structures inside the country and the terrain was fertile for them to operate. The atmosphere in South Africa during the time of Uncle Ahmed's return was vastly different. He had no support structures and had to make decisions on his own. 'Comrade Timol could have laid low from 1970 until the dawn of democracy. Like us. We were not prepared to remain in the camps; were eager to confront our enemy and crush the apartheid regime. We chose to return at great risk and were not afraid to die,' another former combatant said.

From all the documents I have analysed and the hundreds of interviews I have conducted, I strongly believe that my uncle was under surveillance, that his arrest was orchestrated, and that he was tortured.

The police had information that an Anglia motor vehicle had been spotted near the scene of bucket-bomb explosions, and a nationwide operation led them to my uncle. Four days before his arrest he informed Uncle Mohammad that they were both under surveillance and he encouraged his brother to leave town. Uncle Mohammad recalled during his detention that the man watching him conversing with a friend was actually a police officer.

The partial set of records that remain from the 1972 inquest reveal that the last correspondence from Uncle Ahmed to London was in May 1971. By September, his handlers were sufficiently concerned by his silence to raise the matter with Uncle Mohammad. It is highly likely that his mail was being intercepted and forwarded to the security police, Republic Intelligence (RI), BOSS and BOSS's M15 friends in London.

Gloy recorded in his notes that Uncle Ahmed had said: 'I was told not to communicate with other members of the Main Units. I was given instructions from H.Q. in London. Decisions are taken there and policies is [sic] formed.' His training, he told Gloy, 'took place 4 weeks from January 1970 in London at the flat of Jack Hodgson. Took place one night per week. Yusuf Pahad was also present (still in London) ... I had instructions on the forming of the sub-committees. I had to go to schools, colleges and organisations to recruit new members of the Communist Party'.[164]

Magistrate de Villiers said in the 1972 inquest: 'The deceased had a quiet personality, he always spoke softly and gave the impression that he was cooperating, but actually did not cooperate with them, he was not willing to tell the truth.'[165]

I believe that the security police expected Uncle Ahmed to confess to the bucket-bomb explosions and when he did not, this is what led to his gruesome torture and murder.

An intelligence operative, based in Fordsburg at the time, told me that on the day he died, he and a colleague were instructed to assist with Uncle Ahmed's interrogation. They had hoped that by confronting him with certain intelligence on the South African Communist Party, he might reveal more. It did not. He told me in email correspondence, 'Timol was physically still in good shape but obviously not mentally and was stressed.'[166]

He said he and his colleague had an hour with my uncle and left him between 3 pm and 3.45 pm. They saw no marks or bruises on his body and Uncle Ahmed did not complain of any injuries. Upon their return to their Fordsburg office, some minutes away from John Vorster Square, they received a call informing them that Timol had jumped from the building. This contradicts the findings of the second inquest that he died in the morning.

I am convinced that the Fordsburg operative has sensitive intelligence that he is not willing to share. He went on to become a senior member of National Intelligence Service (NIS). My own investigation into that office reveals that it was a covert branch of RI and more of a BOSS covert structure responsible for counter intelligence and counter espionage. Their responsibilities included surveillance and the interception of telephone calls. They were the initial phase of collection and co-ordination with the executive powers stationed at John Vorster Square police station. These intelligence officers received counter intelligence training and were covert RI officers, rather than Security Branch officers. This is why they joined BOSS and reported directly to Hendrik van den Bergh.

Central to the police's version of what led to my uncle's death are the names Quentin, Henry and Martin. They claimed that very soon after an unnamed policeman 'Mr X' entered Room 1026 on 27 October 1971, and told his interrogators that he had found Quentin Jacobsen, Martin and Henry, my uncle jumped to his death. They maintained that the mere mention of this piece of information had left him shocked and panicked.

Who was Quentin Jacobsen, Martin and Henry, and what was their relationship with Uncle Ahmed? Quentin and Martin were twin brothers. While I was not able to find Quentin Jacobsen, I did read his book, *In Solitary in Johannesburg*,[167] in which he describes his South African ordeal.

Quentin Jacobsen grew up in London and left school at the age of 16 to work in Australia. He returned to England to study photography, and after winning the *Sunday Times* photography competition worked as a press photographer for J. Walter Thompson. He freelanced in London and Paris until he came to South Africa in April 1971.

Quentin met a person called Ebrahim when they were on route to London. Ebrahim suggested to Quentin that they should stay together in London. Quentin accompanied Ebrahim to the Anti-Apartheid Movement (AAM) office where he was paying his subscription fees when Ebrahim offered to show Quentin the ANC office which was close by. There, Quentin met Ebrahim's friend Aziz (I suspect that this is Aziz Pahad), who was with Ebrahim's in school in Johannesburg.

A friendly relationship developed between Quentin and Aziz. Quentin borrowed books from Aziz and Aziz advised Quentin to acquire additional books from a bookshop in Chalk Farm. Aziz introduced Quentin to Dr Dadoo and Quentin promoted the idea of making a film in South Africa, keen to know if Dadoo could assist in financing the film. Quentin was not aware that Dr Dadoo was a member of the Communist Party, at this time.

On 2 November 1971, security police raided Quentin's photography studio and arrested him.

In the three months he was held in detention, Quentin was interrogated for up to 72 hours at a time and was questioned about Ahmed Timol, whom he said he had only met once.

Who was Ebrahim that accompanied Quentin to London? My research reveals that Ebrahim's surname was Laher, and was also known as International, Hookah and Mike Todd in the community. He was light in complexion and could easily have been identified as white in apartheid South Africa. Ebrahim was in London during Uncle Ahmed's arrest, the 1972 inquest and Quentin's trial. He returned to South Africa years later and was driving a white Triumph motor vehicle. My investigation reveals no evidence of Ebrahim having been detained upon his return to South Africa. Ebrahim Laher passed away before I could interview him for purposes of this book to get his perspective of events.

Ebrahim's name appears in notes taken by Captain Gloy[168] during Uncle Ahmed's interrogation:

> Ebrahim Essop @ International playboy type was at London with family. He started addressing me as comrade – reasons unknown. He introduced me to the coloured Quentin at the Wits University campus. Social friend – nothing more – does not know others. International is now overseas in London. Don't know if he will come back. Timol cannot confirm about contents of the letter explaining wherein he was warned about the setting up of a studio.

Exhibits M and N presented by the state at the 1972 inquest were two letters from a person called 'International' supposedly found in the Anglia on the night of Uncle Ahmed's arrest. The names Quentin, Henry and Martin appeared on these letters. Colonel van Wyk confirmed that they had determined that Henry was Quentin's twin brother and that Martin was Martin Cohen. The colonel's interpretation was that Quentin and Uncle Ahmed were planning sabotage. Van Niekerk stated that Uncle Ahmed confirmed that the person who signed the letter Exhibit M was the same person who signed the letter Exhibit N as International. A number of other matters were discussed in this regard and Van Niekerk was anxious to find International.

Exhibit R were notes taken by Captain Johannes van Niekerk during Uncle Ahmed's interrogation. The name 'International' appears on the top of the page. Additional information in the notes reads as follows: 'He has been a good friend for a number of years, he is a real playboy with no fixed income; he has many friends and money, but no fixed address or work and he is of dubious origin. He regularly visits Wits and has many friends there; he also knows Quentin, Martin and Henry, etc.'[169]

Notes taken during Uncle Ahmed's interrogation during the

Uncle Ahmed, on a boat at sea, during his stay in London between 1967 and 1970. Courtesy of the Timol Family Archives

Uncle Ahmed at Trafalgar Square in London. Courtesy of the Timol Family Archives

The Janazah *of Uncle Ahmed carried by mourners before being laid to rest at the Roodepoort cemetery.* Courtesy of the Timol Family Archives

Multi-racial crowds queuing outside the Timol flat to pay respect to Uncle Ahmed, 29 October 1971. Courtesy of Saeed Gabru

Amina Desai (Mummy), near the window of Room 1026 after the Timol: Quest for Justice *book launch, 29 January 2005.* Courtesy of Peter McKenzie

Jan Rodrigues being sworn-in before his testimony at the 2017 inquest, 31 July 2017. Courtesy of Oryx Media

Prominent human rights lawyer George Bizos SC with the author, studying documents at South Gauteng High Court in Pretoria at the 2017 inquest, 24 August 2017. Courtesy of Oryx Media

The author in conversation with Uncle Mohammad at the 2017 inquest, 14 August. Courtesy of Oryx Media

The author testifying at the South Gauteng High Court, 14 August 2017.
Courtesy of Oryx Media

Judge Billy Mothle making notes during court proceedings at the 2017 inquest.
Courtesy of Oryx Media

Outside the National Prosecuting Authority offices in Silverton, 19 January 2016 (left to right): Howard Varney, the author, George Bizos SC, Frank Dutton and Moray Hathorn. Courtesy of the author

A pictogram depicting an overview of Uncle Ahmed's operations

morning of 23 October 1971 refers to Quentin and Henry as well as 'International'. Uncle Ahmed stated that International had gone overseas with Quentin. This was a major reason why Van Niekerk wanted to establish more details about International believing that it would lead him to Quentin. Uncle Ahmed claimed that Quentin was coloured, but Van Niekerk did not believe him saying that Uncle Ahmed was protecting Quentin.

Magistrate de Villiers in his findings referred to the contents of Exhibits M and N, letters from 11 Essex House, Links Road, London, written to Uncle Ahmed where he is warned: 'Do not visit Henry and Martin at the studios' and (Exhibit N) dated 9 September 1971: 'Have Quentin contacted you? Stay far from him. I am suspicious'. These letters were signed by the author 'Friend and Brother' in the first case and 'Friend, Comrade, someone called International'. De Villiers argued that if Uncle Ahmed's relationship with Quentin and his friends Martin and Henry were innocent and only on a social basis, there would be no reason to have warn Uncle Ahmed to stay away from them.

Quentin writes in his book about the letters, 'I know nothing about that. I didn't, but it was just possible that Ebrahim had written to that effect. It's one of the awful things about the situation there that nobody trusts anybody.'[170]

The letter dated September 1971 from International is significant. I am quite certain that the last correspondence between Uncle Ahmed and London was in May 1971 from Uncle Mohammad's evidence that Dr Dadoo and London had not heard from his brother for months. This raises the question as to whether this September 1971 letter from International in London was 'manufactured' by the Security Police to add credence to the relationship between Uncle Ahmed and Quentin.

According to Salim, he and Uncle Ahmed had once visited Quentin's studio as they required certain equipment for the production and distribution of propaganda leaflets. There was no other association with Quentin beyond that one visit.

Quentin appeared in court on 21 March 1972 charged under the

Terrorism Act, with two alternative charges under the Suppression of Communism Act. Among the allegations against him was that he had photographed strategic points in South Africa with the intention of committing sabotage and that he conspired with others about committing sabotage. Very little emerged directly linking Timol to Jacobsen through the course of the trial, and Jacobsen himself denied any connection (with a single exception). The state failed to prove its case against Jacobsen, and on 20 April 1972 he was acquitted and discharged – and he left South Africa.

Martin Cohen, a state witness in Jacobsen's trial stated that in Quentin's terrorism trial, there was no suggestion of a subversive link between Timol, Quentin and himself. He added that he had never met Uncle Ahmed and found it strange that his name was mentioned during the inquest.

It is now known that the security police had killed Uncle Ahmed during detention. They needed to come up with a plausible narrative explaining his death. They were perhaps hoping for some connection between Quentin, Henry and Martin, and Uncle Ahmed, in that the mere mention of these three names would trigger Uncle Ahmed to commit suicide. If any of them were involved in Uncle Ahmed's underground operations, there would be evidence that would have resulted in their imprisonment. This never happened as none of them were part of Uncle Ahmed's underground cell.

During the first inquest in 1972, Magistrate de Villiers remarked that the names of Quentin, Henry and Martin were found in the documents the police said they found in the Anglia. He added that my uncle was 'evasive during interrogation when questioned about them and that he did not provide any more information on these people, except to say that they were more occasional friends'.[171]

Colonel van Wyk, a member of the Security Police for over 12 years who had had assisted with the investigations into the Bram Fischer and Rivonia cases, testified at the first inquest said that he had found it strange that Ahmed Timol's name was not mentioned in Quentin's case and that he had, on numerous occasions asked him about Quentin's identity. Van Wyk confirmed that they had determined that Henry was Quentin's twin brother and that Martin was Martin Cohen. It was his interpretation that Quentin and Uncle Ahmed were planning sabotage.

The Timol family's legal representatives argued that Uncle Ahmed's relationship with Quentin Jacobsen was only on a social level. The Jacobsen brothers ran a photographic studio in central Johannesburg that was open to the public and very simple to find. They were not members of the underground, and nor were they particularly close to my uncle. Salim Essop could only recall that one occasion on which he and Ahmed had interacted with Quentin. It was at the studio, where they discussed photography.

It is totally implausible to the point of absurdity that, given these facts, that Ahmed would have considered suicide on hearing that the police had discovered Quentin's whereabouts. He hardly knew him and could not have been shocked when he was identified during the interrogation. I am convinced that the security police fabricated the story about Quentin to cover up the fact that they had murdered my uncle.

IX

The first inquest

Looksmart Khulile Ngudle, an uMkhonto weSizwe operative, was found hanging in his cell at Pretoria Central Prison on 5 September 1963. He was buried in an unmarked pauper's grave and banned after his death. He was the first political detainee to die in police detention in South Africa. By the time my uncle died, eight years later, that number had risen to 22. He was not the last to die – according to the Foundation for Human Rights, 73 political detainees died between 1963 and 1990.[172] No one has ever been held to account.

My maternal grandparents did not have the financial resources to cover the legal costs of an inquest into my uncle's death, but G.H. Bhabha[173] and other members of the Indian community raised funds for the country's best legal brains to try to uncover the truth of what really happened the day he 'fell' to his death.

The Ahmed Timol Inquest (2361/71) began at the Johannesburg Magistrate Court on 24 April 1972 and lasted two months. The legal team representing the Timol family included Cachalia and Loonat who appointed Advocate George Bizos and Advocate Issy Aaron Maisels[174] to argue on the family's behalf, and Dr Jonathan Gluckman was appointed as the pathologist. The police were defended by Advocate S.A. Cilliers; Senior Public Prosecutor P.A.J. Kotze and Magistrate J.J.L. de Villiers presided.

What we know about the first inquest is limited to that part of the court records that still exists. Only 504 of the 1 157 pages have survived – less than half of the full record. This comprises the last part of the record, including the 77-page judgment. Significantly, some of the missing elements include the oral evidence of the police witnesses and certain photographs and other exhibits.

A page is also missing from the sworn statement of Sergeant Jan Rodrigues, who is the last person to have seen my uncle alive. A crucial part of his version of what happened when Ahmed Timol fell from the building has disappeared.

On the first day of the inquest, Magistrate de Villiers ruled against the family's request for a copy of all the documentation. They only received the paperwork when Maisels took the matter on appeal to the Supreme Court which ruled in his favour.

Lt Colonel Willem Petrus van Wyk, who had assisted with the Rivonia Trial and the case against Bram Fischer, testified that at around 3 am on 23 October 1971 he arrived at the office of Captain Dirker in John Vorster Square where Timol was being held. This was Room 1026, a small office that measured 2.5–3 x 4 m.[175]

Van Wyk said that he did not see any obvious injuries on Timol, but that he had not carried out a thorough inspection.

Captains Johannes Hendrik 'Hans' Gloy and Johannes Zacharia van Niekerk both testified that they had interrogated Timol from 6 am to 7 pm on 23 October 1971; on 24 October 1971 from 8 am to 8 pm, and then again on 27 October 1971 from 8.30 am to 3.30 pm. He was free of injuries or wounds, they said, when they took over from Lieutenant Colonel van Wyk at 6 am on 23 October 1971 and also on the morning of 27 October 1971.

Sergeants Louw and Bouwer guarded the prisoner during the nights of 23 October 1971, 24 October 1971, 25 October 1971 and 26 October 1971. They testified that he was not questioned at night and that his sleep was not interrupted and he was taken to the bathroom and toilet when necessary. They said he had used his arms freely when he washed, and could remove his shirt himself. He was given water to drink when he asked for it. They told the court that as it was hot, my uncle had slept in his underwear without a top. They saw his bare torso on several occasions, in good light, but had never seen any marks or injuries on him before he died on Wednesday, 27 October.

Bouwer testified that he did not examine Timol's legs nor did he pay attention to them. He said the detainee rested well and had slept peacefully on a mattress with blankets. His interrogators had hardly conversed with him, except when he wanted to play the card game, Five Card, with them.

Captain Richard Bean participated in Ahmed Timol's interrogation with Van Wyk between 8.30 am and 7.30 pm on 25 October 1971 and again on 26 October 1971 from 8.30 am to 8 pm. He also testified that he had not seen any injuries on my uncle and said that he had made no complaints.

Addressing the question of the ante mortem wounds and injuries on his body, Magistrate de Villiers said there was no reason why he would have been assaulted by any member of the police during his detention. His arrest was 'accidental' and he had proved to be a valuable source of information. Gloy and Van Niekerk testified that they wanted to win his trust and did not want to antagonise him by being unfriendly or by assaulting him.

Magistrate de Villiers said that, except for the injuries to his shoulder blade that could have been older, all the abrasions and other injuries on his body were between four and eight days old and that the bruises were between one and seven days old. He also found it possible that the injuries could have been sustained simultaneously. His impression, from their nature and distribution, was that it was improbable that they were caused by assault. The medical evidence also could not conclude how he had sustained the injuries. The closest explanation was that they had been sustained during a brawl, where he could have been pushed around and had possibly fallen.

The magistrate concluded that his injuries were sustained before his arrest. Surely, if this was the case, his fellow teachers at the Roodepoort Indian High School, his students, family members and Salim, would have noticed them.

The testimony of Warrant Officer Deysel dealt with Timol's fall from the building. He said he was discovered lying on the ground on the southern side of the John Vorster Square building. Upon hearing somebody shouting that he had jumped out of the window, Deysel grabbed two blankets from his office on the tenth floor and rushed downstairs. He saw my uncle lying on his stomach, his right arm under his body, his left arm a little away, his palm upwards, the left leg straight, the right leg bent to the inside, slightly away from the left leg. His right shoe was later seen a little distance from his body.

Deysel added that he had felt for a pulse and had detected one; that his heart was still beating. Deysel rolled him onto the two blankets and he and his colleagues then carried my uncle into the building. In the entrance hall, Deysel again felt for a pulse, but could not detect one. His body was then taken to the office on the ninth floor where Dr V.D. Kemp confirmed time of death as 4.05 pm.

After a fall of this magnitude, he must have been seriously injured but Magistrate de Villiers never questioned why his body was moved.

Gloy's testimony provided insight into the interrogation about Timol's operational activities. They said he had denied having distributed pamphlets on 13 August 1970 in Durban, Cape Town and Port Elizabeth on 14 August 1970. Responding under cross-examination by Bizos, Gloy said that his response was a lie but this did not upset him. He further testified that my uncle gave police very valuable information about himself as well as on the SA Communist Party headquarters in London. He was, however, very vague about information regarding incidents that took place locally.

Gloy found that Timol's response was normal and that he remained confident that the police would get to the truth. He said that the police had obtained very useful facts from the detainee and that they were aware that he had other accomplices in other cities. He claimed that when a detainee provided false information, physical attacks did not help at getting to the truth. Getting angry also did not help the police, rather that 'patience is a virtue'. He maintained that an interrogator needed to win the trust of the detainee and show, in a nice way, that this was a game. The detainee needed to know he was playing a game, one that the interrogator had known about for a long time.

He claimed that Timol and his interrogators had shared several jokes and added that he had thanked him for the exhibits he had given to them. Timol had laughed but his attitude had suddenly changed as he lowered his head and said, 'All you have to do, the prosecutor must just get up and hand over these documents' – he said that the deceased had indicated with his hands – 'one after the other to the Court and I would get at least twenty years'.

Gloy said he replied that Timol should put this idea out of his head immediately and reminded him that the police were not prosecutors and that there were no predetermined sentences. Each case had its own trial. Timol, he said, was not impressed with this response and repeatedly uttered that he would get a long jail sentence. This matter was discussed for an hour or more.

Van Wyk maintained that Timol had repeatedly stated that he was aware that he would go to prison for at least 25 years and that he was not willing to get others into trouble. He had, Van Wyk said, told him that he did not know why he kept the documents when he had instructions to destroy them. This would result in many people and their families suffering because of his behaviour.

Magistrate de Villiers ruled that Timol had committed suicide, not because of having been tortured or ill-treated but for another reason such as self-reproach or for political reasons. He felt there was no doubt that he held a prominent position in the ranks of the SACP as the leader of what the police had referred to as the Main Unit in South Africa.

To bolster his conviction that my uncle had killed himself, he referred to a section of *Inkululeko*, February 1972, no 2, which read: 'Harass your enemy by going on hunger-strikes, act insane, lodge complaints, whether true or false, resort to civil and criminal actions in courts as often as possible, make sure your complaints and actions the suppressors get the utmost publicit.[sic]. Rather commit suicide than to betray the organisation.'

According to the police's version, Sergeant João Rodrigues was the last person in the room with my uncle before his death. Rodrigues was stationed in the clerical division at security police headquarters in Pretoria. He had gone to Johannesburg on 27 October 1971 to deliver certain documents to John Vorster Square and to hand two salary cheques to Gloy and Van Niekerk. Upon his arrival at around 3.30

pm Rodrigues took the cheques and a tray with three cups of coffee to Room 1026 on the tenth floor. He gave the coffee to Captain Gloy, Captain Van Niekerk and Uncle Ahmed which they drank.

A little later, an unknown person arrived and told Gloy and Van Niekerk about a person called Quentin Jacobsen. Timol looked shocked, according to Rodrigues, and turned his head from side to side and looked at him with a wild look in his eyes. The two security policemen then got up and asked Rodrigues to guard the detainee while they went to investigate the information they had just received. They left the room. Rodrigues said he sat down on chair A, closest to the window where Gloy had been sitting in Room 1026,[176] and that Uncle Ahmed was seated in chair B on the opposite side of the table.

A little while after his interrogators left the room, Timol asked to go to the toilet. As he got up, Rodrigues went to his left and his eyes were on chair C. He pushed it and saw Ahmed on the right-hand side of the table from where he was, rushing to the window. Rodrigues said he had first wanted to go to the left, but the chair that Ahmed had just vacated, chair B, was in his way. He then went back to the right, where he had trouble with chair A, which also obstructed him.

Magistrate de Villiers concluded that it was at this moment that Timol had not only reached the open window but he dived through it. As Rodrigues tried to grab him, he stumbled over chair A which prevented him from even touching Timol.

Rodrigues also gave the court another account: that when Timol had asked to go the toilet, he stood up, went to the window, opened it and simply jumped out. And he related another version: that after he had made the request to go the toilet, they both stood up and while Rodrigues was pushing his chair back under the table, he saw Timol going towards the window and as he tried to approach him he stumbled and fell over a chair in his way. When he got to the window, he saw Timol lying on the ground next to the building. He then ran to Colonel Greyling's office and reported the matter to him. Then Greyling and others went down to the street level.

Rodrigues testified that the day Timol died was the first time he had seen him and that he had not questioned him. He also confirmed that he had written a statement on 11 November 1971 in this regard, referred to as 'Statement R' at the inquest, in which he stated that meeting was the first time he had seen Timol and that he had not threatened or assaulted him.

The post mortem report and evidence of the medical doctors who testified in the first inquest is included in the surviving record. The post mortem was carried out by the district surgeon, Dr Nicholas Jacobus Schepers, who recorded the death as consistent with multiple injuries. Later, under cross-examination, he said the cause of death was 'serious brain damage and loss of blood'.

My uncle's body had numerous injuries which appeared to have been sustained ante mortem, in other words, before his death. One was a cracked jaw bone which Schepers suggested could have been the result of him having bumped into furniture. Twenty-seven of the 35 injuries on my uncle's body were said to be ante mortem. He also had a serious injury to his calf, the toes, his hand and his head.

There was considerable discussion in court on the timing of these injuries. The magistrate accepted that they were sustained five to seven days before his death and could, therefore, not have been sustained during his four days of custody.

Magistrate de Villiers issued his findings on 22 June 1972 in terms of Article 16 of Act 58 of 1959. He found that Ahmed Timol was arrested by the South African Police and the interrogation was conducted by members of the Security Branch.

His judgment had the following details:
a. The identity of the deceased is Ahmed Essop Timol, an Asian male, 29 years old, a born South African, teacher of profession.
b. Date of death: 27 October 1971.
c. Cause or probable cause of the death: The deceased died because of serious brain damage and loss of blood sustained when he jumped out of a window of Room 1026 at John Vorster Square and fell to the ground on the southern side of the building. He committed suicide.
d. No living person is responsible for his death.

Magistrate de Villiers said it was absurd that Ahmed Timol could have been murdered because he was valuable to the police. He further ruled that he had been treated in a civilised and humane manner. He accepted, beyond reasonable doubt, that my uncle had killed himself and because he was a communist, this act would have been seen as an order from the SACP that he should 'rather commit suicide than betray the organisation'.

He recommended that, in the future, people detained in terms of Article 6 of Act 83 of 1967, the Terrorism Act, must as soon as possible after an arrest, be examined by a district surgeon to establish their health condition and, in particular, to determine if there were any signs of assault on the body. This could possibly prevent the police from being unnecessarily embarrassed with long investigations like the one about Timol.

The Terrorism Act of 1967 had given extraordinary powers to the police to extract information from a detainee relating to terrorism, which was defined as anything that might endanger the maintenance of law and order. The Act authorised detention without trial for purposes of interrogation for 60 days renewable.[177]

The apartheid state began giving itself wide-ranging powers of detention without trial of political opponents from 1963 when the General Law Amendment Act was made law. It allowed detention in solitary confinement, without a warrant, of suspects for 90 days, renewable for another 90 days.

The *Rand Daily Mail*[178] reported that Papa and Ma had sat stoically throughout the inquest proceedings and, in the end, Papa left the court sobbing, shaking his bowed head muttering, 'I can't believe it, I can't believe it'. Ma could not hide her tears and was supported by her son Mohammad. 'We are all very sad. But can only turn to Allah

The first inquest

– He knows better than anybody else who is right and who is wrong,' said Papa. He also thanked all those, white and black people had stood by him. He also thanked his relatives who had assisted with the huge financial burden of the inquest.

Spending time with both Ma and Papa during school holidays as I was growing up, it became evident to me that they had been deeply scarred by the loss of their son. They hardly spoke about him and I had to keep probing Ma to share any details with me.

The De Villiers findings starkly contrasted with evidence emerging from the so-called Case of the Four, the trial that had started on 8 June, shortly before the first inquest ended. The four trialists were – Mrs Mummy Desai, Moe Essack, Indhrasen 'Indres' Moodley and Mohammed Salim Essop, who was arrested with my uncle, and was tortured for three days at John Vorster Square

They had been detained in October 1971 and all of them, apart from Mummy, who was released on conditional bail, had been held in solitary confinement until they appeared in court on 13 June 1972, less than 10 days before Magistrate de Villiers handed down his judgment in the inquest. They were all accused of conspiring with the South African Communist Party and/or the banned ANC and/or the dead detainee, Ahmed Timol.

The four accused appeared in the Supreme Court of South Africa (Transvaal Provincial Division) sitting at the Old Synagogue in Pretoria. The Honourable Mr Justice Snyman presided. The state was represented by Advocate J.E. Nöthling SC assisted by Advocate K. von Lieres. Salim was defended by Advocate J. Browde SC assisted by Advocate P.J. Hare instructed by Cachalia and Loonat, Jhb. Essack and Moodley were represented by Browde SC assisted by Advocate I. Mahomed instructed by Bugwadeen, Durban. Amina Desai was represented by Advocate J. Coaker SC assisted by Advocate E.M. Wentzel instructed by N. Kades.

The state described the arrest of Ahmed Timol and Salim Essop and the discovery of ANC leaflets and documents in the boot of the car and said the police had also found a list of names, addresses and envelopes in Salim's room. He testified that he and Uncle Ahmed were going to a party and knew nothing of the pamphlets in the boot. Ahmed had paid him to type the names and addresses on the envelopes for a soft goods mail order business. Salim had not typed the envelopes, but had glanced at them before putting them aside. He confirmed his opposition to communism and violence.[179]

The state produced evidence that Indres had handed copies of *Inkululeko* to two people in Durban. He testified that he and his wife had received them through the post and had not read them. He gave them to the two witnesses to demonstrate that the South African Communist Party was not inactive, as they had thought. He also said he had asked the witnesses to destroy the pamphlets.

Mummy, who was a widow and living alone, was alleged to have allowed Uncle Ahmed to store materials in her home where, it was claimed, he had experimented with the preparation of gunpowder. Bottles containing substances required to decipher secret letters were found in her pantry. In her yard was a plastic bucket containing the residue of material, which expert evidence concluded, was the result of gunpowder having been exploded in the bucket. It was also found that her typewriter had been used to type envelopes found to contain ANC leaflets. Mummy denied any knowledge of any of these incidents and said Uncle Ahmed was like a member of her family, a regular visitor who had access to the entire house. She spent time out of her home to attend to her own business. She confirmed to the court that Uncle Ahmed had borrowed her car on the night of his arrest, 22 October 1971.

The testimony of Yousuf Hassan Essack (21), known as Moe, is critical for the investigations into Uncle Ahmed's operations. His name was never mentioned in Uncle Ahmed's correspondence with London, and nor does the name appear to have come up during Uncle Ahmed's interrogation. Who was Moe and why was he arrested and charged?

He was born in 1950 in the Durban suburb of Morningside. Anti-apartheid activist Dr Monty Naicker lived at 195 Percy Osbourne Avenue. He was banned and his home was regularly raided by the security police. Despite his banning order, Moe was his regular visitor.

As a youngster growing up in South Africa, Moe was not politically active prior to experiencing his family's forced removal from Morningside because of the Group Areas Act, which declared the area as 'white', forcing his grandfather to sell the family property. Moe had grown up in a house with a big garden, surrounded by extended family and friends; now the family was confined to an apartment on Queens Street.

Moe's grandfather owned a hardware shop which predominantly traded with members of the African community. Moe became a fluent isiZulu speaker while helping out at the shop. He also witnessed the dignified and respectful interactions his grandfather had with his clients. He was told to look after them as they looked after his family; it was due to them that the family had food on its table.

At the age of 15, Moe came into contact with brothers Subash and Sarath Maharaj. They were university students and intellectuals who were politically inclined in their thinking. His relationship with the brothers shaped Moe's political thinking. Moe also met 'Old Man Docrat', called 'Commie Doc', who lived in Victoria Street. Although he was officially banned and couldn't see visitors, Docrat's library was accessible to Moe and his friends.

Moe completed matric in 1968 at Sastri College in Durban. After school, he took a job at a chemical factory called NCP where he witnessed workers being deprived of protective clothing. A single mask had to be shared between two workers. He found the working conditions so atrocious that Moe resigned. For a short period thereafter, Moe worked on a factory assembly line in the hope of becoming a technician but when this seemed impossible, he resigned once again.

Still in his teens, Moe had witnessed the exploitation of workers in South Africa and developed a keen understanding of the plight of African workers in particular. He relocated to Johannesburg in 1969, where he was employed at Skye Products. As a people's person, Moe quickly integrated in his new community. He became friends with Hoosein Moola, known as Langes, who was associated with the Dynamos Football Club. Having a passion for soccer, Moe became involved in the activities of the club and was well known to all the members. It was here that he came into contact with the Pahad brothers, Zunaid and Naseem (brothers of Aziz and Essop who were in exile in London).

After a stint back in Durban, Moe returned to Johannesburg in December 1970. He was re-employed by Skye Products, living with friends in Lenasia, and commuting to work in Johannesburg. It was around this time that Moe heard that Naseem (known as Nas) Pahad's wife was going abroad. Naseem, knowing Moe from his earlier stay in Johannesburg, agreed to his request to lodge at his apartment, 11 Orient House, in Becker Street, a few minutes' walk from the former John Vorster Square.

Moe was outspoken in his political beliefs and was aware of the Pahad family's involvement in the anti-apartheid struggle. He recalls: 'I once asked Naseem, "How can one get involved in the struggle?"' Naseem responded: 'The organisation will find you.' Well, it certainly did.

Uncle Ahmed was a frequent visitor to Naseem's flat, and it was here that he met Moe. Moe's immediate impression of Uncle Ahmed was that he was a very pleasant and calm person, easy to get along with and highly intelligent. A friendship quickly developed. Moe felt that their personalities were mutually complementary; Uncle Ahmed was cool and rational, the counterpoint to his own aggression, hot-headedness and street savvyness. Moe's life was quickly falling into place. Coming to Johannesburg for the second time, meeting Uncle Ahmed and living at the Pahad's flat surrounded by photographs of struggle heroes like Sisulu and Kathrada… There was even a photograph of Nelson Mandela on Naseem's bedroom wall. Mandela was a banned person and surely having a photograph of him would bring you to the attention of the security police. Was Naseem not afraid?

Regular meetings took place on the corner of Becker and Market streets, in central Johannesburg, and at the Dynamos Social Club, on the corner of Commissioner and Bezuidenhout streets. The social club was run independently from Dynamos Football Club, but they shared most of the same members. Naseem Pahad was the treasurer and Uncle Ahmed the assistant secretary of Dynamos Football club.

The Dynamos Social Club was a hive of activity. Members played table tennis, chess, Scrabble and card games; there were lots of parties and social events, and movies were screened on Sunday evenings. Due to Naseem's wife being abroad, his apartment also became a regular party venue – and the site of many deep political discussions.

Moe recalls about one Sunday evening early in 1971: 'Ahmed collected me and we went to the Roodepoort Moslem Club. Arriving at the club, I found thousands of *Inkululeko* pamphlets on the table. Ahmed asked me to commence stapling them. After I read the *Inkululeko* pamphlet, I commented to Ahmed that this was rhetoric. Ahmed responded that the pamphlet was aimed for the masses and not the intellectuals. The intention was to send a message that we are alive in the country; and give the people hope that the organisation is alive. I put the pamphlets in the envelopes and Ahmed asked me to post them.'[180]

Moe took the pamphlets to Naseem's apartment, where he was living. Uncle Ahmed and Moe had agreed not to post all the pamphlets at the same time. Moe put the pamphlets in a knapsack and on his way to work posted them in batches. Moe later recruited his friend Yusuf 'Chappies' Adam to assist him with the posting.

Although Moe showed Yusuf one of the pamphlets they were posting, he never disclosed any link to Uncle Ahmed. This aspect is critical to the unfolding story.

According to Moe, Uncle Ahmed never spoke to him about his political training or activities in London. However, it was pretty obvious to Moe that Uncle Ahmed had made contact with the ANC.

Moe understood the necessity of operating on a need-to-know basis; it was not necessary for him to ask Uncle Ahmed detailed questions. They divided their relationship between conducting underground activities and socialising as friends. When they weren't working, they constantly teased each other. But under no circumstances could they expose their secret underground activities, and they tried not to create the impression that that they were too close.

Correspondence between Uncle Ahmed and London (Reference SPECIAL 3/3/71), stated: '(4) Also urgently needed are documents of the following type: (a) reference books (b) tax receipts and exemptions (c) any other travel documents especially for Africans (what does an African get if he wishes to travel for a short while to and from one of the ex-protectorates?) (d) any other internal documents which blacks need for travel and survival.'

It was to Moe that Uncle Ahmed turned to identify discreet individuals who could help without revealing his identity. Moe had developed strong networks in African townships, partly due to his love of soccer. He regularly accompanied Orlando Pirates official Goodenough Majija on the train journey from Westgate Station to Orlando Stadium in Soweto to watch Pirates play.

In response to Uncle Ahmed's need for assistance, Moe identified a gentleman working at the Department of Bantu Affairs who smoked marijuana. Through his contacts in Durban, Moe arranged delivery of a roll of marijuana. In return, his new contact supplied Moe with reference books that were passed on to Uncle Ahmed. Moe had no idea what Uncle Ahmed intended to do with the reference books. According to evidence provided in subsequent court proceedings, reference books were found in Uncle Ahmed's locker at Roodepoort Indian High School.[181]

The court heard damning evidence against Moe, which demands close scrutiny as it indicates that Uncle Ahmed's underground activities had been compromised.

The first inquest

First of all, one of the state witnesses in the case was Dinesh Naik (a cousin of Dr K.C. Naik who was detained shortly after Uncle Ahmed). Dinesh led evidence to the effect that Moe was to do a favour for Timol and/or Accused Number One, Mohamed Salim Essop, with regard to obtaining reference books, travel documents and permits, apparently for urban Africans who had documentation problems.[182]

Then, evidence from Fatima Burgers and Mahomadi Milansi was heard, relating to an incident at the Roodepoort Moslem Club. They testified that because Uncle Ahmed and another Indian male person were busy in the kitchen of the Roodepoort Club one Sunday evening they were asked to leave the premises.[183]

The state presented envelopes (Exhibit 101B, date stamp 3 August 1971) addressed to L. Kamohi and Kamohi Cash Store, which contained *Inkululeko* pamphlets, and led evidence that Moe's finger prints were found on both the envelopes. The date stamp confirms that mail was intercepted confirming the capacity of the security police to intercept mail.

Why was Moe's mail intercepted? Did the security police know of the relationship between Moe and Uncle Ahmed? Were Moe and Uncle Ahmed under surveillance?

A newspaper reported that a witness in the 'Essop trial' in Pretoria claimed that he was afraid of what the police might do to him.[184] The witness, Mr Naseem Pahad, also claimed that the police had been harassing him since February 1972.

Examined by Mr von Lieres for the state, Naseem confirmed that he had known Uncle Ahmed for a very long time.[185] He had met accused number 1, Salim Essop, sometime in 1971 with Uncle Ahmed and accused number 2, Yousuf Essack (Moe) in January 1971. Naseem had known Moe well as he had lodged with him in his flat from around January to December 1971. When asked about Moe's arrest and subsequent death of Uncle Ahmed and his relationship with Moe, Naseem's response was: 'Well, this is something from the questions that Captain Gloy put to me. I was able to recollect but I can't be 100% certain, but to the best of my knowledge the gist of it was that he worked with *Inkululeko* at my flat and at the Roodepoort Club. Naseem could not remember and was not certain if he heard this from Yusuf. Von Lieres persisted wanting to know if Naseem was told this by Moe and where was this. His response was, 'I think so, to the best of my knowledge, well from what I can remember and to the best of my knowledge, at my flat.'

Judge Snyman intervened and asked Naseem for clarity regarding 'to the best of my knowledge'. His response was that he had a lingering doubt as to the circumstances and all. I have not been able to recollect properly. Naseem continued, 'Captain Gloy gave me circumstances under which this had taken place. Captain Gloy mentioned to me that it was Saturday morning, the morning on which they raided Cajee's Commercial College that I was standing on the corner with Moe and thereafter we went up to our flat and it is then that Moe mentioned that to me.'

Naseem continued to testify irking Judge Snyman and Advocate Von Lieres with answers such as, 'well from what I can remember and to the best of my knowledge'. He confirmed that the gist of his conversation with Moe was that Moe worked at his flat with *Inkululeko* and also at the Roodepoort club. When asked by Von Lieres to recollect the exact words spoken by Moe about *Inkululeko*, Naseem responded that they had correlated *Inkululek*o at his flat and that he could not remember the actual discussions taking place.

Judge Snyman asked Naseem if he wanted to give evidence and his response was that he was subpoenaed to give evidence and that he was reluctant to give evidence. The judge was not impressed, 'You see, I don't want to waste my time or have my time wasted with a witness who is qualifying his evidence to such an extent that it is useless to the Court. You must make up your mind whether you want to give evidence or not. I am not here to compel you and nor will you be compelled in my court to give evidence.'

Advocate Browde intervened saying that Von Lieres must be confined to examining-in-chief and not to cross-examine. Judge

The first inquest

Snyman understood Von Lieres's difficulties and allowed him a certain amount of latitude. Von Lieres continued examining Naseem who stated that he received *Inkululeko* in the post sometime in June or July 1971 and added that he was not certain of himself. He confessed to His Lordship that he was afraid of the police as they had been harassing him since February when a statement was taken from him. Between four and five times they came to his place of employment. Naseem testified that he received a call from Van Tonder accusing him of having orgies at his flat while his wife was away.

During cross examination, Advocate Browde confirmed with Naseem that Captain Gloy had given facts to Naseem, 'painted a picture' and that he could not confirm if he had an independent recollection of facts or whether they came from Gloy or if he misunderstood what Moe had told him. Naseem concluded his testimony that maybe it was just a figment of his imagination.

Naseem's testimony was further pursued when Moe testified.[186]

Nöthling asked if Moe could explain Naseem's evidence. 'Well I think everybody makes a mistake sometimes is a fact and this must be one of his mistakes… I wouldn't know, but like I said because this is most probably what Captain Gloy suggested to him,' Moe responded.

> Nöthling: 'Yes, very well. Accept for a moment that Captain Gloy had asked him whether that did not happen. Is he the type of person who will simply say yes, it did happen, if it did not in fact happen?'
> Moe: 'Well he may have.'
> Nöthling: 'Is he that type of person?'
> Moe: 'Well where the security police are concerned, yes.'
> Nöthling: 'Why?'
> Moe: 'Well, everybody is afraid of the security police.'
> Nöthling: 'But was Mr Pahad ever detained by the security police?'

Moe: 'Not that I know of.'

Nöthling: 'Then why should Mr Pahad simply agree with everything that the security police says?'

Moe: 'Because he said so in this Court, he was afraid, the security police were harassing him.'

Nöthling: 'You think he would have been prepared to tell a lie like that?'

Moe: 'Well I wouldn't know.'

Naseem was adamant that the source of his information about *Inkululeko* and Uncle Ahmed was his lodger Moe. But he also said that this might have been a 'figment of his imagination'.

Dinesh Naik's testimony as a state witness incriminating Moe contributed to him been found guilty on the main count under the Terrorism Act. Naseem Pahad was subpoenaed to testify, meaning that he did not appear on his own free will, but was forced to do so. Captain Gloy coerced Naseem to a narrative on what had transpired about the *Inkululeko* pamphlets. What is unknown is if Dinesh and Naseem had been in contact with the Security Police prior to their testimonies sharing information on Uncle Ahmed's political activities.

Naseem's testimony at the Rodrigues criminal case will hopefully shed more light on his testimony during the Case of the Four in 1972. He will be testifying for the state and is listed as a witness on the indictment served on Rodrigues. It will be interesting to hear his testimony and get more clarity from his perspective on what transpired and his relationship with Uncle Ahmed. Hopefully, Naseem will provide context to the harassment he endured from Gloy and how he survived this ordeal for so many years.

Judgment on the Case of the Four[187] was handed down on 30 October 1972, a year after Uncle Ahmed's death. Judge Snyman convicted all four accused on the main count under the Terrorism Act. He found that it was unnecessary for the prosecution to establish whether that they had been in direct communication with one another. Anyone who conspired with an organisation to commit an offence became a conspirator with every individual who acted in the same way, he said. Judge Snyman added that it had become obvious to him during the trial that, as a result of the interrogation of the accused and the evidence of some state witnesses, a good deal of information and statements obtained by the police were prevented from being placed before him by reason of the law and rules of evidence.

Under the judges rule of evidence, an accused person had to be warned and informed of his rights before he could be questioned by the police. Any confession made had to be done freely and voluntarily. The Terrorism Act had given extraordinary powers to the police to extract information from a terrorist or an individual withholding information relating to terrorism, and prosecuting counsel was prevented from placing such evidence before the courts.

PART IV

The Second Inquest

X

Culture of torture

During the struggle against apartheid the ANC observed certain days to mark important past events. One of those days, 26 June, was called South African Freedom Day,[188] the day the Freedom Charter was adopted in 1955. It was also the day on which the Anti-Apartheid Movement was formed in 1959.

This is a red-letter day for me too; it was the day on which the inquest into my uncle's death was formally reopened in 2017. It was a turning point in the story of my journey to discover the truth about how Ahmed Timol died. It marked the first time that a death in custody of an anti-apartheid activist was to be re-examined in democratic South Africa.

It was almost exactly 45 years since the first inquest had ended with its devastating ruling of suicide. We had never accepted that finding and my family deserved to know the truth, just as much as anti-apartheid activists and the millions of South Africans who suffered under the system of racial oppression did. I also wanted Uncle Ahmed's legacy to be corrected and safeguarded.[189]

I was excited, but anxious to attend a court hearing for the first time in my life. My years of battling to have my uncle's inquest reopened had not been in vain. I had left my home in Pretoria that winter morning with my bag packed. I was to stay with my cousins, Yusuf and Fatima Vania, in Mayfair so I would not have to commute from Pretoria to the South Gauteng High Court in Johannesburg. The month of Ramadan had ended the day before and we were celebrating

Eid al-Fitr (the end of fasting celebrations). I parked my car at my cousin's house and performed the Eid prayers at the Mayfair Jumma Masjid.

I could hardly believe that it had been 11 years since I had first requested the National Prosecuting Authority to reopen the Ahmed Timol case. I showed them a note in my uncle's TRC file reporting that investigator Piers Pigou had been told by João Rodrigues's daughter that the police version of what happened to my uncle was not true.

The early years had been tough on me, reflected in this internal prosecuting authoritiy memorandum I had seen:

> 2.2.1 Death in detention Ahmed Timol. This death in detention matter goes back to 1971. The nephew of the deceased requested that an allegation that one of the police officers who had interrogated the deceased had confessed to a journalist be investigated. The DSO traced and interviewed the journalist who denied the allegation. There was no evidence to prove that the deceased had definitely been murdered and other crimes had prescribed. The matter was therefore closed.[190]

I wrote to the National Director of Public Prosecutions, Bulelani Ngcuka, in December 2003 informing him that my uncle's main interrogators, Captain Johannes Hendrik 'Hans' Gloy and Captain Zacharia van Niekerk, were still alive. 'Persons who failed to apply for amnesty are liable for prosecution. None of the persons involved in the Timol case applied for amnesty,' I added. 'I have established that some of these policemen have died whilst others are still alive. I hereby request your office to re-investigate the Timol case as I feel sufficient evidence exists indicating that Timol did not commit suicide, but was murdered.' I concluded by informing him that I was sending a copy of this letter to the Minister in the Presidency, the Minister of Intelligence and the Minister of Safety and Security respectively, in view of the important issues at stake in this case. No one has ever responded to this correspondence.

Some five years later, in 2009, I contacted Yasmin Sooka, a former commissioner at the Truth and Reconciliation Commission. While she was keen on meeting me, I did not feel ready. The 13 years in which I had been struggling to get the inquest reopened had taken its toll and I simply did not have the energy.

It would be another six years before we finally met and began working together. Sooka quickly found core funding and established a team, which included human rights lawyer Advocate Howard Varney; the private investigator Frank Dutton and former TRC investigator Piers Pigou. Moray Hathorn from Webber Wentzel, a Johannesburg law firm, agreed to work pro bono. In them I found people of integrity to help light the way.

Our initial goals were to reverse the inquest findings into the deaths in detention of my uncle and Dr Neil Aggett, medical doctor and trade unionist. They had died at the notorious John Vorster Square 11 years apart. Sooka and her team had been in contact with the Aggett family and Dutton had already conducted some investigations around his death. Aggett[191] was an organiser of the Transvaal branch of the African Food and Canning Workers' Union when he was detained under the Terrorism Act on 11 December 1981, initially at the Pretoria Central Prison. On 5 February 1982, 70 days after he was arrested, he was found hanging in a cell at John Vorster Square while in the custody of the South African Police.

The police claimed that Aggett, aged 28, the first white activist to have died in police detention, had killed himself. He was the 51st person to have died in detention in South Africa since the 1963 introduction of the 90-day detention law. He was also the fifth political captive to die at John Vorster Square.

Workers from various trade unions had downed tools on 11 February 1982 in solidarity with Aggett and in protest against his death.[192] An estimated 15 000 people attended his funeral.

On 19 January 2016, a year after my initial meeting with Sooka, our team, bolstered by the presence of South Africa's most celebrated human rights lawyer Advocate George Bizos SC, made a presentation to the National Prosecuting Authority. Gathered at their Pretoria office for that meeting were the National Director of Public

Prosecution Advocate Shaun Abrahams, Senior Deputy Director of Public Prosecutions Nomgcobo Jiba and Senior Deputy Director of Public Prosecutions Dr Torie Pretorius. Varney and Dutton told them we wanted the inquest reopened because the security branch's claim that they had treated Ahmed Timol with care and consideration was untrue.[193] There was prima facie evidence that he was tortured and that important witnesses were not made available to the 1972 inquest. Our contention was that, if this evidence had been presented, it was likely that the inquest court would have arrived at a different finding.

Jiba undertook to instruct the police to conduct additional investigations to allow the NPA to make a decision about whether to recommend to the Minister of Justice that the inquest be reopened. At that time, three former Security Branch officers involved in my uncle's case, Neville Els, Seth Sons and João Rodrigues, were still alive. They were not located and interviewed. Jiba, however, recommended to the Minister of Justice and Correctional Services that the inquest be reopened due to the new evidence presented by our team. This comprised of an affidavit by Salim Essop of his horrendous torture at the hands of the security police. If it had been possible for him to testify at the 1972 inquest, he would have provided a powerful contradictory view on the conduct of the security police.

Minister Michael Masutha forwarded the recommendation to the Judge President of the Gauteng Division of the High Court of South Africa, Judge President D. Mlambo who, in turn, designated a judge to reopen and preside over the inquest proceedings.[194]

On 25 October, the day before it was announced to the public, I received a call from Advocate Shaun Abrahams who told me the inquest would be reopened. Advocate Abrahams must be commended for taking the decision to reopen the inquest. I was ecstatic. As always, I thanked the Almighty for having given me the strength and patience to continue to pursue my aim.

The Ahmed Timol Family Trust issued a press release on 26 October 2016:

'BREAKTHROUGH IN AHMED TIMOL CASE 45 YEARS AFTER HIS DEATH IN POLICE CUSTODY – NPA agrees to reopen inquest into death of Ahmed Timol.' It said, inter alia, that the National Prosecuting Authority believed there was 'compelling evidence' to reopen the inquest.[195]

On the morning of 27 October 2016, 45 years exactly after my uncle died, I was at O.R. Tambo International Airport waiting to board a flight to East London. The Steve Biko Foundation was hosting the Ahmed Timol Exhibition and I had been invited to speak at the opening. During a radio interview, I was asked about the announcement that the inquest would be reopened. Did I really believe it? My response was that I always had faith that it would be reopened.

For the first time in South Africa, 23 years after the advent of democracy, a High Court judge would reconsider the findings of an inquest that probed the death in detention of an anti-apartheid activist. I was confident that the truth would emerge.

I had operated solo for years and had only started working with Sooka's team the previous year. Now we all threw ourselves into preparations for the inquest, including following up with witnesses and obtaining their affidavits. The inquest commenced on 16 July 2017 but a few weeks prior to this, I was politely informed that as a client in the proceedings I needed to exclude myself from the team. My involvement could raise objections and precautions needed to be taken to ensure that no technicalities could be raised during proceedings.

Generous donations made to the Ahmed Timol Family Trust, allowed me to hire Adil Bradlow, an award-winning television cameraman, to film the entire inquest. Enver Samuel, the director of the documentary *Indians Can't Fly*, would also be filming at the hearing. Justice Billy Mothle was to preside over the reopened inquest at the South Gauteng High Court. A few weeks later it moved to the North Gauteng High Court in Pretoria which had a bigger court room available. I was delighted as the change of venue meant I could stay in my own home and not worry about travelling to or making sleeping arrangements in Johannesburg.

Varney, with Musatondwa 'Musa' Musandiwa as his learned junior, represented the Timol family. Varney was instructed by Moray

Hathorn of Webber Wentzel Attorneys assisted by Marcia Haffejee, Michelle Sithole, Sicelo Blose and Kukhanya Msomi, and from the Legal Resources Centre (LRC) by Naseema Fakir assisted by Mutondi Mulaudzi.

The National Prosecuting Authority was represented by Senior Deputy Director of Public Prosecution Dr Torie Pretorius, Advocate Jabulani Malotwa and Advocate Shubnum Singh. Advocate Connie Lithole was appointed as a watching brief on behalf of SAPS. I am eternally grateful to the former director general of the SSA, Arthur Fraser, for granting me special leave to attend court proceedings. He understood the importance of my journey in preserving Uncle Ahmed's legacy and my fight for truth and justice.

On day one, Judge Mothle authorised the issuing of subpoenas to order all police officers who were involved in the arrest and interrogation of Uncle Ahmed and Salim to testify. He ruled further that they be represented by the state attorney.[196] This meant that Els, Sons and Rodrigues were now compelled to give evidence at the inquest. Advocate Stephanus Johannes Coetzee, from the High Court Chambers of the Pretoria Bar, was instructed to represent the former police officers and was present in court with Mr Ben Minnaar from the state attorney's office. Minnaar subsequently resigned and is now representing Rodrigues in his criminal case.

'There is no doubt in my mind that during these proceedings we, as South Africans, are about to enter a door that will rekindle painful memories,' said Judge Mothle in his opening remarks. 'A door that invites us to embark on a journey which will cause all of us to confront the sordid part of our history. That door will only close, once the truth is revealed.'[197]

Varney said that not only should the legal profession hang its collective head in shame,[198] but that South Africa had largely abandoned the Timol family and so many other families of victims of apartheid era atrocities.

> Why did these families have to wait 45 years for this day? Why had the promises of the constitutional compact to victims not

been met? Why have virtually all the cases from the past been abandoned by the authorities? Why did the Timol family have to move heaven and earth to get this inquest off the ground? In particular, why had the real decision makers behind police atrocities and death squads not have to face justice? Why have pitiful reparations been handed out to apartheid era victims and why have the vast majority been excluded all together from any benefit, simply because they were unable to get to see statements taken from the TRC?

Varney concluded[199] that Uncle Ahmed had given his young life for South Africa's democracy with its enshrined freedoms.

He was a selfless man who sought no riches or advantage for himself. The family lost a beloved son and brother. His girlfriend Ruth Longoni lost a soul mate. Ahmed's comrades lost a gentle freedom fighter. A man who was always there for them. South Africa lost a visionary young man who could have helped us through our troubled journey. We owe it to the family and friends and comrades to uncover the real truth of what happened to Ahmed Timol. But most of all we owe it to Timol himself.

Pretorius noted the historic status of the case, which he called 'legal precedent'.

Captain Ben Nel, the investigating officer in the Timol case, testified that he had traced the whereabouts of the other police officers involved in the case and confirmed that only three of the 30 directly involved in his arrest, detention, torture and assault, were still alive. They were Neville Els, Seth Sons and João Rodrigues.[200] He did not mention how Rodrigues was located probably because his daughter, Tilana Stander, had contacted me directly.

All the known members of my uncle's interrogation team, some of whom I had tracked down and spoken to over the years, had died. I had practically begged Gloy,[201] to come clean and clear his conscience while he still could. I told him that we were not seeking vengeance, but the truth – that I was not on a mission to see him locked up in jail. But he chose to take his secrets to his grave.

The judge's job was not eased by the fact that more than half the records of the original inquest proceedings had mysteriously vanished, including the cross-examination of security police witnesses and photographs. Fortunately the portion of the record that remained, included the 77-page judgment, quoting what the magistrate would have regarded as the most salient details of the police's evidence.

By the time the second inquest convened, I was confident that we had accumulated the body of evidence necessary to undermine the key foundations of Magistrate de Villiers's judgment and prove, beyond reasonable doubt, that my uncle was murdered.

We were convinced that the security police's story was a fabrication. My uncle was not arrested at a random police roadblock on the evening of 22 October 1971. The allegation that the Communist Party had instructed its cadres to commit suicide, rather than to betray their comrades was a blatant lie. It was the norm for political detainees to be routinely tortured and assaulted. The testimony of detainees and affidavits of other activists would confirm this. My uncle was so severely assaulted before his death that he may have been unconscious when he fell from the window. Had he committed suicide and dived out of the window as described by the police, his body would not have landed just a few metres from the building. It would be our case that he had not committed suicide, but was murdered by the police.

Dr Salim Essop had come from London to testify at the inquest. He was the first of several witnesses to tell the court of their experiences under torture. His account of being gruesomely tortured at John Vorster Square after being arrested with Uncle Ahmed drew gasps from the gallery during his three days of testimony from 26 to 28 June 2017.[202] He also identified uncaptioned photocopied photographs of members of the South African Police in a Security Branch Officer Identity Photograph Album.

Three days after his arrest, while Uncle Ahmed was still under interrogation, Salim was admitted to hospital in a coma. He told Judge Mothle:

By this stage Kleyn had already managed to pick, to pull out tufts of my hair, my hair was relatively long you know, growing over my ears. This guy does it even more viciously, the tufts of my hair are coming out and I can see my hair on the ground ... And then he throws me, he literally lifts me, he was a strong guy, bigger than me, far bigger, probably maybe close to six feet or maybe you know even more ... And once he had thrown me to the ground, landing on my head and this is devastating. Right, then he comes back to these knocks like on my face. At one stage he gives me such a knock here on my right side, just on my temple here, it is devastating. I am actually – my eyes started to go and I cannot see now in my right eye. My vision is gone. And I am just wondering, and I was a medical student, I am just wondering ... God, has my ... you know eyeball become dislocated, has the nerve, you know, going into my eyes ... you know become separated and I am absolutely worried and I am in terrible pain already.[203]

Salim told the court that on the third day of his interrogation he was convinced that he saw Uncle Ahmed for the last time. 'This is when I last caught a fleeting sight of Timol. He had a black hood placed over his head and was being dragged along by two Security Branch officers.' He said that he knew immediately that this was his friend and comrade – he recognised his physique and his height. What he saw alarmed him, 'He was not able to walk normally and was being held up by security officers on either side of him who were holding onto the sides of his trunk. I got the impression that the Security Branch had 'worked on him' in the same manner as they had on me, perhaps with even greater savagery.'

Salim said that he had assumed that they had taken my uncle to the toilet and were walking him back from the bathroom. It was, 'probably the same toilet that I was also taken to a few times to urinate and wash the blood off my body, and this may have been a reason they had taken Timol to the toilet. Although I could not be [a] hundred percent certain, I believe that the day I saw Timol was Monday,

25 October 1971.' Imagine if he had been able to testify at the first inquest? He said, 'Even today, when I reflect on my last sighting of him I feel a sense of overwhelming sadness knowing that the Security Branch probably singled him out for the most vicious and sadistic treatment.'[204]

Before Salim continued with his testimony on Tuesday, 27 June 2017, Judge Mothle informed the court that someone attending the proceedings had came forward to say that his brother had also been detained and had been thrown out of the building.[205] He asked Advocate Pretorius to investigate the matter further. I established that it was Lasch Mabelane who came forward referring to the death of his brother Matthews Mabelane who was held for 25 days at John Vorster Square. He died on 25 February 1977 at the age of 23. His inquest concluded, 'Cause or likely cause of death: MULTIPLE INJURIES – Sustained by the deceased while questioned by police jumping through a window and walking along a ledge on the outside of the building at the tenth floor losing his balance and falling to the ground below – Accidental. Nobody was responsible for his death'.[206]

Despite Judge Mothle's request on 27 June 2017, there has been no progress on the investigation on the death of Matthews Mabelane. His father, Phillip aged 96, passed away in May 2018 hoping that the mystery around his son's death would be explained, and that the people responsible, for what he believed was his son's murder, would be brought to justice.[207]

Later in the day, an *in loco* inspection took place at the Johannesburg Central police station, formerly John Vorster Square. During the tour of the scene of the crime led by Salim, he described to Judge Mothle and the legal teams his recollection of events during his ordeal.

Professor Kantilal Naik[208] had earlier testified on Thursday, 28 June 2017 at the South Gauteng High Court in Johannesburg that he knew Uncle Ahmed as they were both from Roodepoort and had both taught at the same school. Naik was arrested on 23 October 1971 and was taken to John Vorster Square where he was was tortured by the so-called helicopter technique until he suffered paralysis of his hands. He described his agony:

They had actually, tied my hands like this and put the thing over the knees and then they put a broomstick in between where, you know, you could actually put the broomstick in such a way that, you know, you are hanging and they started rotating … it actually went [on] for quite a while, I would say between one to two hours. And with that, you know, I mean the hands got totally immobilised.[209]

He said in an affidavit to the court that the police had instilled in him such fear that he was too afraid to talk to people after his release. The worst torture for him was that people suspected him of being an informer.

My uncle Mohammad[210] testified on Thursday, 28 June 2017 about the training he received in London before his return to South Africa. This comprised political and security training, as well as instructions in the production and distribution of leaflets, including through bucket bombs. He described the leaflet bomb as 'a plastic bucket with a small explosive device, with a timing mechanism in a small platform inside the bucket'. Activists would place the buckets in carrier bags and ignite them in areas of high pedestrian traffic.[211]

He then described his return to South Africa and Uncle Ahmed's insistence that he leave for Durban after discovering that they were both under police surveillance, and then his arrest by security police in Durban on 25 October 1971. He described being in the holding room and then being taken to an office on one of the floors of the building. A group of between three and five security policemen arrived and caught him completely unwares. They were telling him, 'We have got you, we have got your brother, we have got the big fish and we have got all of you. Right, now is the time to sing!'[212] They wanted to know what he was doing in London and who he met upon his return to South Africa. As he tried to respond, he was told that he was talking lies.

A brick was placed in front of me, I was not made to sit at all, a brick was placed on the ground, a brick was there, a brick was placed on the ground, I was made to stand on the brick and then I was given two telephone directories and told to hold them up and I had to stand on the brick ... I got punched in the face, I got smacked, I got kicked and this continued on and off. It continued for hours on end, different questions, interrogation continued, until about 11 o'clock that night, that was the Monday night ... Between standing on this brick and holding up the telephone directories ... you can only keep it up to a certain point, and then made to sit on an imaginary chair. Actually you are sitting on a chair which is not there, in a squatting position, and if you relaxed you got kicked, you got beaten up, you got smacked, you had to sit up again, sit on the imaginary chair – and there would be laughter around and they continue. They just continued.[213]

At around 11 pm that evening, Uncle Mohammad was taken to the Berea police station and locked up for the night. 'It gave me time to try and recollect what happened the last 12 hours ... I also had training in interrogation methods and what happens during interrogation. So I was not sure if Ahmed was arrested or not, right?' He said he had tried to hold on for as long as he was able. One of his thoughts was that, following his training, if Uncle Ahmed had was not yet been arrested [it] would give him time to get away.[214]

The following morning, Uncle Mohammad was collected by the security police and taken to Fisher Street. 'This was around 8 am, 8.30 am when the usual interrogation started. There would be three or four guys, they would change, other guys would come – and standing on a brick and hitting me in the stomach'. At some point, he broke under interrogation. 'I could not take the beating up and I told them that I had received training and that somebody was supposed to have contacted me, but that did not happen, right?'

He worked out that what was important for his interrogators was the identity of the people he was in contact with in South Africa.

These were all innocent people, these were my relatives, my friends ... And I mentioned whoever I could remember, I mentioned them and subsequently I learnt each and every person that I mentioned was caught by the security police or the security police had interviewed them, to corroborate my story. That was on Tuesday, it continued till about 11 o'clock Tuesday night as well.

On Wednesday, 27 October, on the third day of his arrest – at about 6 pm – the interrogation suddenly stopped. Uncle Mohammad was informed that his brother had died and that he was not permitted to attend the funeral. He did not know if it was true, or if he was being deliberately misinformed to break his resistance. On Friday, on the way from his police cell to the security police offices, he saw a newspaper poster, 'Death plunge, Vorster speaks'. In the lift, an Indian policeman expressed his condolences – but still he could not be sure.

After a month in custody, Uncle Mohammad was transferred from Durban to John Vorster Square where he was held for three months in solitary confinement. He was released on 13 March 1972. Before leaving the building, he was interviewed by a detective, Major Fick. 'They wanted to know whether Ahmed had any tendencies of suicide, they wanted to know whether he had any mental problems,' Uncle Mohammad said. 'It was basically such questions and then they took me home. It was the CID that took me home and my mother, everyone, was surprised when I was released.'[215]

Uncle Mohammad told Judge Mothle:

Ahmed died a week before his 30th birthday. He had a whole life in front of him and he did not have to leave England. He had a girlfriend that he introduced me to, and I met her on numerous occasions – and she has kept in touch with us in this 45 years. She married after Ahmed's death. Ahmed enjoyed his stay in the UK, he enjoyed his teaching, but the calling, the calling to the return to South Africa during the most difficult days of Apartheid … and in a small way, begin the process of building the underground resistance movement against the Apartheid system. Because, post-Rivonia, the trial, the

Mandela and Sisulu trial, both the trial of Braam Fisher and others, underground activities had virtually come to a stand and the resistance against Apartheid came to a standstill. So, Ahmed, for him it was a calling.[216]

Varney asked Uncle Mohammad if, during the training he received in the United Kingdom about dealing with interrogation, he was ever advised to commit suicide rather than to betray others. He said his instructions had been that in the event of arrest, he had to hang on for as long as he could. The longer he held out, the interrogators would not get information on other members of his unit. This would give them time to get away. At no point was he told to commit suicide or to take his own life. It was well understood that for a political operative fighting against apartheid, arrest meant going to jail.[217]

Dr Dilshad Jetham was the last witness to testify on Friday, 30 June 2017. She had attended school at Roodepoort Indian High School where Salim was her contemporary and Uncle Ahmed had been her History teacher. She was arrested on the 23 October 1971, a day after Uncle Ahmed. She told the court:

> Initially it was just the one fellow smacking me and then the other – and then they took turns. Somewhere along the line, because I think I had drank water when I broke my fast in Greyling's office, I needed to relieve myself and I asked to go to the bathroom. They would not let me. I still feel the pain, I still feel the humiliation, I still feel awful when I think of urine running down my legs. Here I was, a decently brought up young lady, at medical school, and this happening to me, it was humiliating. They thought this was a huge joke.[218]

Early in the morning on Uncle Ahmed's last day of life, 27 October 1971, Dilshad said she overheard a prisoner screaming under the pain of torture – then, suddenly, the screaming stopped.

When that screaming stopped, it was so sudden, I kind of

thought to myself, 'Ah, poor devil'. Anyway, suddenly there was a lot of ... somebody came into our office and there was a sort of hive of activity on that floor and there were people running up and down the corridor. The office door, the office in which I was, was left open for people were going in and out. The reason I know the time is I would guess about 30 to 40 minutes after this event occurred, the morning call to prayer went out.[219]

Dilshad is convinced that it was the last assault on Uncle Ahmed that she heard.

Stephanie Kemp, my former colleague from the Alexandra Health Centre testified on 24 July 2017. She had worked for the South African Communist Party and the British Anti-Apartheid Movement in London during her 24 years of exile from 1966 to 1990. She was responsible for facilitating secret communications between London and Uncle Ahmed after his return to South Africa. She told Judge Mothle of her experience under arrest in 1964:

He started hitting me, on both sides of my head ... and then he grabbed me, I had long hair then, he grabbed me by my hair and pulled me down to the floor and bashed my head on the floor until I was unconscious. Then I woke up, I was incoherent so there was no way they could take a statement from me. I do not, in any case believe that that was the purpose of all this. They appeared to have as much information as I could get [sic] them. Some of the leading people in this organisation had already made statements. I think they wanted me to give evidence for the state but ... there is a feeling they just want to break you, to control you, to have complete power over you.[220]

Former security policeman Paul Erasmus testified on 24 July 2017 and referred to a culture of torture that he had seen. 'When I joined as a young security policeman ... I witnessed the first torture that I ever saw ... on the tenth floor at John Vorster Square where this man's testicles, and I ask forgiveness if I can give any details, were being crushed by Colonel Cronwright, who was then Major Cronwright.'

What had struck him most was 'the severity of this attack and I often wondered if I would be called on to do things like that … I think one either had the stomach for it or you did not. My own role was, I would say, more common assault or creating a fear factor by slaps and stuff like that.'

He confirmed that, 'Yes, torture was standard procedure and the basis of this was sleep deprivation if there was time permitting.' Police would ensure that detainees would be given meals at irregular times to confuse their body clocks. 'And then of course – like you see in the movies – there is always the good guy, bad guy.' Erasmus described how 'one guy would go in there and beat the hell out of the detainee and two minutes later a gentle soul would come in and say, "No man, you cannot carry on like this, you are going to die in this place. Just tell me this".'

XI

A different picture

Evidence at the 2017 inquest created a different picture of the police interrogation from what Gloy and Van Niekerk had portrayed in the first inquest.[221] Both security policemen had been accused of assaulting detainees before the Timol-Essop detention in 1971. In May 1960, Van Niekerk had been convicted on two counts of assault where a detainee later died from his wounds. Complaints had also been filed against Gloy for assaulting detainees in 1970 and 1971.

The 1971 inquest's depiction of how police handled detainees continued to unravel as the testimony by various expert witnesses built a totally different case. Professor Don Foster had served three times as the head of the Department of Psychology at the University of Cape Town over the course of an illustrious career of over four decades. He has published books and more than 160 academic papers. In the 1980s, Foster led an empirical research project on the psychological consequences of security legislation in South Africa, particularly pertaining to the holding of political detainees for interrogation. 'I was a psychologist, it was apparent that psychological techniques were being used in security-related detention, and it became incumbent on us to hear from detainees themselves what psychological and physical aspects pertained to their experience of detention,'[222] the professor told Judge Mothle on 27 June 2017.

His research covered the decade from 1974 to 1984, and involved interviewing 158 individuals, some of whom were detained more than once. The project culminated in 1987 with the publication of the book, *Detention and Torture in South Africa: Psychological, Legal and Historical Studies* – written by Foster, with the assistance of Dennis Davis and researcher, Diane Sandler.

Foster elaborated on what he termed the closed system of detention.[223] He said it was founded on three key points: Firstly, that detainees had no legal recourse and lawyers had no recourse to access their detained clients. Secondly, detainees were entirely at the mercy of the security system, not only the security police but also the handful of doctors and other personnel that served their needs. They could be held incommunicado for lengthy periods, which could be renewed. In other words, they could be held virtually indefinitely without ever being brought before a court. And thirdly, detainees felt enormously vulnerable in such a situation. Very often they were held in solitary confinement or in places away from other detainees, without seeing anyone else besides their guards and interrogators.

Foster said that 83 per cent of the detainees interviewed reported being physically tortured in some way. The most common forms of torture reported were beatings, maintaining abnormal postures, like sitting in an imaginary chair, forced to do gym exercises, suspension, including the so-called helicopter method, bags on heads, electrocution, strangulation, starvation and sleep deprivation.[224]

Turning to psychological torture, the professor listed four categories: distorted communication, mental weakening, psychological terror and degradation. Distorted communication meant, for example, any form of lie meant to cause alarm to the detainee, such as threatening to harm family members or claiming to have obtained a statement containing damning evidence against him or her. Mental weakening, involved, for instance placing a gun to a detainee's head and threatening to pull the trigger. Psychological terror could be caused by unanticipated levels of physical brutality; and degradation was caused when, for instance, a detainee was forced to undress, to endure electric shocks to the genitals and being bitten by dogs.[225]

Foster said the study revealed that interrogation was conducted by relatively large teams of security police, working in relay. After an eight-hour stint, fresh interrogators would take over and the weary would take time off to rest. This ensured there was no rest for the detainees, who became increasingly exhausted and debilitated.[226] His testimony provided empirical evidence of systematic torture inflicted on political detainees. It was under these circumstances that interrogation took place and statements were taken from detainees and often used in court cases.

The testimonies of Salim Essop, Kantilal Naik, Uncle Mohammad, Dilshad Jetham and Stephanie Kemp support the argument about police brutality and torture. Their testimonies were bolstered by Paul Erasmus who had described the culture of torture within the security police. How was it possible that Ahmed Timol, leader of his underground cell, could not have been tortured?

Affidavits sworn to by activists who had been severely tortured in police detention were also submitted to the inquest. They did not testify, but their statements were crucial in exposing the culture of police torture of political detainees. They are Abdulhay Jassat, Snuki Zikalala, Shanti Tweedie, Gadija Chothia, Laloo Chiba and Peter Magubane.

The first witness to testify at the North Gauteng High Court in Pretoria on Monday, 24 July 2017 was Advocate Ernest Matthis,[227] who was living in retirement in KwaZulu-Natal. He had contacted me through my website on 30 July 2016 in response to my post about the 'Breakthrough' in the Ahmed Timol case, the news that the inquest was to be reopened.[228] He wrote: 'I am a retired advocate. I saw Ahmed Timol fall to his death from John Vorster Square and I am willing to testify at a reopened inquest.' I immediately made this information available to the legal team.

Matthis was involved in the prosecution of a client named A.N. Kramer of Auto Protection and was at John Vorster Square police station either on the fourth or sixth floor on the day my uncle died. He testified that he had been standing a distance from the window, 'And I saw a person fall ... he landed in a prone position with his arm bended beyond his head. I looked up and I could not see anything, I could not see an open window. I saw him lying about a metre and a half from the building, in a prone position'. He said that he did not see any police rushing to the body or any indication that an ambulance had been called. He said that he was unsure of the time of the fall but would guess that it was in the morning.

He then telephoned a member of parliament, Harry Schwartz, and informed him of what he had seen. Schwartz told him that this announcement would cause some consternation in government ranks.

Muhammed Ali Thokan,[229] a businessman, testified on 3 August 2017. He told the court he was at a petrol station called Dollars, directly across from John Vorster Square police station on the morning of Wednesday, 27 October 1971 when he heard a loud thud. He was uncertain as to where exactly it had come from, but he heard from a pedestrian that a person had fallen from John Vorster Square. As he walked across to the police station, he saw police officers coming out of the building and quickly cordoning off the area. He was aggressively chased away. Thokan later read in the newspapers that the deceased was Ahmed Timol.

Abdullah Mohammed Adam,[230] a bookkeeper who worked at Dollars garage, testified on Thursday, 10 August 2017 that at around tea time, 10.15 am on 27 October 1971, he was informed by his boss that there was some commotion taking place across the street. When he walked over, he saw a body lying on the shrubs. He had joined a crowd which was looking at the body when the police chased them from the scene. He later read in the newspaper that the dead body lying on the shrubs was that of Ahmed Timol.

The testimonies of these three independent witnesses – Matthis, Thokan and Adam – confirmed that a body had fallen at John Vorster Square in the morning. None of them had been asked to testify at the 1972 inquest. This calls into question the security police's version of events that the fall had taken place in the afternoon. How could there be such a huge time difference? Was this coincidental or planned?

Collin Woodall Savage, an architect, testified on 3 August 2017 about the original plans of the exterior and landscaping of the outside of John Vorster Square, which were drawn up in the early 1960s. He confirmed that there had been no significnt change to Room 1026 since then.

A different picture

Professor Ken Boffard, a surgeon who had received extra training in trauma surgery, took the stand on Tuesday, 25 July 2017. He testified[231] that during the period 1966–1973, when he was studying medicine at the University of the Witwatersrand, he also worked for the Sandton and Johannesburg Ambulance Services. He said that in the 1960s and 1970s, ambulance personnel were primarily drivers who were trained in first aid to an advanced level. He confirmed that the South African Police, on the other hand, were trained only in very basic first aid. All first aid training recognised the severity and danger of neck injuries in patients who fell from heights or were involved in motor vehicle accidents. The recommendation, at the time, was that a badly injured patient was not to be moved until an ambulance arrived.

Uncle Ahmed was badly injured yet, according to Deysel's testimony in the first inquest, he had rolled him onto two blankets. Then, after he had noticed a light pulse, my uncle was transferred to the foyer of John Vorster Square where it was discovered there was no pulse and he was taken upstairs and pronounced dead.

The extent of his injuries, based on the report and the 1972 testimony of Dr Schepers, meant that he should have been rolled onto his side allowing him to breathe. Boffard added that it was critical that when a patient had fallen from a height, they should not be picked up by their arms and legs. They had to be rolled onto a board or stretcher to support their spine and bones. He concluded, that due to the type of injuries he had sustained, Timol should not have been moved until an ambulance arrived. The ambulance depot was close to the police station and could have got there quickly if it had been called.[232]

On the 11th day of the reopened inquest, forensic pathologists Dr Shakeera Holland and Dr Steve Naidoo testified. Working independently of each other, they reached a similar conclusion – Ahmed Timol was assaulted before he died. They had studied surviving photographs of his body, notes from the post mortem and medical references in the surviving portion of the 1972 inquest record.

In his testimony, Naidoo, a former chief specialist and Professor of Forensic Medicine at the University of KwaZulu-Natal in Durban, said:

I believe at the best scenario that the deceased was desperately ill. He would have hardly been in a position, if he was conscious that is, to be able to ambulate and walk to the window or get out of the chair, walk to the window, and even place an attempt to achieve that effort of heaving himself out – that is the best case scenario. He would not have been able to walk unaided with the ankle and calf injuries that I believe are ante mortem. At the worst-case scenario I believe that he would be ... prostrate or unconscious ... Rather than heaving himself out the window would he have been able to dive through? I think the Court will accept that my opinion would be that ... unless assisted he would not have been able to dive through the window.[233]

Dr Holland, a senior specialist based at the Forensic Pathology Services in Gauteng and a Forensic Pathology lecturer at the University of the Witwatersrand, is responsible for conducting medico-legal investigations into unnatural deaths.

She listed many bruises – scabs, contusions, abrasions and fractures – that she said could not be associated with my uncle's fall. These included a depressed skull fracture that may have rendered him unconscious, three jaw fractures and a broken nose – injuries that would have made drinking coffee virtually impossible. The extent of the bruising on Timol's leg would have made it difficult for him to stand.

She told Judge Mothle:

The post-mortem findings indicate multiple fatal injuries consistent with a fall from a height. However, there are a number of injuries that are not consistent with a fall from a height. The implication is that these injuries must have been present prior to the fatal fall and that the injuries were sustained during the time that the deceased was in police custody, which include the following as previously discussed: The multiple diffuse well defined patterned bruises. The multiple external wounds with scab formation. Histological analysis on the wounds indicate that there were many wounds that were sampled which were estimated to be 4–6 days old which confirm that these wounds were present before the fall from a height. The multiple facial fractures that do not appear to be related to the base of skull fractures sustained in the fall. The isolated depressed skull fracture, which is rare in a fall from a height. A tear of the soft tissues around the hyoid bone a fracture of the first rib.[234]

In concluding her testimony, Dr Holland said that the multiple injuries that were present on my uncle could not be ascribed to the fall from a height. These injuries indicated that he sustained physical assault while in police custody before his death.

These findings call into question the conclusion of the original inquest process that the manner of death was suicide. How could independent pathologists come to the same conclusion that there were 27 ante mortem wounds inflicted on Uncle Ahmed's body and that they were caused by assault? During inquests held in the apartheid era about deaths in police detention, state pathologists covered up the extent of injuries inflicted. There was routine open collusion at the time that gave the security police carte blanche to continue torturing political detainees with impunity.

Tivesh Moodley, an aeronautical engineer who specialises in trajectory calculations, testified on Friday, 28 July 2017 that if a fully fit Ahmed Timol had jumped from the tenth floor window, as police claimed, he would have landed 13 metres from the face of the building. If he had stepped through the window he would have landed four metres from the building. He said:

> The distances are beyond what the police versions are claiming – 3 metres – as well as [what] his orientation and direction would be ... he would be landing leg first and his head would probably have fallen forward because he had a horizontal force pushing him forward, so his head would lay in the direction of the road and his legs would lay in the direction of the building. So, in the complete opposite direction of what Deysel found him.[235]

Another scenario Moodley described was that if my uncle had been pushed from the window from a seated position on the edge, facing in or out, his body would have landed between 3 to 3.1 metres from the building. If he was thrown off the roof above the tenth floor he would have landed 4 metres away from the building and he was rolled off the roof, he would have landed 1.25 metres from the building, he said. If he was carried to the window, his legs carried out and then the rest of his body pushed, he would have landed 3.1 metres from the building.

Moodley's calculations led him to conclude that my uncle was either pushed out from the tenth-floor window, or off the roof immediately above it. This is the most likely explanation as his body landed approximately 3 metres from the building. If he had jumped or dived, he would have landed much further from the building.

Frank Dutton joined the South African Police in 1966 and worked as a detective from 1971. In 1992, he led the team investigating political violence in KwaZulu-Natal on behalf of the Goldstone Commission into public violence and intimidation before South Africa's first democratic election in 1994. In 1996 he was seconded to the United Nations International Criminal Tribunal to investigate war crimes and crimes against humanity in Bosnia and Croatia. He has received South Africa's highest honour, the Order of Baobab, in recognition of his police work in the country and abroad.

After retiring as a policeman, when he led South Africa's elite crime fighting unit The Scorpions from 1999 to 2004, he has worked as a consultant and was one of the professionals Yasmin Sooka brought onto the team to fight for justice for Ahmed Timol and Neil Aggett.

Dutton told Judge Mothle on Thursday, 27 July 2017 that his review of available literature on Ahmed Timol's death bore all the hallmarks of a police cover-up. The police did not follow their own administrative procedure by conducting an internal investigation into what was clearly a major incident, the crime scene investigation was totally inadequate and key witnesses were not called to testify at the inquest. In addition, the head of detectives in Pretoria, General C.A. Buys, who led the police investigation for the inquest, demonstrated his lack of objectivity by telling *Rapport* newspaper right at the beginning of his investigation that Timol had committed suicide.[236]

He testified that there had been a detention order issued for Uncle Ahmed and Salim which specified that both of them were to be held in the cells at John Vorster Square. However, they were held illegally in offices on the tenth floor, which allowed the security police to torture them, including depriving them of sleep.

> And if one examines the reason for that, one can only come to the conclusion it was for reasons of torture and it was for reasons of sleep deprivation. Because, instead of putting two guards at night as Gloy and Van Niekerk say they did to guard the prisoner, who slept on a mattress, they could quite easily have just taken him down a couple of storeys and lodged them in the police cells and it would have been a very easy way to deal with it. But the reason they couldn't do that is because they were beating these men. They knew that if they took them to the cells, the person in charge of the cells would see their injuries and it was practice as well, that at least once a day, an officer had to visit the cells. He would see the injuries and he may even have ordered that these people be taken to the doctor. And I am not saying that was a foolproof system. It was far from a foolproof system. But it created an element of risk for them, so they kept them on the tenth floor.[237]

Dutton said that, in his view, the alleged secret agent, referred to as 'Mr X' at the 1972 inquest, who interrupted Uncle Ahmed's interrogation to inform his interrogators of a breakthrough in the search for the Jacobsen brothers – the development that police say triggered his decision to commit suicide – was a police concoction. He could find no evidence of a connection between Timol and Quentin Jacobsen, and Timol had not featured in the evidence at Quentin Jacobsen's subsequent trial.[238]

Further evidence, supporting his view that the police covered up the facts about Uncle Ahmed's death, emerged from the contents of the police file on Sergeant João Rodrigues, the lowly police clerk who claimed to have been alone in the room with Uncle Ahmed in the last minutes of his life. Rodrigues had bought his discharge from the police on 5 June 1972, having managed, in his 16-year career, to climb just one step up the police hierarchy from constable to sergeant.

He was an administrative clerk based at police headquarters in Pretoria. There was nothing in his file that indicated any special achievements; on the contrary, he had taken a large amount of sick leave. Yet on 20 June, two days before Magistrate De Villiers delivered his judgment exonerating the police, Rodrigues had received a letter of commendation from National Commissioner General Joubert which read, 'Your conduct has been determined as exemplary. The achievements of this distinguish [sic] is proof that you always served with an unblemished record in a faithful and competent manner'. [239]

In his whole career in the South African Police he had hardly come across many instances of the commissioner providing a letter of commendation, Dutton told Judge Mothle. If such a letter was issued, it was normally done at a provincial or district level.

> So that would be the first point. But the second one that I find curious with [sic] this is that Mr Rodrigues joined the SAP on 9th February 1956, and on 27th June 1956 he was convicted of statutory perjury for contravening Section 9 of Act 16 of 1914 and given a suspended sentence for five years, provided he was not again convicted of an offence involving dishonesty.

Rodrigues's certificate of service described his career as 'exemplary' but Dutton said that, in his experience, very few members of the police received such a glowing report. His conclusion was that Rodrigues was specially commended for his role in my uncle's case.

Finally, he informed the court about a number of files he had perused on a visit to John Vorster Square. These included references to previous allegations of torture and assault against security policemen involved in Uncle Ahmed's interrogation – Captain J.Z. van Niekerk and a Captain Gloy.

Advocate George Bizos SC testified on Wednesday, 28 June 2017.

A senior counsel at the Johannesburg Bar and employed at the Legal Resources Centre in Johannesburg, he placed Ahmed Timol's death in its appropriate historical and legal contexts. Bizos had been admitted to the Johannesburg Bar in 1954 and had represented victims of apartheid atrocities throughout his career. He had represented the Timol family as a junior advocate at the 1972 inquest, and is a hugely respected and widely beloved member of his profession.

He presented Judge Mothle's court with overviews of South Africa's security laws, detention, deaths in detention and inquest hearings, facts and figures, and analyses drawn from his deep well of experience. He said that inquests held in the apartheid era into the deaths of detainees were usually heard before a white senior magistrate who invariably accepted the police's versions.

> Most of these explanations were lacking in credibility. In my considered view, the majority of these magistrates had no real desire to reach the truth. Indeed it appeared that some of these magistrates saw it as their duty to protect organs of the state, such as the police. Magistrates tended not to interrogate police versions that vigorously. By way of example, magistrates invariably never asked police the most obvious question: 'Why should a detainee commit suicide when he had the option of remaining silent under interrogation?'[240]

His affidavit also included a distillation of key evidence presented to Magistrate De Villiers at the 1972 inquest, and the magistrate's findings.

> In my respectful view there was no basis for Magistrate De Villiers to exonerate the police involved in the interrogation of Timol. There was sufficient indication that Timol had been brutally tortured during his police detention. The Magistrate uncritically accepted the police version, even though it flew in the face of forensically established facts and the probabilities. In doing so he did what was expected of him by the apartheid regime. The interests of justice and truth demand that this

deeply flawed finding be overturned.[241]

Essop Pahad,[242] a veteran member of the ANC and the SACP, testified on Tuesday, 25 July 2017. He told the court that his formal involvement in politics began during the Defiance Campaign in 1952, when he was 13 years old. He became an executive member of the Transvaal Indian Youth Congress in 1958. In 1964 both Essop and his brother Aziz, received banning orders; they were not allowed to continue their studies at the University of the Witwatersrand and they were not even permitted to speak to each other. They left South Africa in December of that year. With Thabo Mbeki and others they established the ANC Youth and Student Movement in the United Kingdom.

In 1966 Essop was asked to join the South African Communist Party, which one could only become a member of by being recruited, which he considered to be a great honour. Although it had a small number of members, the party recruited those considered to be the best cadres in the liberation movement. Essop was based in the party's underground London unit – only members of the unit knew of its existence, he said.

He went on to serve on both the National Executive Committee of the African National Congress and the Central Committee of the SA Communist Party. He returned to South Africa in 1990 and was later elected as a member of parliament, and appointed as a member of President Mbeki's cabinet.

'Ahmed was one of my best friends,' Essop wrote in his affidavit submitted to the inquest court. He told how their grandfathers had come from the same village in India and that their parents were also friends. 'We had known each other for a very long time but we became closer when Ahmed came to study to be a school teacher in Fordsburg, Johannesburg. When I was banned, Ahmed gave me money for personal expenses and when I eventually left South Africa, Ahmed bought me an overcoat to wear in London.'[243]

He confirmed that Uncle Ahmed had shared an apartment with him and his brother Aziz, where they had numerous political discussions. He said Uncle Ahmed was recruited to the SACP by Dadoo, and that he had attended the Lenin Party School in Moscow with Mbeki. He had also received training from Jack Hodgson before Dadoo sent him back to South Africa. While working underground in South Africa, Uncle Ahmed was involved in the reproduction and distribution of materials sent to him from London. He said they would also have been given the task to mobilise people in the Indian community.[244]

'When Ahmed left for South Africa, I was the last person to talk to him before he left for the airport from our flat in North End House, West Kensington,' Essop said. 'I discussed with him what would happen if he got arrested. We agreed that there was a high likelihood that he may get arrested as the Security Branch was infiltrating our units. We discussed how he should respond.'

He said that the first thing a detainee in that position should do would be to give a name and an address. 'Secondly, he should know that breaking under torture is not an act of treachery and may be unavoidable. It is likely to happen, but he should try his best not to give away the names of others, and in the event he did, he should try to limit the number of names.'

Essop had told Uncle Ahmed to: 'Give names as gradually as possible to allow implicated comrades time to leave the country or hide. In other words, he must hold out for as long as possible after his arrest to allow comrades to take the necessary steps to protect themselves from arrest.' Other advice he gave my uncle was that if the police had incriminating evidence against him, 'Accept that it is yours and let them charge you ... You could even agree to give evidence against others to stop the torture, but in court you should then testify about the torture you sustained and then refuse to give evidence against any comrade that is charged.'[245]

Contrary to evidence that had been accepted at the 1972 inquest, Essop said:

> Suicide was not, and has never been, the policy of the SACP or the ANC. There was never any such protocol nor was any such instruction issued. It was a common understanding in the movement that there is a limit to human endurance. Abdulhay

Jassat and the late Laloo Chiba withstood torture of high magnitude and never spoke, but we fully understood that others may not have been able to do so. In our last discussions, we had agreed that Ahmed should not commit suicide.

He added that, as a Muslim, Uncle Ahmed could not have considered suicide, anyway. 'He may have given information but he would have refused to give evidence against others and would have rather been imprisoned. Indeed he would have welcomed going to the prison in the cause of resisting the vicious system of apartheid.'

The instruction to comrades to commit suicide, contained in the publication, *Inkululeko* No. 2 of February 1972 and used as evidence in the first inquest was manufactured by the police, Essop said. 'The listing of names on page 7 of the document is further evidence of an inept fabrication since the SACP in those days never referred to anyone by name in its publications, with the exception of a few of those serving on Robben Island and in leadership positions,' he said.

Ronnie Kasrils became a member of the African National Congress and its armed wing uMkhonto weSizwe in the early 1960s. He worked in Dar es Salaam for a while before undergoing military training in the Soviet Union and was deployed to London in 1966 to work with a strategic committee of the SA Communist Party headed by Dadoo and Slovo. Kasrils went on to lead uMkhonto weSizwe's intelligence service in the 1980s, and was appointed Deputy Minister of Defence and later Minister of Water Affairs and Forestry by President Nelson Mandela and Minister of Intelligence Services by President Thabo Mbeki.

His evidence to Judge Mothle on Thursday, 3 August 2017 provided the context for the work of the London Recruits, and undermined another critical link in the police chain of evidence. He also accused the police of having forged the alleged communist propaganda exhorting communists to commit suicide to avoid giving information to police under interrogation.

Kasrils said the London committee's mission was to reorganise the underground structures of both the African National Congress and the SA Communist Party within South Africa. This also entailed the creation of a support network for uMkhonto weSizwe. From 1966 they focused on sending literature and leaflets into the country so that the people of South Africa would know and understand the programme, policy and the directive of both the ANC and the Communist Party. Recruits had to be found to carry out the propaganda distribution and recreation of the underground network.

They had to firstly identify South Africans, particularly younger people, who were studying in Britain or were passing through Britain, and who were inclined to want to serve the movement. He added that they identified such people and would then recruit them into the underground of both the ANC and the SA Communist Party and, in some cases, simply the ANC. Their training was related to how to survive in a police state such as South Africa, and in relation to that training, there were particular methods which are referred to as Trade Craft. How do you survive? How do you remain anonymous?[246]

Among the people identified for recruitment were Raymond Suttner, Alex Moumbaris, Tim Jenkin, Dave and Sue Rabkin and Ahmed Timol, Kasrils said. He confirmed that Uncle Ahmed received training from Jack Hodgson.

By 1970 or 1971, there was a peak in the mass distribution of leaflets in South Africa through the use of so-called bucket bombs. Newspaper reports at the time made it clear that the police were not aware of who was conducting the campaign, and that the leaflets were a significant concern to the apartheid state.

Kasrils said recruits were specifically prepared for how to behave if they were arrested.

> What we believed in was a world-view approach, Your Lordship, in which we understood then and now that an individual involved in struggling for a just cause against an invader, against a police state, against tyranny, has a powerful weapon on their side which is a moral issue, and a question of giving them strength to confront any form of danger. Whether it comes in a form of arrest, whether it comes in the form of assault, or even torture. Whether it comes in the form of facing a Court as Mr Mandela,

Sisulu and others did in terms of possible death sentence. So it was based on strengthening the moral fibre of an individual in the belief in the cause that we were fighting for. That was the platform or the basis on which to prepare a person.

Secondly, would be an understanding, an analysis, of the kind of methods that your captors would use against you. We had plenty of examples by 1970 of how the South African Police or Special Branch were behaving in terms of their interrogation methods, in terms of even torture. In relation to torture, Your Lordship, you cannot simply prepare a human being and know that that person will break or not, that is an impossibility, but the question of infusing a person with the belief and that strength arising out of belief is the best that you can do. However what to do then if one is caught and you have been part of a structure in which two or three other people have been working with you? We have all heard of the Gestapo and the kind of torture that people had to face, so we made sure that our recruits understood that. If they felt that they just could not withstand even capture then we would not force them into an underground or illegal situation. That had to come over time and patience, the politics, and the training, but we had to face and they had to face this crucial question: If I am captured how do I behave? We would go through the trauma of that, and we would go through the shock one would experience, and how to try to survive that in terms of inner strength, and so on. We would stress the need to withhold the most sensitive of information, and we knew this was something that could not hold out indefinitely because of the threshold of pain if under assault, or torture.

So a key thing if one was a Mr Timol or a Member of his Unit would be, comrades, try and hold out if you are captured, try and hold out for at least 24 hours, 48 hours if possible so that those who you have been working with … would be alert to the fact that individual A, B or C has disappeared, is likely to be under arrest. Then everybody is under instruction to not be a hero; that is the time to run for it. We would have prepared people with the ideas of how to disguise and how to make for the border, and we knew our borders very well, Your Lordship. So we would say such and such places or where you could quite easily cross into a neighbouring African state. So the question of holding out 24 to 48 hours is the key factor of time. We did not say that you should hold out indefinitely, but we did say if you can do that, and there were many instances of comrades who did resist to the point of being beaten unconscious. That if you have got that strength, by all means, but if not, hold out for that minimum period of time.[247]

Kasrils said recruits were trained to, in the first place, reveal what the enemy already knew, and then to try to limit themselves to those parameters – 'knowing that once you give a little bit they also are not fools they would pressurise you for a little more, but that is a particular tactic in that battle of wits'. The recruits knew ultimately to expect lengthy prison sentences, and were prepared for that eventuality.[248]

Turning to the publication, *Inkululeko* No. 2, on which Magistrate De Villiers relied as the basis for his conclusion that Uncle Ahmed had committed suicide, as instructed by the Communist Party, Kasrils said while the overall document appeared to be authentic, the passage encouraging comrades to commit suicide was 'a complete fabrication and a forgery'. This section had evidently been drafted by someone not comfortable with English, as the language was inconsistent with that used throughout the rest of the document and it referred to the South African Communist Party by its old name, 'Communist Party of South Africa', which was not a mistake a real communist would have made. The security police contention that communists were encouraged to commit suicide was a fabrication.[249]

The security police had to explain Uncle Ahmed's death and turned to manufacture their own *Inkululeko* pamphlet. This narrative was presented as an explanation for my uncle taking his own life.

XII

Police witnesses

Having heard the evidence of former detainees, comrades from London and expert witnesses, the time had arrived for Judge Mothle to hear from the security policemen associated with Ahmed Timol's case.

Three of the surviving policemen had been subpoenaed to testify. They were Neville Els, the security policeman on duty on the night of Uncle Ahmed's arrest; Seth Sons, one of the security policemen who visited the Timol home after his arrest; and João 'Jan' Rodrigues, who, according to police, and the judgment of the first inquest, was alone in the room with Uncle Ahmed in the moments before his fatal fall.

While none of the police named as members of the interrogation team were still alive, I continued to harbour the hope that those who remained would be able to cast new light on the events that led to my uncle's death. My hope was heightened by the evidence the inquest had already heard, particularly from the expert witnesses. In the face of this evidence it did not seem feasible that the police could continue to insist on their innocence.

I was particularly optimistic that Rodrigues would have had second thoughts about the evidence he had given to the 1972 inquest that my uncle had showed no signs of having been assaulted. Rodrigues, who had created a new life for himself as a game ranger and author after leaving the police soon after Uncle Ahmed's death, had fallen into the inquest's hands after his daughter Tilana Stander had read a media release about the inquest and made contact with me to report his whereabouts.

Neville Els, who testified on Monday, 31 July 2017, was the first of the Security Branch officers to take the stand. I greeted this frail and bald-headed 82-year-old man and promised him a copy of my 2005 book. I honestly believed that he would speak the truth. How wrong I was.

He confirmed that he was the security policeman on duty on the night of Ahmed's and Salim's arrests, and that he had been asked to come from the Newlands police station to the roadblock to view subversive literature he was told had been found in the boot of the car they had been travelling in. After seeing it he called his John Vorster Square colleague Captain Dirker to collect the detainees. Els left the Newlands police station after Dirker arrived, and said he played no part in Uncle Ahmed's interrogation. He described Dirker as 'a gentle person'.

My wish that he might assist the inquest to establish the truth quickly evaporated. The essence of his testimony was that in his extensive career as a security policeman he saw, spoke and heard no evil – and said that he certainly had not participated in any evil, himself – ever. He referred to his advanced age and that the matter under the microscope had occurred many years before. He could recall some details of the events in October 1971, but only those that did not involve him deeply in Ahmed Timol's case. Thus, for example, he could definitively remember that he was not 'involved in the arresting of anybody after that'.

Els told the court that he had heard allegations of torture being discussed by his peers, and had read allegations of it in the newspapers, but he had never seen a detainee being assaulted or tortured in any way, and had never seen a detainee who appeared to be injured or in distress. When it was pointed out that he had participated in Professor Kantilal Naik's interrogation, Els said: 'I may have been involved in sitting in during questioning in … if it is on record, yes, but the detail regarding that I cannot remember.'

Below is a short extract from the transcript of Els's cross-examination by Advocate Varney.[250]

Varney: We will be submitting to this court that the sleep deprivation that the detainees sustained at the time, sometimes up to several days, constitutes a severe form of torture.

Els: Of torture, I cannot comment on that, M'Lord. My opinion is that I would have interrogated a person to within reason, whereby if answers are given, I follow it and proven what I wanted to know, yes I would have stopped. But for four or five days; I supposed that length of time it can be torture, it can be extreme.

Varney: What about sitting on an imaginary chair?

Els: I have heard of that, yes, but I have not seen it.

Varney: Are you aware of any security branch officer who had been involved in applying electric shocks to a detainee?

Els: No, I am not aware.

Varney: The placing of a hessian or a plastic bag over the head of a detainee?

Els: No, I cannot recall that.

Varney: Mr Els, have you heard of a practice referred to sometimes as the helicopter treatment, sometimes the aeroplane?

Els: I have heard of that this morning, M'Lord.

Varney: So you know that it is about being suspended between two tables with a broomstick which is tied between hands and knees?

Els: I have not seen that, M'Lord, and I am not aware of it, M'Lord.

I really believed that Els was going to speak the truth and literally, 'spill the beans'. This was purely optimitism on my part but I was disappointed in the vagueness of his testimony and the fact that he said he could not recall anything.

Seth Sons, a security policeman who was based at John Vorster Square police station, at the time of my uncle's detention testified[251] on Thursday, 16 August 2017. This frail, but towering figure, wearing spectacles came across to me as slightly arrogant. I could only imagine being in the room with him during detention. As a member of the so-called coloured population group, although he was nominally in charge of a small group of coloured and Indian security policemen, he would not have been held in high esteem by his white colleagues. Sons, who had risen to the rank of colonel, was among the most senior black members of the repressive apartheid security police.

Judging from the feedback received following his testimony, he had brutally tortured detainees in the coloured and Indian communities around Johannesburg who both feared and despised him.

Sons, who said he bore the rank of sergeant in 1971 after joining the police in the 1950s, told Judge Mothle that he accompanied Captain Dirker and a team of security policemen to the Timol residence on the day of Uncle Ahmed's death. But he was not with his colleagues inside the house; he said his function was to drive the van. He noticed that when Dirker returned to the van he was carrying a typewriter.

On the team's return to John Vorster Square, Sons noticed a disturbance and was told that someone had fallen out of a window. He did not stop to look at the body but immediately took a lift up to his office on the ninth floor. He had no need to look at the body and did not want to be called as a witness, he said.

In common with his colleague Els, Sons told the court he had no knowledge of Timol's interrogation and knew nothing of torture being practised at John Vorster Square. He had heard allegations, and knew that some former political detainees had launched civil suits against the police, he said. He acknowledged that he was aware that detainees were deprived of sleep, but did not see it as a form of torture.

Acting special director of public prosecutions, Advocate Pretorius put it to Sons that, as a security policeman, he must have known about the assault of prisoners, to which Sons responded that it might have been the case had he been a more inquisitive person.

Varney asked Sons if he had ever, in his career as a policeman, been personally or involved in any assault or any abuse of any detainee at any time. He responded 'no', adding that his brains must be rusted – like his age.[252] Sons did confirm, however, that he knew a Security

Branch officer by the name of Billings, a coloured officer he had worked with. Billings, like Sons, had been involved in the arrest and questioning of suspects. Sons also confirmed working with Mr Harry Persad. He denied knowing a white officer named Mr Smit. He was questioned about his interrogation of a detainee, Hanif Vally, who had been arrested by Billings and Persad.

> Varney: I want to return to a name that was put to you by Mr Pretorius, Hanif Vally. You testified earlier that you could not recall this particular name.
> Sons: Well I cannot remember the name, but it rings a bell.
> Varney: So do you recall that Mr Billings and Mr Harry Persad arrested Mr Vally in 1980?
> Sons: I cannot remember that.
> Varney: We will be putting up an affidavit from Mr Vally and he will say that you actually searched his house, and following the search you took him back to John Vorster Square.
> Sons: I cannot remember that M'Lord.
> Varney: And on arrival at John Vorster Square, when you began to question him, you took away his spectacles, his glasses.
> Sons: I cannot remember that.
> Varney: Mr Vally will say that while in that interrogation room with you and your colleagues he was forced to stand naked.
> Sons: I cannot remember that.
> Varney: Did you ever require anybody to stand naked during interrogation?
> Sons: Not that I can remember.
> Varney: Mr Vally says that thereafter he was assaulted by way of being slapped and kicked.
> Sons: The answer is, again, I cannot remember that M'Lord.

A few days after Sons's appearance at the inquest, the Ahmed Timol Family Trust released a media statement[253] saying that five former political detainees – Hanif Mohamed Vally, Alwyn Musson, Ismail Momoniat, Kevin Martin and Jesse Duarte – had come forward to contradict Sons's contention that he was not aware of the torture and assault of captured anti-apartheid activists. The affidavits of four of the activists, which were filed at the North Gauteng High Court in Pretoria, were used as evidence in the reopened inquest.

All five former detainees allege that Sons played a role in their humiliation and assault.[254] Hanif Mohamed Vally, the Deputy Director of the Foundation for Human Rights, deposed to an affidavit about the events following his arrest in 1980 during protests against unequal education. He was taken to John Vorster Square, where he was detained for two weeks. 'I was stripped naked in that first session. Paul Erasmus was present. I distinctly remember Sons taking off my spectacles and as I was looking at him, other police started slapping and kicking me,' he wrote.

Alwyn Musson, a former youth activist from Bosmont, was arrested when he was a student at the University of the Witwatersrand in 1983, and was taken to the tenth floor of John Vorster Square where a 'burly white man' threatened to throw him out of the window. 'Captain Sons returned to the office after about half an hour and became angry when he noticed that I had not written anything down. He then slapped me on the sides of my head with an open hand,' he said.

The writer of the third affidavit, Ismail Momoniat,[255] said he was arrested while campaigning in Lenasia against the government-sponsored South African Indian Council. 'I was then taken to the tenth floor where Major Cronwright and Major Arbee ... started assaulting me. Sons was with me at that point. The assault took place in the presence of Sons. Aside from striking me in my face, Major Arbee grabbed my hair and banged my head on the desk.' The former organiser for the Transvaal Indian Congress, and later the United Democratic Front, Momoniat testified about his detention in 1980 in connection with school boycotts. On his way to John Vorster Square, Captain Sons, knowing that he was of Muslim extraction, threatened to force him to eat pork while giving praise to Allah. 'I understood this as a threat and a clear attempt to humiliate and intimidate me,' he said.

Kevin Martin, the author of the fourth affidavit, was a young student activist who was arrested in 1975 while on the school bus. He was taken to the ninth floor of John Vorster Square. 'I sustained torture at the hands of Lt Sons and others,' he said. 'Once on the ground Lt Visser and Lt Sons each took an arm and a leg and lifted me off the ground and then repeatedly dropped me on my back. Lt Sons then held me down and Lt Visser sat on my chest and kicked me repeatedly on my head with the heel of his shoe. Thereafter, Lt Sons pulled my pants down and squeezed my testicles saying as his "grandmother" would do.'

Several of the affidavits make the point that, although Sons was an enthusiastic, dedicated and relatively high-ranking security policeman, he remained subordinate to all his white colleagues. 'He was still junior to the most junior of the white security policemen. The black security policemen never did the primary interrogation, which was the preserve of the white security policemen,' one said. Another said that Sons and his black henchmen appeared to mostly do 'menial' work. 'It appeared they were always under pressure to prove their commitment to their white security police colleagues,' he said. A few hours after Sons's appearance, ANC Deputy Secretary General Jesse Duarte labelled him a 'torture master' in a lengthy social media post. 'Sons would definitely have been aware of the beatings or torture at John Vorster Square. This is because one could easily hear people when they were being assaulted or tortured, and sometimes one could even see assaults taking place through stained glass partitions. He forgot that he made me kneel next to my brother Achmat [Dangor] as his goons from the SB searched our house for 6 hours.'[256]

Of all the witnesses who testified at the reopened inquest, the one who had claimed direct knowledge of what occurred in Room 1026 in the moments before Uncle Ahmed's death was João Rodrigues. He testified on Monday, 31 July 2017; and on Tuesday, 1 August and Wednesday, 2 August 2017.

Rodrigues was pivotal to the police version of events on a number of counts. He was said to have been, quite by chance, alone in the room with Uncle Ahmed. So he was the only eyewitness to have seen him fall to his death. He said he had travelled from Pretoria to deliver cheques and a document to the interrogation team at John Vorster Square. As he was doing so, a mysterious person, referred to as 'Mr X', came into the room to inform the interrogation team of a breakthrough in the search for three individuals: Quentin Jacobsen, Martin and Henry. Their version was that it was Timol's fear of being exposed by them that led to him committing suicide.

When he testified in 1972, Rodrigues was within what Professor Foster had described to the court as the 'closed' security domain controlled by apartheid police, prosecutors, doctors and magistrates. Although the family argued that my uncle had been assaulted, Magistrate De Villiers ruled that he could have incurred various injuries before his detention.

But when Rodrigues testified in 2017, he could no longer rely on the protection of a closed system. His evidence followed that of a pair of highly qualified and experienced forensic pathologists who presented independent reports finding that Uncle Ahmed had been so badly assaulted before his death that he might have been unconscious when he fell. Besides a depressed skull fracture that could not be associated with the fall, he had an ankle injury that would have made walking extremely difficult.

This time, his evidence also followed that of a trajectory expert who found that if Timol had jumped from the window, as the policeman claimed, he could not have landed on the ground where he did. And Rodrigues's evidence followed that of a group of witnesses, detained more or less the same time as Uncle Ahmed at John Vorster Square, all of whom told the court of being brutally assaulted.

Rodrigues had two choices: He could either stick to his version, implausible as it was, and hope for the best, or he could take the court into his confidence about his role in the police cover-up of murder. Neither strategy was risk-free. If he stuck to his story and was found by the court to have lied, he could face criminal charges. If he admitted that he had lied in 1972, he would be admitting to perjury, and would have to implicate others. I hoped he would opt for the latter. If he exposed the police cover-up it would not only be important for truth and justice in the Timol matter, but also for the families of other comrades whose murders were disguised as accidents and suicides – including the families of Bantu Stephen Biko, Chief Albert Luthuli, Dr Hoosen Haffejee, Mapetla Mohapi, Nicodemus Kgoathe, Ashley Kriel and Dr Neil Aggett.

Then aged 78 years old, João Rodrigues walked with a stick due to recent surgery, but he was tall and strong. A former rugby player, athlete and wrestler, he would have been a foot taller and 20 kilograms heavier than my uncle. Judge Mothle explained to Rodrigues the predicament in which he found himself:

> Judge Mothle: Now, Mr Rodrigues, you have been subpoenaed here to come and assist us with this inquest. Now, according to your own version, your own version that you gave to the 1972 inquest, is that you are the last person to see Mr Timol alive.
>
> Rodrigues: That is correct.
>
> Judge Mothle: Now, there is evidence that has come in, as I said to your previous colleague, which raises questions about the correctness of that statement. Now, you are here to help us understand what happened, but then in terms of the Constitution today, I need to inform you that at the end of this inquest should I find that there has been some role that people have played – in particular, you, that caused the death of Mr Timol – that may put you at risk for prosecution. Do you understand?
>
> Rodrigues: I understand.

Rodrigues told the court that he had joined the police in 1956, and its Security Branch in 1969. He did administrative work, such as maintaining vehicle log books and handling post, and provided 'support services' to the families of security policemen carrying out investigations or interrogations.

On the day in question, he was called by Captain Gloy to deliver his and Captain Faan van Niekerk's salary cheques to John Vorster Square, where they were working. He was later called to bring an envelope, with him, too. It was the first time he had gone to John Vorster Square. He took the lift to the tenth floor, where he was told to hang on for a bit because Gloy and Van Niekerk were busy with an interrogation. After a while he was told he may enter the room they were in.

On his way in he was intercepted by a man with a tray containing three cups of coffee, who asked him to take the tray into the room because he was not allowed inside. When he entered the room he said that the atmosphere was calm, and the two security policeman and the detainee, who he later learned was Timol, had proceeded to drink their coffee. One of the forensic pathologists had earlier told the court that Uncle Ahmed had fractures to his jaw that would have ruled out drinking coffee.

Rodrigues testified that:

> Gloy opened the envelope, took out the contents and started reading. I wanted to leave but he asked me to stay for a moment. At that moment, somebody entered the room and said aloud that three of Timol's collaborators had been arrested. He mentioned the names but I cannot remember the names … The person who came in and made the announcement then left … Van Niekerk and Gloy looked at each other, and I saw that Timol – who I now know was Timol but didn't know at the time – got a massive fright. I saw that he got a massive fright, *hy het geweldig groot geskrik*. His eyes were big and he was shaking his head, and he was looking at the three of us.

At that point, the interrogators looked at each other and asked him if he could mind the prisoner for a few minutes while they had a chat outside, Rodrigues said. He was left alone with Uncle Ahmed who sat in a chair staring in front of him. They did not speak to each other.

> We were alone in the office and a few minutes later, Timol asked me to take him to the toilet. It was a very reasonable request to me, it was very reasonable and I got up from the chair and he got up from his chair also. I moved to the left around the table.

The chair on which Van Niekerk had been sitting was in the way and I pushed it back under the table. My eyes were on the chair. At that moment, I saw a movement out of the corner of my eye ... I looked up quickly to see Timol moving fast around the other side of the table. It all happened in a split second. I had to decide whether I am going to follow him on the left hand side of the table, but saw that the chair on which Timol had been sitting would obstruct me. You must please understand, Your Honour, that all this occurred in a fraction of a second. I immediately realised that I would not make it, and moved towards the right of the table as quickly as I could. I wanted to stop Timol but my chair was in the way. I lost my balance and tumbled to the ground. Before I could reach Timol I saw him opening the window. I saw him dive out of the open window.

I tried my best, I tried my best. I moved as fast as possible but I could not reach him before he was through the window.

He testified that he ran into the passage shouting that Timol had jumped. People streamed out of the offices and rushed to the window, and then to the ground floor. He saw people taking Uncle Ahmed's pulse and heard someone say he was still alive; then they rolled his body onto a blanket and took him inside.

After the incident, he could not remember precisely when, Rodrigues said he was pressured by General Buys, Gloy and Van Niekerk to include in his affidavit to the 1972 inquest that he and Uncle Ahmed had wrestled with each other prior his suicide. But that was not true and he declined to include it. The confrontation he had with the officers over what to include in his affidavit led to him resigning from the police, he said. He realised then that he had no future in the police force.

A few months later, he re-joined the police to complete specialist counter insurgency training. 'I wanted to receive the specialist training that the men got in order to do duty on the borders ... which was very good training,' he said, before returning to his job, as a journalist on the Pretoria afternoon newspaper, *Die Hoofstad*. He later became an editor for the South African National Parks. Some game parks are located close to South Africa's borders, so his counter-insurgency training may have become useful.

Rodrigues refused to amend his affidavit as requested by Buys, Gloy and Van Niekerk, who were then all high-ranking officers in the security police. Why he did not report this to his superiors? The fact that he resigned and was re-employed in the police raised further questions. Interestingly, the fact that he was not re-employed to conduct administrative tasks, but selected to undergo counter-insurgency training raises further questions.

Varney questioned him about his claim that my uncle had been drinking coffee with his interrogators.

> Varney: Mr Rodrigues, if the injuries were ante mortem as not related to the fall as Doctor Holland concludes, there would have been quite a bit of swelling around the jaw, and you do not have to be a specialist to notice that somebody's jaw is swelling up.
> Rodrigues: No, I cannot say that I have seen this swelling on Timol's jaw because I did not know him before, and I did not see him before now at that point in time as it is now being put to me by Counsel.
> Varney: And you testified that when you brought the coffee in he then enjoyed a cup of coffee.
> Rodrigues: All three men that were inside that room drank the coffee.
> Varney: Because it is also the evidence of both the forensic pathologists for the family, that with these kinds of injuries it would have been extremely difficult if not impossible to drink coffee.
> Rodrigues: I cannot comment on what the pathologist or the examinations of the pathologists results are saying as I am not an expert.

Advocate Pretorius added his own questions:

> Pretorius: I put it to you that you did not know Mr Ahmed Timol from a bar of soap.
> Rodrigues: Ja, I did not know Timol before, but all I can remember is that he was shocked. His eyes were big and he was looking from one side to the other.
> Pretorius: You could see no injuries?
> Rodrigues: I did not see any injuries sustained on his body.
> Pretorius: Not on his nose, not on his jaw, not on his temple?
> Rodrigues: No, I did not see such injuries.

Judge Mothle reminded Rodrigues that if he accepted his version, he would have to reject the findings of the autopsy saying that there were no such injuries and vice versa. If the judge accepted the autopsy, this meant that Rodrigues's evidence was false and must be rejected.

> Judge Mothle: Do you realise where I stand now?
> Rodrigues: Yes.
> Judge Mothle: That is why I say I want you to through your comment, to help me out. What should I do?
> Rodrigues: I can't remember sir. I can't remember seeing any marks on his face. Let me put it that way and maybe you will understand that.
> Judge Mothle: You cannot remember seeing any marks?
> Rodrigues: No I can't remember.
> Judge Mothle: So there could have been marks on his face?
> Rodrigues: It is possible, but I didn't see it. I can't remember.
> Judge Mothle: You can't remember seeing it, or you can't remember?
> Rodrigues: I can't remember. I can't remember seeing it on his face.

After a discussion with Benny and Roger from Oryx Media, I proposed to our legal team that they should ask Rodrigues to get out of the box from which he testified; to stand in front of the gallery with a member of the public of the same height as Uncle Ahmed and demonstrate how he 'attempted' to block him from diving to his death. This was simply to get Rodrigues out of his comfort zone as he appeared to be too comfortable answering the questions posed to him. The proposal was not supported.

As I was not involved with the legal team in their preparation of the witnesses, I had had ample time to study the demeanour of all of them, specifically the former security police officers. Rodrigues had always appeared jovial and smiled for the cameras. He appeared to be unmoved after, in his own words, seeing Ahmed Timol diving to his death.

XIII

He was murdered

Judge Mothle said he had wanted to afford me the opportunity to be the last witness to testify[257] at the historic reopening of the Ahmed Timol's inquest. This was, however, not to be as Sons's testimony could only be heard after mine, after he was traced and subpoenaed. Nevertheless, his gesture made me extremely grateful. I obtained special permission from Judge Mothle to wear my Ahmed Timol T-shirt that was printed by Foundation for Human Rights (FHR) and I testified on Monday, 14 August 2017, a day after my birthday.

'I am truly humbled that 46 years after the inquest into the death of my uncle, that the Timol family has an opportunity to present evidence in a democratic South Africa and for that we are eternally grateful, M'Lord,' I began. Then, led by Advocate Varney, I told the court of the journey I had undertaken to discover the truth about the death in detention of Ahmed Timol.

> I can recall travelling in the middle of the evening with my late mother from Standerton, Mpumalanga, to my maternal grandparents' flat in Roodepoort. It was in the early hours of the morning, M'Lord, and I can remember family members all crowded together in the small kitchen that they had, around the table, and they were all whispering to one another in a very, very hushed tone and then there was this knock on the door and there was silence.

And then I could picture these huge white men all walking around the flat, and this is the image that remains imprinted in my mind. And subsequent to that, M'Lord I have an image of my grandmother standing at the balcony of their flat, and this huge crowd standing on the road, and only subsequently did I learn that that was obviously the day of my uncle's funeral.

M'Lord, my grandfather died a broken man in 1981 after the loss of his eldest son; I spent quite a bit of time with my grandfather. I would accompany him to the local cemetery in Roodepoort where we would go and visit my uncle's grave and I would recite versus from the Quran paying tribute to my uncle, and when I would return to the flat, my grandmother would always ask me, 'Did you pray for Uncle Ahmed', and I would politely say, 'Yes Ma, I prayed for Uncle Ahmed'. But my grandfather passed away in 1981, and he died a broken man after the loss of his eldest son.

During the school holidays I would take out the newspaper cuttings that the family have kept from the time, from my uncle's death and the subsequent inquest. I would go through these newspaper cuttings and I would place a picture in my mind, at a very tender age, to try and comprehend and find out what had really transpired – and then I would relentlessly pursue my grandmother. I would tell her, 'Ma I want to know about Uncle Ahmed', and she would always ask me, M'Lord, 'but why do you want to know about him?' I just said, 'Look, I want to know about my uncle, tell me about him, give me as much information as possible.' And then we would sit and she would relate to me the sequence of events, M'Lord. She would start from the final moment when she had seen him, he had stared at her for a very long time; he was concerned about her health. Then, the subsequent visits from the Security Branch, numerous raids that they would conduct at the flat. She would ask a family relative, the late Mr Iqbal 'Baboo' Dindar and his wife, Jameela Dindar to take food for him at John Vorster square police station.

She told me of how she was admonished by the Security Branch officers for not giving her son a hiding. And then, when she was broken on the news that Ahmed was dead, and she had informed my grandfather, Papa had to come and identify the body. And with grief, sorrow and pain in her eyes she would then narrate to me the condition of his body which was then returned to the family.

She reminded me that my grandfather performed the final *Janazah* prayer, which is a final funeral prayer, as part of our Muslim belief, and that was bidding farewell to Uncle Ahmed.

M'Lord, my late mother would narrate to me that after Uncle Ahmed's death, and this is a period when Uncle Mohammed is still in police detention which we then subsequently heard, he was in solitary confinement. The security police would approach my grandfather in Roodepoort and they would want him to convince Uncle Mohammed to work for them. So, in other words, they wanted him to be an informant, they wanted him to be a collaborator or, as we say in the townships, they wanted him to be an *impimpi*. This is after the killing of his brother and I think that just demonstrated the audacity of the apartheid regime, and my grandfather, obviously, with the contempt it deserved, dismissed them.

But in addition, M'Lord, I remember specifically that the Security Branch officers would visit our home in Standerton, Mpumalanga, and they would then ask my dad, this particular motor vehicle, this car registration number, this colour of this vehicle, does it belong to you? And my dad would say, 'yes', it does belong to us. They would then want to know why, on these specific dates, this car was seen at this residence in Azaadville. And my dad would concur and say, 'Yes, we were at that particular residence because it is the residence of my in-laws'. And again, M'Lord I [deduced] very, very quickly that my grandparents' home was under surveillance, they will be monitored, and more importantly, there were police informants within the community that were reporting to the security

Branch of any people that were visiting the residence of my grandparents.

M'Lord, my grandmother simply refused to appear in front of the Truth and Reconciliation Commission in 1996, but I had a very special bond with her, M'Lord and she would always listen to me and I convinced her. I said: 'Look, Ma, even it is 25 years after Uncle Ahmed's death, it is important that you go and testify. That not just the country, but the world should know that what happened to Uncle Ahmed.' And, very reluctantly, she appeared before the Truth and Reconciliation Commission, I think it was on the 30th of April 1996, at the Central Methodist Church in Johannesburg.

M'Lord, unlike all the other conversations that we used to have in the comfort of our home, when I sat and listened to her – in front of the commissioners, accompanied by her sons, Uncle Mohammad and her younger son, Uncle Haroon – I was filled with emotion. Unlike all the other conversations that we had, M'Lord, I had to hold back my tears, and on that particular day, M'Lord, I made a silent vow to myself that from this day onwards I am no longer just going to speak about Uncle Ahmed. I am going to do something constructive in memory of my beloved uncle, uncertain as to what it was and how it was going to unfold, but very clear in my mind that I am not just going to speak about him, I am going to do something constructive in preserving the legacy and memory of my uncle, and most importantly to find out what really happened to him.

I once again visited the newspaper cuttings, but this time much more focused. I started researching, I started analysing, I started identifying individuals whose names had appeared in the newspaper cuttings. With no academic qualifications I started this process of conducting research, conducted numerous interviews and, already at that particular point, M'Lord, we are talking of 1996, I had known within myself that this was my calling in life, that I was sent specifically to find out about the life of my uncle and more importantly to establish what really happened to him during his police ordeal.

I told the court of my attempts to track down and speak to those security policemen who were involved in Uncle Ahmed's detention and torture.

I managed to make contact with Captain Gloy ... I would just like to put it in context that all the years that I have been through this particular journey, I have always been polite and very respectful, including with many of the other detainees who were arrested with Uncle Ahmed. There were instances where they would refuse to see me, and I respected their wishes, M'Lord, including close friends of his were not willing to give me an interview. But at all particular times I have remained dignified, I have remained respectful and I have accepted the decisions that they had made in cases where they were not prepared to see me.

M'Lord, it was in this particular context that I had a number of telephonic conversations with Johannes Hendrik ['Hans'] Gloy, who, I had established, was very pivotal in the interrogation of my beloved uncle. My conversations with him, M'Lord were in Afrikaans, as I am fluent in Afrikaans.

On the first occasion when we had spoken he indicated to me that I must look at the inquest records. Very clear, 'look at the inquest findings', and then stated that I should call him again to make an appointment if I needed to see him, and again I respected his wishes, M'Lord. During my second telephonic conversation with him, Mr Gloy informed me that he was advised by his lawyer not to meet me, in other words not to have a meeting with me, and he also added, M'Lord, that he was suffering from Parkinson's disease.

Then he went on a bit further, M'Lord. He then stated that my grandparents had spoken a bunch of lies during the inquest, claiming that my Uncle Ahmed was beaten and tortured, and he said very categorically that that was not true. And in my final conversation with him, M'Lord, I informed Mr Gloy that I had read the inquest records and he claimed to me that he had no reason to apply for amnesty as the courts had already ruled and that I had no case against him.

In conclusion, he reminded me that if I continued calling him, he was going to ... he was going to get a court order against me. I respected his wishes, M'Lord. However the urge for me to pursue the matter [remained] and in 2007 I wrote him formal correspondence. I sent him a letter ... an old fashioned proper letter through the post office where once again I made an appeal to him. I said, look, the years are passing on, his time on the earth is coming to an end and will he not reconsider the facts. That, you know, we can meet and find some levels of closure. But unfortunately, M'Lord, I had no response from Mr Gloy.

I told Judge Mothle that Captain van Niekerk had died in 2006, and that Captain Gloy had followed him in 2012. I highlighted to the court my futile attempt in 2004 to persuade the National Director of Prosecutions to re-look at Ahmed Timol's death. And I highlighted Mr Justice Legodi's 2008 judgment in *Nkadimeng and Others versus the National Director of Prosecutions and Others*. Judge Legodi said: 'Crimes are not investigated by victims. It is the responsibility of the police and prosecution authority to ensure that cases are properly investigated and prosecuted.' I told Judge Mothle I believed that Judge Legodi's judgment spoke profoundly to the Timol family, the family of the slain Nokuthula Simelane, the families of the Cradock Four, and all the other families who suffered terribly as a consequence of violence committed by the apartheid state.

Closing arguments from the respective legal teams was heard on Thursday, 24 August 2017 and judgment day was set for seven weeks later on Thursday, 12 October 2017.

While I was waiting for Judge Mothle's ruling to be pronounced, I took the bold decision to go for therapy. I felt the need, not from having listened to the harrowing testimonies of detainees, but because of all the attention I had received from the media and the community more broadly. I visited a clinical social worker and held a number of sessions which assisted me in preparing for the judgment.

Similar to the 19 days of the inquest, I arrived at court early on judgment day. I met veteran freedom fighter Comrade Laloo 'Isu' Chiba, who had provided an affidavit to the inquest about his own ordeal of torture in police custody. He complimented me for preserving my uncle's legacy and for my efforts to reopen the inquest.

The public gallery was packed to the rafters. My thoughts throughout the inquest had been of Ma and Papa. I wondered how they had survived sitting through the 1972 inquest listening to the security police witnesses fabricating evidence, which was ultimately unequivocally supported by Magistrate de Villiers. There was a large contingency of media, local and international eagerly awaiting the judgment, taking pictures and filming the court gallery.

In his judgment,[258] Judge Mothle very graciously acknowledged my work and remarked that it was through my persistent efforts that this historic sitting of the inquest had taken place. My efforts, he said, should be emulated as an example of how citizens have to assert their rights.

He said that the evidence placed before the inquest revealed the complicity of certain prosecutors, magistrates and medical doctors in the declaration of the so-called war against the anti-apartheid movement. 'These persons betrayed and demeaned their respective oaths of office by participating in inquest proceedings that became a sham; concealing the atrocities committed by the Security Branch and ensuring that the judicial system finds no one to blame, he said.

Judge Mothle rejected Rodrigues's evidence as lacking merit and credibility. In one of his criticisms of his testimony he said it was 'strange' that of the approximately 20 police officers who testified in the 1972 inquest, or who had provided it with affidavits, only five had mentioned Rodrigues. 'The mystery around the presence and role of Rodrigues at John Vorster Square at the time Timol fell supports the contention that his version has been conjured up to conceal the truth,' he said.

This, and other evidence, supported the view that the statements of members of the Security Branch, the police officers investigating the death of Timol and the proceedings in the 1972 inquest were all part of an attempt to cover up or conceal the truth concerning his death. This view was supported by the evidence of Dutton and Erasmus as well as the contradictions and improbabilities appearing in Rodrigues's version.

Evidence placed before the reopened inquest had unmasked the cover-up, he said:

> But due to the absence of the interrogators who had all passed on, the real events leading to the push could not be established. However, the evidence prima facie and logically points out that at the time Timol was pushed either out of the window of Room 1026 or from the rooftop, he was in the company of members of the Security Branch in charge of his interrogation. He could obviously not have been in a cell. These members were at least Gloy and Van Niekerk, as their police file records show and the evidence of Bouwer and Louw confirms. They were on duty at that time. The Court is unable to establish on the evidence whether there was anyone else with them.
>
> It is the Court's prima facie view that the push occurred during interrogation under circumstances where the Security Branch involved, resorted to torture. The torture on Timol was applied with a view to extract information. Counsel for the family of Timol submits that the Security Branch are guilty of murder. Murder is committed intentionally (direct intent) or through *dolus eventualis*. There is no evidence supporting the view that the Security Branch had direct intent to commit murder. There are theories suggesting that possibility but no evidence to back that up. However, the evidence supports murder through *dolus eventualis*. *Dolus eventualis* is present in instances where 'the perpetrator foresees the risk of death occurring, but nevertheless continues to act appreciating that death might well occur, therefore 'gambling' as it were with the life of the person against whom the act is directed.

Judge Mothle concluded that as all the others arrested with [him] and detained at John Vorster Square, my uncle was tortured by the interrogating members of the Security Branch. The torture included physical assaults which resulted in severe injuries. The injuries he referred to were those sustained before the fall and were distinct from those he sustained in his fall.

Magistrate de Villiers's conclusion that my uncle had been treated in a civilised and humane manner was not correct, Judge Mothle ruled. The trajectory evidence excluded the possibility of his having either dived or jumped from the window of Room 1026 on the day he fell. Instead, it supported the view that the cause of the fall was that Timol was pushed either from the window of Room 1026 or from the roof of the John Vorster Square building. Three independent witnesses had put the time of my uncle's fall as mid-morning on 27 October 1971. This directly contradicted Rodrigues's evidence that the fall took place between 3.45 pm and 4 pm. The court accepted that my uncle fell in the mid-morning and that Rodrigues, if ever he was in Room 1026 later in the afternoon, was brought there to legitimise the cover-up narrative; and that the substandard and sloppy manner in which the investigation of his death was conducted by Buys and his team, supported the view that there was a clear intent to cover up the incident through a fabricated version of suicide.

Timol's fall to the ground was as a result of being pushed from window of Room 1026 or from the top of the roof of the John Vorster Square building. Consequently, he did not take his own life. He died as a result of having being pushed to fall, an act which was committed by members of the Security Branch with *dolus eventualis* as the form of intent, and prima facie amounting to murder.

He said the evidence from my uncle's comrades as to how they were tortured in detention reveals 'an element of recklessness' on the part of the police. He said of the ante mortem injuries on Ahmed Timol's body 'demonstrates that there were no boundaries of respect for human life'.

He found that all members of the Security Branch involved with my uncle's interrogation or guarding him in Room 1026 were collectively responsible for the injuries sustained ante-mortem. They had failed to exercise the duty of care they had over him, and their denials of knowledge of the ante mortem injuries on his body constituted a cover-up. The Security Branch involved in his interrogation had intentionally and unlawfully inflicted these injuries through systematic and continuous torture.

The court's prima facie finding was that members of the Security Branch who were interrogating Uncle Ahmed on the day he died, through an act of commission or omission, murdered him. This they committed through *dolus eventualis* as the form of intent. Rodrigues placed himself on the scene as a party to the cover-up to conceal the truth. He, thereby, prima facie, by his conduct became an accessory after the fact of murder.

Judge Mothle ruled that Els should be investigated for misleading the court by claiming only to know of the allegation of assault on detainees through the media. Police records reflected that he was in attendance as one of the interrogators when Professor Naik was subjected to the helicopter method of torture. Sons was also to be investigated for testifying under oath that he had only heard of the assault of detainees through the media. Rodrigues was to be investigated for making contradictory statements whilst under oath. He had a previous conviction on perjury.

The judge ruled that the evidence of Rodrigues and the other police witnesses was 'clearly fabricated to conceal the real truth as to what caused Timol to fall'.

The fact that the police moved the injured man without calling for an ambulance was done 'clearly to conceal the crime' and it may have 'accelerated' his death.

The police went out of their way to cover up the incident by fabricating suicide.

Judge Mothle said that there was prima facie evidence implicating Gloy and Van Niekerk who were on duty and interrogating Ahmed Timol at the time he was 'pushed to fall to his death'. He said that Rodrigues:

On his own version participated in the cover-up to conceal the crime of murder as an accessory after the fact of that murder, and went on to commit perjury by presenting contradictory evidence before the 1972 and 2017 inquests. A recommendation is made to have him investigated and prosecuted for these offences.

Forty-six years after the first inquest found that there was no one to blame for my uncle's death, Judge Mothle said: 'Timol did not jump as alleged. He was pushed by someone and there is thus a case that members of the Security Branch conducting interrogation at that time had to answer.'

Then came the words from Judge Mothle that we, as a family, had longed to hear: 'He did not commit suicide but was murdered.'

A poignant moment in the hearing was when Judge Mothle made the decision to return to my uncle the dignity that was taken away from him by Magistrate de Villiers in his judgment when referring to him as 'An Asian male'. Judge Mothle consequently changed the inquest finding to read: 'The deceased is Ahmed Essop Timol, a South African citizen.'

Judge Mothle recommended that other families seeking closure on the unanswered questions concerning the death of relatives in detention be assisted at their initiative, to obtain the records and gather further information with a view to have the initial inquest reopened. The Human Rights Commission, working in consultation with the law enforcements agencies, should be sufficiently resourced to take on this task, he said.

This was critical as the outcome of reversing an apartheid-era inquest judgment did not only impact the Timol family. There were many other families throughout the length and breadth of South Africa who are still seeking closure and justice for the death of their loved ones, like the Mabelane family. The fact that the 2017 judgment reversed the 1972 findings should serve as a motivation to the state to reopen other inquests into the deaths of anti-apartheid activists.

I had arranged with Benny Gool and Roger Friedman to hold

an impromptu press conference for the media, both local and international, who had attended the judgment. This was a victory not only for the Timol family, but for all apartheid-era victims' families who yearned for similar closure. We felt it appropriate that Uncle Mohammad chair the press conference and that speakers include George Bizos, Yasmin Sooka, Thoko Mpumlwana, chairperson of the Foundation for Human Rights, and Nkosinathi Biko, the son of Bantu Stephen Biko, the slain Black Consciousness leader.

As the inquest drew to an end, I drew parallels between the first and the second – 45 years apart. They were, the legal representation, the public support and the role of media.

Papa and the Timol family did not have the financial resources to cover the legal costs of an inquest. They were assisted by the generous donations from the Indian community in the Transvaal, to be able to appoint the best legal team to represent the family at the 1972 inquest. In 2017, it was the efforts of Yasmin Sooka and the FHR that the Timol family was legally represented without having to bear the costs in the second inquest. Sooka's team made history with the reversal of the 1972 inquest finding from one of suicide to murder.

There was overwhelming public support offered to the Timol family from the moment we heard of Uncle Ahmed's death on 27 October 1971. This support continued until the end of the first inquest findings in June 1972. South Africans of all backgrounds condemned the apartheid regime for his brutal death as well as the arrests of detainees throughout the country. They expressed their outrage by attending protest meetings and writing letters to the newspapers. Similarly, the South African public stood by the Timol family throughout the 2017 inquest. Messages of support and solidarity poured onto social media platforms from far and wide.

The media covering and reporting the 1972 inquest kept my uncle's tragic death in the public eye. Despite the fact that it took place in a period of severe repression in the country, journalists and media houses continued to bravely disseminate extensive coverage of his death and the arrest of other detainees throughout the country. It was this coverage that I, as a teenager, diligently read in the family album about my uncle. It allowed me to piece together a picture about what had happened and this set the foundation for me to pursue the truth.

The media in a democratic South Africa continues to help promote the legacies of our fallen heroes and heroines. I sincerely appreciate the efforts of all the journalists and media houses, for covering the second inquest into the death of Ahmed Timol and for keeping his name alive in a new era.

XIV

The wheels of justice turn slowly

My uncle Ahmed Timol was not, as police claimed, fortuitously arrested at a random roadblock; he was under surveillance, and he had been hunted down by the police. He was aware that he and his brother Mohammad were both being watched, and he had asked his brother to leave town five days before his own arrest.

Uncle Ahmed was not treated with kid gloves in detention, as police said; he was kept awake and brutalised for more than four days. The testimony of detainees arrested with him, as well the affidavits from other activists, all confirm the practice of police brutally torturing detainees.

He did not follow an instruction from the SA Communist Party to commit suicide rather than to betray his comrades, because there was no such instruction. It was fabricated by the security police. My uncle knew, before his return to South Africa to conduct his underground activities, that there was a high probability that he would be arrested and tortured. He was trained for this eventuality, and as a committed cadre he would have been prepared to serve a lengthy term of imprisonment, if necessary. The security police had fabricated that there was a doctrine within the Communist Party for committing suicide if captured.

He did not skip around the table in the interrogation room, outmanoeuvring his guard to reach the window, as Rodrigues said. By then they had hurt him so badly that it is doubtful he would have been able to stand up, let alone walk. He did not dive out of the window, as they claimed; had he dived it would not have been possible to hit the ground where he did.

He did not commit suicide, contrary to the findings of the first inquest magistrate, J.J.L. de Villiers. This was a cover-up for his murder at the hands of the security police. The entire version of events accepted at the first inquest was concocted by the security police to conceal the fact that he had been killed in custody.

Magistrate de Villiers was not only complicit in the pretext; he rubbed salt in the family's wounds by callously insulting our grieving Ma, labelling her as a poor witness and a liar. His lack of humanity contributed to Papa dying of a broken heart. The police killed Ahmed Timol, and then the magistrate did his best to strip the family of its dignity.

My uncle was the 22nd detainee out of 73 political detainees to die in police detention since 1963. Not one police officer has been convicted for any of these deaths.

Justice Billy Mothle's official reversal of De Villiers's 1972 inquest finding that nobody was to blame vindicated Ahmed Timol's family's insistence that he had been murdered. It reinforced his dignity and that of my grandparents. And it vindicated all those who believed that justice would prevail in the democratic South Africa for which Uncle Ahmed and so many others paid the ultimate price. As senior advocate Dumisa Ntsebeza SC said in reaction to the unprecedented judgment, this was truly a case that proved the old adage: The wheels of justice turn slowly but grind exceedingly fine.[259]

After Judge Mothle's historical judgment on 12 October 2017, I sent letters of appreciation to all the witnesses who had testified at the 2017 inquest, individual members of the legal team, the private investigator and the Foundation for Human Rights (FHR), which was pivotal in the reopening of the inquest. I was profoundly aware of the courage it took former detainees to re-live the trauma of their torture. The brutal assaults of those linked to Uncle Ahmed such as the late

Amina 'Mummy' Desai, Hassen Jooma, Indres Moodley and others were not mentioned during the inquest. Their sacrifices, however, must never be forgotten.

On 24 October 2017, Member of Parliament Xitlhangoma Mabasa moved that the House of Assembly:

> welcome the judgment that Ahmed Timol did not commit suicide, but that he was murdered; note that the judgment affirmed the long-held view of the progressive forces and the freedom loving South Africans that Ahmed Timol was murdered; believes that the judgment paves the way for justice to run its full course, and that those who committed the murder must now face the music and be held accountable in accordance within the rule of law; trusts that the verdict will lead to the National Prosecuting Authority prosecuting former members of the police, who sought to evade justice through perpetuating lies; and supports the Timol family's undertaking to deepen its campaign towards a wider programme that seeks justice for other political activists who disappeared at the behest of the apartheid regime.[260]

More than 46 years after the reversal of the ruling of the 1972 inquest and 26 years since the dawn of democracy, I had imagined that it would be a mere formality for Judge Mothle's recommendations to be urgently implemented. Rodrigues would be charged with murder and for defeating the ends of justice; and that Neville Els and Seth Sons would be charged for perjury. It did not happen, but rather led to the start of another epic struggle.

Soon after Judge Mothle's ruling was handed down, I communicated with Advocate Pretorius, the Acting Special Director of Public Prosecutions, who had represented the state at the second inquest. I wanted to be updated on the Rodrigues, Sons and Els investigations. He informed me that dockets had been opened: João Rodrigues's case number 798/10/2017 had been opened at the Johannesburg Central police station; Seth Sons's case number 798/10/2017 and Neville

Els's case number 822/10/2017 had been opened at the Pretoria Central police station. This was positive news and I anticipated the investigations to be speedily concluded and to be quickly followed by the start of their court cases.

I was at a function of the Islamic Unity Convention in Cape Town on 24 October 2017, where I was to address the 48th annual commemoration of the killing in detention of Imam Abdullah Haron. There, I was informed by a lawyer that during apartheid, Pretorius had successfully prosecuted anti-apartheid activist Imam Achmat Cassiem, with whom I had the honour of sharing the platform that night.[261]

I had not been aware of Pretorius's past work on behalf of the apartheid state but I soon learned that he had also represented the state in the unsuccessful prosecution of the chemical warfare expert, Dr Wouter Basson. Nicknamed Dr Death, Basson was once the head of the apartheid government's secret chemical and biological warfare project, Project Coast.

In an interview with Cape Talk[262] on 25 October 2017, the Hawks spokesperson Hangwani Mulaudzi confirmed that the bulk of the work had been done during the inquest but the unit was looking at tying up a few loose ends before taking the case back to the NPA to prosecute. He added, 'It is unclear whether Rodrigues will be arrested considering his age.'

The reality was that there had been no real progress on any of the investigations.

I continued my interactions with victims' families throughout the country trying to assist them on their journeys to find closure. The families included that of Chief Albert Luthuli, who died in 1967 after being struck by a train; Suliman 'Babla' Saloojee, who police claimed committed suicide in 1964; Nicodemus Kgoathe, Solomon Modipane and Jacob Monakgotla, who died in police detention in 1969; Imam Haron, who the police allege died after falling from a flight of stairs in 1969; Matthews Mabelane, who the police said committed suicide in 1977; Dr Hoosen Haffejee, who police said took his own life in 1977; Ashley Kriel, a 20-year-old South African activist, who was shot dead by police in Cape Town on 9 July 1987 (Policeman, Jeffrey Benzien was granted amnesty from prosecution by the TRC for his part in the killing.); and Coline Williams and Robbie Waterwitch, who died in 1989 in Cape Town following an explosion.

My interactions with their loved ones were extremely difficult and painful as I witnessed the dynamics and challenges around their pain. Families have not healed and they still carry the scars of their losses. They have been frustrated by having not had their cases genuinely investigated. I hope to continue working with these families and to help them overcome the challenges they face in finding out what really happened to their loved ones and to finally get closure.

The *Argus* newspaper[263] on 7 February 2018 reported that the sister of Ashley Kriel, Michelle Assure, had been visited by members of the Hawks in 2016 and notified that they planned to reopen the case into his death. Despite her leaving messages for them and the National Prosecuting Authority, no one has come back to her. The Kriel family's experience, and that of other victim's families, has convinced me that the private and public commitments made by the NPA and the Hawks officials were disingenuous. I am of the opinion that the information that is retrieved from victims' families is not done with a view to using it to assist the investigations, but it simply allows officials to determine the extent of available evidence. The investigations are stalled; victims' families lose hope and the matters are forgotten.

Advocate Shaun Abrahams announced in Parliament on 9 May 2018[264] that the NPA would prioritise the prosecution of those who were linked to the murder of anti-apartheid activists. The 15 cases considered for possible prosecution included the murders of Victoria Mxenge, that of the Cradock Four and Dr Neil Aggett. Aggett's case was indeed reopened in January 2020. I still have my doubts that there is a political will to investigate all the deaths in detention. Apart from the Aggett case, there has been very little progress made on these investigations to date.

The docket was referred for a decision to the office of the director of public prosecutions in South Gauteng, Advocate Andrew Chauke. Extensive further investigation was undertaken by a handpicked team of investigators after the matter was enrolled. Advocate Chauke must be commended for taking a bold decision to charge Rodrigues.

Nine months after the Mothle judgment, Rodrigues was to appear in court on 30 July 2018 and Oryx Media issued a press release about it. Within seconds, I received numerous telephone calls from the media seeking my comment. What remains entrenched in my memory is a question from one of the journalists, 'Is Rodrigues really being charged, is this true?' That evening I received a call from a comrade asking if I would attend the court proceedings. He was concerned that I should not attend on my own as he was afraid that there could be a threat on my life. I laughed it off – nothing was going to deter me from attending this historic court proceeding.

It took me back to how Rodrigues was found. It was not the NPA or the Hawks that traced him; it came about after an email I received on 4 June 2017 from his daughter Tilana Stander. She said that for many years she had had an urge to expose the man who had sexually abused her as a child and had belittled her over a long period. When she grew up and left home, Tilana married Drikus Stander, who supported her to recover from her horrific ordeal at the hands of her own father.

One evening, the couple watched a news broadcast about the reopening of the Timol case, which said that all the police officers involved in the matter had passed on. Tilana recalled:

> I had this overwhelming excitement of knowing I can actually help this family to find Rodrigues. My husband and I immediately started to search the web for journalists, until we came upon the Timol website where I left a message. Due to the uniqueness of the spelling of his surname, they got it wrong. Also by going under the name 'Jan', it made it difficult to find the man. I saw pictures of a mother crying at the TRC. She wanted to know what happened to her child. My own experience on what happened to me through the hands of my biological father, inspired me to help this family. I am a mother of two boys and can understand that a mother and her family and will go to the end of the world to find out what happened to her son in order to get closure.[265]

The wheels of justice turn slowly

Tilana's message to her father is clear, 'You are now 80 years old and it's time for you to come clean and tell the truth. Take responsibility and apologise for all your wrong doings.' She doubts, however, that he will because she believes that he is too arrogant and self-centred. While he tried to apologise to her in an email many years ago, he continued to attempt to manipulate her. Her message to her father was:

> What is happening to him is because of the choices he made earlier in his life and thinking he is untouchable. I want him to know he is not above anybody or better than anyone else. I believe whatever you do in life that is wrong against anybody – apologise – be sincere about it. These things creeps up on you and life has a way of bringing this to the surface so that you can learn the lessons that you need to in this lifetime. It will come back and haunt you forever. You won't heal if you don't feel.

Why did Tilana take so long to come forward? Was she being vindictive against her father? I honestly do not think so. According to research into abuse,[266] the answer is complicated. There are a wide range of reasons people do not report to the authorities their experiences of sexual harassment and assault, often hiding them from friends and family members even. The announcement of the reopening of the inquest and information in the media, that all the security police officers had passed on, was the trigger Tilana needed to open up publicly.

I left home at around 5 am on Monday, 30 July 2018 to head for the Johannesburg Central police station, the renamed John Vorster Square building. My early departure was aimed at missing the chaotic morning traffic between Pretoria and Johannesburg. Enver Samuel, the film producer, wanted to get footage of Rodrigues for his documentary on the reopened inquest. I got to the building, did an interview with Enver, and then we waited for Rodrigues to appear.

I first caught sight of him walking down Commissioner Street towards the police station flanked by his legal representatives, Advocates Ben Minnaar and Fanus Coetzee. It was an historical moment. To see Rodrigues on his way to being charged for murder at the same building where, 46 years before, my uncle was killed. I was excited and took many photographs and video clips of him in the charge office to upload onto various media platforms.

Rodrigues was charged, taken to the holding cells and driven by police to the Johannesburg Magistrate Court where he applied for bail.

After giving several telephone interviews, I also went to the court, ironically the same building where the 1972 inquest had been held. There I waited for more than an hour, with a large contingent of journalists. The delay was caused by Rodrigues's legal team discussing with the magistrate and the state attorney how he would enter the courtroom. They claimed that their client was not able to climb the flight of stairs from the cells up to the dock. After a lengthy consultation, Rodrigues finally surfaced, climbing the steps without assistance. The MEC of Basic Education and ANC Deputy Chairman, Panyaza Lesufi, was in court, supporting the family of a South African teacher and activist. No other family representatives were present.

Rodrigues was charged for murder and defeating the ends of justice, and released on bail of R2 000. A pre-trial date was set for 18 September 2018. Outside the court I addressed the media with Phindi Louw, the spokesperson of the National Prosecuting Authority. She hailed the 2017 inquest judgment as affirming the rule of law. 'The judge ruled that it is both in the interest of justice and that of society that the people who are alleged to have perpetrated violent crimes against humanity must be brought to book,' she said.

I had been due to take part in studio interviews that evening with the SABC and eNCA but they had to be cancelled when I received the tragic news that my cousin Sabera Jassat had passed away in Azaadville. She had bravely fought cancer for a number of years, never complaining about her illness and the pain that she bore. This was an important lesson for me. It was an emotional day witnessing

Rodrigues being charged and laying Sabera to rest the same evening.

Rodrigues's court appearance was only the beginning of a new journey. Some of those who had been supportive of the reopening of the 2017 inquest suddenly disappeared. Questions began to be posed, such as: Why is Rodrigues being pursued? Who approved this? How can it be stopped? All trustees of the Ahmed Timol Family Trust, consisting of Uncle Mohammad, Mahomed Chothia, Fatima Areff and Ahmed Timol (son of Uncle Haroon) resigned from the body, the Ahmed Timol Golf Day was abandoned and I became the victim of a smear campaign. These were just some of the new challenges I was faced with.

My part in this 46-year journey to set the record straight formally began on 30 April 1996, the day of Ma's testimony to the Truth and Reconciliation Commission. On 12 October 2017, when Judge Mothle pronounced his verdict, we had summited a major peak.

His ruling broke important new ground: For the first time, an apartheid-era inquest into the death of an activist was reopened and exposed as a fraud. And, for the first time, members of the feared Security Branch were forced to emerge from the safety of anonymity and publicly account for their actions. I also hope that my investigation has brought us closer to understanding the security environment in apartheid South Africa, and the events leading to Uncle Ahmed's arrest – and that of many others.

The revised inquest finding was a significant milestone in my quest to honour my uncle. But, I couldn't help think that the journey was not over.

Forty-six years after Ahmed Timol's murder, and 26 years since the birth of the democratic South Africa, the political landscape, nationally and globally, has dramatically altered. Apartheid has been consigned to the rubbish bin of history, where it belongs, and Cold War relationships have thawed. As Archbishop Tutu put it, 'We marched in Cape Town and the Berlin Wall fell'.[267] We now call the world a 'global village', and increasingly understand that this comes with global responsibilities and challenges – huge challenges of inequality, resource depletion and environmental degradation.

Addressing a group of school pupils celebrating Nelson Mandela International Day in 2011, Ahmed Kathrada, a stalwart of the anti-apartheid struggle who served 26 years in prison, said, 'You can have all the wealth, all the riches in the world, but it wouldn't mean anything without dignity, which is the most important thing in the world. Apartheid robbed our people of dignity and our biggest achievement is that, after 300 years of oppression, we have won dignity for our people.'[268]

The system that my uncle, and many others, opposed did not just racially divide South Africans and ensure that white people owned the best land and all the mineral wealth; it also deliberately under-educated black people, deprived them of basic services and infrastructure. It split families and communities through, amongst others, the migrant labour system, crushed their dignity and forced them into subservient poverty – for nearly 350 years. Today we are living with the material result: We are one of the most unequal societies in the world.

I am often confronted with questions like: What did my uncle die for? Was it worthwhile? Less than a generation after being freed from the tyranny of apartheid, it already feels as if we take our democracy for granted and require constant reminders that it didn't come cheaply or easily. As we confront our new challenges, we can be emboldened by the knowledge that we do have the power to effect change; our hard-fought freedom was achieved because of the selflessness of ordinary men and women – most of whom were only armed with the strength of their argument and the courage of their convictions. Ordinary people, teachers and factory workers, entrepreneurs, professionals and the unemployed. People like Ahmed Timol. People like you and me.

The last white president of South Africa, F.W. de Klerk, was awarded the Nobel Peace Prize with Nelson Mandela in recognition of their roles in the political transformation of our country. But make no mistake, De Klerk did not suddenly wake up one morning in a generous mood and hand freedom to the oppressed masses on a golden platter. He, himself, is implicated in the deaths of the Cradock Four.[269]

It was the deeds of the people, across the length and breadth of the country – supported by the actions of the armies of liberation, and international economic sanctions – that eventually forced the apartheid regime to negotiate with the people it had dismissed as terrorists and communists. Most of these selfless comrades involved in the protracted struggle for our freedom have never been acknowledged. But their struggles were not in vain.

When I am asked if my uncle's sacrifice was worth it, I think of the words of the celebrated MK combatant Basil February who said, 'A guerilla is one who fights to free his people from bondage and enslavement. The prospect of death does not even arise in his mind as his life will go on in the hearts of a nation that will remember him.'[270]

Was my uncle's death worth it? It depends on what measure you choose to use. Has post-apartheid South Africa reached nirvana? The answer is obviously no. Have we built a culture of human rights and equal justice for all? Once again, considering such factors as the levels of violent crime perpetrated by men against women and children, and the grinding poverty, the answer would have to be no. Was it worthwhile to actively oppose apartheid? If one had to pose this question to the opponents of fascism in Pinochet's Chile or in Hitler's Germany – or to those seeking justice for the people of Palestine – the answer would be a resounding yes.

I suspect that what many people would really like to know is, if Ahmed Timol was still with us today, would he be satisfied with the nation's progress? What would he have thought, said and done? Similar questions are asked in respect of other slain activists such as Chris Hani, Matthew Goniwe and Bantu Stephen Biko. I have learned that some questions don't have answers and am disinclined to speak on my uncle's behalf.

Having been able to help to have his inquest reopened has given me a sense of contentment and achievement. I feel as if I have finally succeeded in removing the pebbles from my shoe. The journey was arduous; and it sometimes felt as if I was peeling an onion that had an infinite number of layers – but it was worth it. It was ultimately revealed that Uncle Ahmed's arrest was orchestrated by the apartheid security system before the police brutally tortured, assaulted and murdered him.

My journey has taken me to some pretty dark places, including the murky world of the security establishment. Neither the roles of BOSS and Hendrik van den Bergh, nor the departments of Justice and Internal Affairs featured in either of the inquests. While the extent of the intelligence on Uncle Ahmed obtained in London is not known, Dr Niël Barnard[271] has confirmed that the SACP was a permanent feature on the National Intelligence Service's radar, and that the agency acquired sources in its highest council chambers. This intelligence would have provided the state agency with direct knowledge of the SA Communist Party's strategies, tactics and plans.

In my heart and in my mind I have now found closure and I do not believe that my uncle's murder will ever be forgotten. But over the course of the investigation I picked up new pebbles in my shoe: Firstly, the role and control of its agents by apartheid-era security structures in the democratic era has never been revealed. We do not know if, around the time of the first democratic elections in 1994, all the books were closed and the agents released of their responsibilities. Which of these agents who informed on liberation movements later assumed important political positions in the new dispensation? If they were not loyal to their liberation movements, could they be loyal to South Africa's constitutional democracy? These are important questions that, if addressed, would shed light on some of the current challenges the country is grappling. So, that's the first new pebble. Perhaps I will have to learn to live with it.

My wish is that our progress in this case has given hope to the other families whose mothers, fathers, sons and daughters were murdered by apartheid police. I am very grateful that reopening the inquest into Uncle Ahmed's death has made history. I am also very conscious of the responsibility it has created. My new priority is to use whatever knowledge and experience I have picked up on this journey to assist these families. The state is morally, ethically and legally obliged to help bring closure to all who lost loved ones in the struggle for freedom.

A former uMkhonto weSizwe combatant friend of mine, known as China, tells me I have been brave in my quest; other friends and comrades warn me that I could be murdered.

I feel that I have been more resolute than brave. I tell China and the others that it was, in fact, comrades such as themselves who were the 'brave ones', who left their homes and loved ones and were willing to sacrifice their lives for the freedom of the people of the country – with no certainty of when or if they would return to a democratic South Africa, and if they did, how they would survive the dangers they faced.

As for me, the day Allah calls me to return to Him, I will do so without any qualms. Not a day earlier or later, only as He prescribes will I reunite with my beloved uncle.

Aluta Continua – The Struggle Continues

Ahmed Timol timeline

3 November 1941: Born in Breyten, Mpumalanga, South Africa

1949: Moves to the suburb of Roodepoort with his parents

1955: The Timol family moves to Balfour, Mpumalanga

1956: The Timol family returns to Roodepoort and Uncle Ahmed finishes his education at the Johannesburg Indian High School

1960: Starts working as a bookkeeper in Johannesburg

1961–3: Trains as a teacher at the Transvaal Indian College in Fordsburg (also referred to as the Training Institute for Indian Teachers; Teacher's Training College and Johannesburg Training Institute for Indian Teachers).

9 September 1964: Suliman 'Babla' Saloojee dies in police detention after falling from the seventh floor window of Grays Building. His death is ruled as suicide. Timol attends his funeral.

1964–1966: Begins teaching at Roodepoort Indian High School

25 December 1966: Travels to Mecca in Saudi Arabia to perform hajj

April 1967: Arrives in London, via Egypt

1969: Undergoes political training in the Soviet Union with Thabo Mbeki and Ann Nicholson

1970: Returns to South Africa and works underground for 18 months

10 April 1970: Resumes teaching at the Roodepoort Indian High School

22 October 1971: Is arrested with Salim Essop at a police roadblock in Coronationville

27 October 1971: Dies in police detention, aged 29

29 October 1971: Is buried in Roodepoort

24 April 1972: The first inquest into his death begins

22 June 1972: Magistrate J.J.L. de Villiers rules that his death was by suicide

October 1973: The Ahmed Timol Memorial Trust is established shortly before the anniversary.

1987: uMkhonto weSizwe names a unit after him

30 April 1996: His mother, Hawa Timol, testifies at the Truth and Reconciliation Commission

29 March 1999: Nelson Mandela renames the Azaadville Secondary School as Ahmed Timol Secondary School

2005: Imtiaz Cajee's book, *Timol: Quest for Justice* is published

2005: Broadcast on eTV of the first documentary on Ahmed Timol's death, entitled *Indians Can't Fly* produced by Debora Patta

2009: Imtiaz Cajee calls for the reopening of the inquest into his uncle's death

11 December 2009: Ahmed Timol is posthumously awarded the Order of Luthuli in Silver for his 'excellent contribution and selfless sacrifice in the struggle against apartheid'. His brother, Mohammad accepted the award on his behalf.

2015: A team is established to apply for the reopening of the inquest.

2015: Broadcast on SABC of the second documentary on Ahmed Timol's death entitled *Indians Can't Fly* produced by Enver Samuel

1 September 2015: The Ahmed Timol Family Trust is established.

19 January 2016: A formal application is made for the reopening of the inquest.

26 October 2016: The National Directorate of Public Prosecutions announces that the inquest will be reopened.

4 June 2017: Tilana Stander, the daughter of João Rodrigues, confirms that her father is still alive and she tells Imtiaz Cajee where to find him.

26 June 2017: Judge Billy Mothle opens the second inquest

12 October 2017: Judge Billy Mothle finds that Ahmed Timol was murdered. He calls for charges to be laid against three former policemen.

29 July 2018: A warrant of arrest is issued for João Rodrigues.

30 July 2018: João Rodrigues is charged at the Johannesburg Central police station, formerly John Vorster Square, with murder and defeating the ends of justice. He is formerly released on R2 000 bail at the Johannesburg Magistrates Court from where the first inquest was held.

18 September 2018: João Rodrigues applies to the High Court for a permanent stay of prosecution

Acknowledgements

I would like to express my gratitude to Yasmin Sooka, the former CEO of the Foundation for Human Rights (FHR) for setting up a formidable team comprising the Legal Resources Centre (LRC), Webber Wentzel (WW), Howard Varney and Frank Dutton, which helped to have the inquest into be uncle's death reopened. I am also grateful to the Khulumani Support Group and the South African Communist Party for support during the 2017 inquest, and to Bongani Ntuli from KwaZulu-Natal for his support.

I thank the local and international donors who contributed to the creation of the Ahmed Timol Exhibition in 2015 at the Apartheid Museum as well as for the funds for filming of the 2017 inquest. Gabi Mohale and the staff of Historical Papers at the University of the Witwatersrand were tremendous in providing me with vital archival assistance.

Thanks are also due to Omar Badsha of South African History Online (SAHO) and Faizel Cook for their help in the publication of *Timol: Quest for Justice*; Adams and Adams for assistance in setting up the Ahmed Timol Family Trust and for registering the copyright of the Ahmed Timol name; the subscribers to my mailing list, Facebook and Twitter. I want to thank members of the media for preserving the legacy of Ahmed Timol in a democratic South Africa and my selected group of special advisors who prefer to remain anonymous. I am grateful to Ronnie Kasrils and Uncle Mohammad for their assistance in the initial phases of this book, and to Benny Gool and Roger Friedman for their assistance. Thanks also to Tilana and Drikus Stander for helping to locate João Rodrigues.

Over the past two decades I have been honoured and privileged to play a small role as a member of the post-apartheid security establishment. It has enabled me to constructively contribute to building our beloved country and, in a way, to continue my uncle's work. One would think that working in such an environment would have given me an advantage in my hunt for information about my uncle's death. It has not, although I am very grateful that my employer, the State Security Agency, has not stood in the way of my long quest for justice. I hope they will agree that I have never neglected my duties and responsibilities to my country.

My deep appreciation goes to those who never abandoned me and, at huge cost to themselves, continued to support me.

As always, our Creator gave me the strength, patience and perseverance in the most difficult times to remain steadfast in preserving the legacy of Ahmed Timol and also assisting other families in their quest for justice.

Endnotes

1 Mandela on 5 August 1962 and Biko on 18 August 1977 were arrested in roadblocks; the Cradock Four (Matthew Goniwe, Fort Calata, Sparrow Mkhonto and Sicelo Mhlauli) were captured at a roadblock on 27 June 1985 and murdered by police.
2 George Lardner Jr. and David B. Ottaway, 'CIA linked to Mandela's 1962 ARREST', *Washington Post*, 1990, https://www.washingtonpost.com/archive/politics/1990/06/11/cia-linked-to-mandelas-1962-arrest/9163094c-6a68-4f7e-8087-730720879bd7/, accessed on 28 March 2015.
3 Feliks Garcia, 'Former CIA agent admits involvement in Nelson Mandela's arrest', *Independent*, 2016, https://www.independent.co.uk/news/world/africa/nelson-mandela-cia-arrest-south-africa-a7030751.html, accessed on 15 March 2015.
4 ABC (Australian Broadcasting Corporation), https://www.abc.net.au/news/ Former CIA spy Donald Rickard claims his tip-off led to Nelson Mandela's 1962 arrest; Updated 15 May 2016 – https://www.abc.net.au/news/2016-05-16/cia-spy-claimed-his-tip-off-led-to-mandela-arrest-report-says/7416446, accessed on 10 June 2016.
5 Nelson Mandela, *Long Walk to Freedom: The Autobiography of Nelson Mandela*, Back Bay Books, 1995.
6 Performed after *Isha* (obligatory night prayer) and before *Fajr* (obligatory morning prayer)
7 Leeds United Club News, 'Blue Plaque tribute to Albert Johanneson', 2019, https://www.leedsunited.com/news/club/24382/blue-plaque-tribute-to-albert-johanneson, accessed on 11 November 2019.
8 Steven Bantu Biko, aged 30, founder of the Black Consciousness

Movement (BCM), died due to brain injury during a scuffle with the police on 12 September 1977. He was the 41st person to have died in police detention.

9   Peter Gordon, 'Timol's whereabouts a mystery', *The Citizen*, 7 January 1978.
10 Lungelo Mkamba, 'Capital Radio bid to restart', *The Mercury*, 1989, https://www.iol.co.za/mercury/capital-radio-bid-to-restart-1366991, accessed on 8 January 2018.
11 He later became a lawyer and the MEC for Transport in Mpumalanga.
12 Email correspondence, dated 11 June 2019 with Haroon Cajee.
13 A non-aggression, good neighbourliness pact on the border between both countries. South Africa would cease to support Renamo forces in Mozambique and in return Mozambique would not allow liberation movements such as the ANC and Pan-Africanist Congress (PAC) to establish bases in Mozambique.
14 Kevin A. O'Brien, *The South African Intelligence Services: From Apartheid to Democracy, 1948–2005*, New York: Routledge, 2012.
15 An annual association football award given to the world's best male football player by the sport's governing body FIFA.
16 Tom Mashland, 'Protesters rally again in S. Africa', *Chicago Tribune*, 1989, http://articles.chicagotribune.com/1989-09-16/news/8901130442_1_march-in-cape-town-milelong-march-protest, accessed on 27 April 2016.
17 Between the South African government and the ANC were held on 2, 3 and 4 May 1990. They were followed by the Convention for a Democratic South Africa (CODESA) in 1991 and 1992. http://www.sahistory.org.za/dated-event/talks-between-government-and-anc-negotiations-proceed, accessed on 25 April 2017.
18 South African History Online (SAHO); , http://www.sahistory.org.za/people/stephanie-kemp, accessed on 25 April 2017.
19 A legal clerk and political activist, aged 32, Saloojee was the fourth detainee to have died in police detention on 9 September 1964.
20 The South African Truth and Reconciliation Commission was set up by the Government of National Unity to help deal with what happened under apartheid. The conflict during this period resulted in violence and human rights abuses from all sides. No section of society escaped these abuses. The TRC was based on the Promotion of National Unity and Reconciliation Act, No 34 of 1995. For more on its work, see http://www.justice.gov.za/Trc/

21 TRC case number: GO/O173, https://www.justice.gov.za/trc/hrvtrans/methodis/timol.htm, accessed on 10 April 2016.
22 https://www.sahistory.org.za/archive/speech-renaming-ahmed-timol-school-29-march-1999, accessed on 26 August 2012; see also, Imtiaz Cajee, *Timol: Quest For Justice*, Pretoria: STE Publishers, 2005, pp 188–89.
23 There were desks that were established at the Security Branch for Indians, coloureds, Africans and whites. These desks focused on activists that were identified as a threat to the state.
24 Dictionary.com, https://www.dictionary.com/browse/those-who-cannot-remember-the-past-are-condemned-to-repeat-it, accessed on 10 December 2019.
25 Former members of the SACP Central Committee exiled in London sought to reconstitute themselves, linking with those in Dar Es Salaam. Attempts to recreate the party underground in South Africa was given to a specialist sub-committee headed by Dr Dadoo, together with Joe Slovo and Jack Hodgson, and included Ronnie Kasrils who arrived from Tanzania to join them at the end of 1965. This committee recruited and trained young activists such as Ahmed Timol for clandestine work back in South Africa; and organised the secret distribution of literature for the ANC as well as the Party. For this work they also recruited foreign activists for mainly the clandestine distribution of leaflets in South Africa, referred to as London Recruits.
26 Interview with Meg Pahad in 2004. See, Cajee, *Timol: Quest For Justice*, 2005, p 75.
27 The CPSA was the name of the party before it was banned. The one he belonged to was the SACP, South African Communist Party.
28 A copy of the autobiography, obtained from Lenin University, is available with me.
29 Salim Essop's interview with Ruth Longoni in 2003. Cajee, *Timol: Quest For Justice*, 2005, p 76.
30 Debora Patta produced the first documentary *Indian's Can't Fly* for eTV. It was first broadcast in 2005. Enver Samuel produced another, with the same name, for the SABC in 2015.
31 Vladimir Shubin, *ANC: A View from Moscow*, Cape Town: Mayibuye Books, 1999, p 48.
32 Shubin, ANC: *A View from Moscow* p 43.
33 Mark Gevisser's research papers for *Thabo Mbeki: The Dream Deferred*,

South African Historical Archives (SAHA), http://www.saha.org.za/collections/the_mark_gevisser_collection.htm-E7.3.11; Interview with Alexandra Rodionova (Comrade Shura), former interpreter, instructor, chair of Social Psychology at the Lenin School, 25 October, http://www.saha.org.za/collections/AL3284/e7311.htm, accessed on 5 May 2016.

34 Norman Levy, *The Final Prize: My Life in the Anti-Apartheid Struggle*, 2011, South African History Online, https://www.sahistory.org.za/article/trial-state-versus-abram-fischer-and-thirteen-others-norman-levy, accessed on 27 August 2019.

35 Mark Gevisser's research papers for *Thabo Mbeki: The Dream Deferred* SAHA, http://www.saha.org.za/collections/the_mark_gevisser_collection.htm AL3284_E7.1.5.pdf, accessed on 30 August 2015.

36 Interview with Wolfie Kodesh, 28 August 1994, Tape # 2 of 3, Tape MCA6 – 339b: Nicholson, Ann (2), Mayibuye Centre Audiotape.

37 South African History Online (SAHO), https://www.sahistory.org.za/people/percy-john-jack-hodgson, accessed on 10 December 2019.

38 Interview with Uncle Haroon in 2003. See, Cajee, *Timol: Quest for Justice*, 2005, p 88.

39 Fakir Hassen, 'Role of Lenasia scholar in Ahmed Timol's activities revealed', *Lenasia Times*, July 2017.

40 Ronnie Kasrils, *Armed and Dangerous*, London: Heinemann Books, 1992, pp 78–79.

41 Partial set of the 1972 inquest records obtained from Cachalia & Loonat, exhibit in 2017 inquest records. Now available at the Ahmed Kathrada Foundation; and Wits Historical Papers: Inventory for AK3388, http://www.historicalpapers.wits.ac.za/?inventory/U/collections&c=AK3388/R/9141 TIMOL, Ahmed Inquest, records, 1971–1972, accessed in October 2017.

42 Interview with Essop Pahad in 2004. See, Cajee, *Timol: Quest For Justice*, 2005, p 85.

43 A/J/1/24/4/70, http://www.historicalpapers.wits.ac.za/inventories/inv_pdfo/AK3388/AK3388-B7-01-jpeg.pdf, accessed on 10 May 2017.

44 A/J/2/12/5/70, http://www.historicalpapers.wits.ac.za/inventories/inv_pdfo/AK3388/AK3388-B7-01-jpeg.pdf, pp 2–3, accessed on 10 May 2017.

45 J/S/1/17/5/70, http://www.historicalpapers.wits.ac.za/inventories/

Endnotes

inv_pdfo/AK3388/AK3388-B8-01-jpeg.pdf, p 5, accessed on 10 May 2017.

46 A/J/3/4/7/70, http://www.historicalpapers.wits.ac.za/inventories/inv_pdfo/AK3388/AK3388-B7-01-jpeg.pdf, p. 4, accessed on 10 May 2017.

47 A/J/1/10/11/70, http://www.historicalpapers.wits.ac.za/inventories/inv_pdfo/AK3388/AK3388-B7-01-jpeg.pdf, pp 8–9, accessed on 10 May 2017.

48 3/3/71, http://www.historicalpapers.wits.ac.za/inventories/inv_pdfo/AK3388/AK3388-B8-01-jpeg.pdf, p 22.

49 A/J/1/24/4/70, http://www.historicalpapers.wits.ac.za/inventories/inv_pdfo/AK3388/AK3388-B7-01-jpeg.pdf, accessed on 10 May 2017.

50 A/J/3/4/7/70 http://www.historicalpapers.wits.ac.za/inventories/inv_pdfo/AK3388/AK3388-B7-01-jpeg.pdf, p 7, accessed on 10 May 2017.

51 A/J/2/12/5/70 http://www.historicalpapers.wits.ac.za/inventories/inv_pdfo/AK3388/AK3388-B8-01-jpeg.pdf, p 4, accessed on 10 May 2017.

52 Interview with Indres Naidoo in 2004. See, Cajee, *Timol: Quest for Justice*, 2005, p 101.

53 A/J/2/12/5/70 http://www.historicalpapers.wits.ac.za/inventories/inv_pdfo/AK3388/AK3388-B8-01-jpeg.pdf, p 3, accessed on 10 May 2017.

54 C/3/29/12/70 http://www.historicalpapers.wits.ac.za/inventories/inv_pdfo/AK3388/AK3388-B8-01-jpeg.pdf, p 21, accessed on 10 May 2017.

55 A/J/1/10/11/70 http://www.historicalpapers.wits.ac.za/inventories/inv_pdfo/AK3388/AK3388-B7-01-jpeg.pdf, p 9, accessed on 10 May 2017.

56 A/J/4/17/8/'70 http://www.historicalpapers.wits.ac.za/inventories/inv_pdfo/AK3388/AK3388-B7-01-jpeg.pdf, p 7, accessed on 10 May 2017.

57 Email from Dr Dindar in 2003. See also, Cajee, *Timol: Quest for Justice*, 2005, p 108.

58 Interview with Yacoob Adam in 2003. See also, Cajee, *Timol: Quest for Justice*, 2005, p 108.

59 Interview with Yunus Cajee in 2003. See also, Cajee, *Timol: Quest for*

Justice, 2005, p 108.
60 http://www.historicalpapers.wits.ac.za/inventories/inv_pdfo/AK3388/AK3388-B2-01-jpeg.pdf, p. 16, accessed on 10 May 2017.
61 Interview with Salim Essop in 2003. See, Cajee, *Timol: Quest for Justice*, 2005, p 110.
62 Interview with dressmaker in 2002. See also, Cajee, *Timol: Quest for Justice*, 2005, p 108.
63 Interview with Irene on 11 June 2016 in Johannesburg.
64 Email correspondence with Jane in June 2016.
65 The family insisted that an inquest be held, where it emerged that the imam had been badly injured prior to his death. As a consequence, the family sued the Minister of Police, who eventually paid them an ex gratia payment of R5000.
66 Tim Clarke, 'Biggest probe since Rivonia', *Sunday Express*, 31 October 1971, https://www.ahmedtimol.co.za/downloads/archive/articles/1971NewspaperArticles/19711031SundayExpressBiggestExpressbiggestprobesinceRivonnia.pdf, accessed on 10 February 2017.
67 International Defence Aid Fund, *BOSS: First Five Years*, London: IDAF, 1975, as quoted in the *Rand Daily Mail*, 22 November 1971.
68 http://www.historicalpapers.wits.ac.za/inventories/inv_pdfo/AK3388/AK3388-B2-01-jpeg.pdf, pp 1–2, accessed on 10 May 2017.
69 SAHA, *Between Life and Death: Stories from John Vorster Square*, commissioned by SAHA as part of the Sunday Times Heritage Project and filmed by Craig Matthews of Doxa Productions, https://www.google.com/culturalinstitute/beta/exhibit/detention-without-trial-in-john-vorster-square/gQ-1o9MM?hl=en-GB; http://www.saha.org.za/news/2010/August/remembering_a_darker_time_when_john_vorster_square_was_opened.htm, accessed on 13 August 2017.
70 Marius De Witt Dippenaar, *S.A. Police Commemorative Album: The History of the South African Police 1913–1988*, Silverton, South Africa: Promedia, 1988.
71 A scanned copy of the original article can be found at: https://www.ahmedtimol.co.za/downloads/archive/articles/1971NewspaperArticles/19711029RandDailyMailwindowshavesteelgrilles.pdf
72 SAHA, *Between Life and Death: Stories from John Vorster Square*, commissioned by SAHA as part of the Sunday Times Heritage Project and filmed by Craig Matthews of Doxa Productions, http://www.

saha.org.za/publications/between_life_and_death.htm, accessed on 5 March 2020

73   Interview with Baboo Dindar in 2002. See, Cajee, *Timol: Quest for Justice*, 2005, p 125.
74   http://www.historicalpapers.wits.ac.za/inventories/inv_pdfo/AK3388/AK3388-B3-01-jpeg.pdf, p 6.
75   Fast breaking time in the month of Ramadan.
76   Interview with Salim Gabba in 2003. See, Cajee, Timol: Quest for the Truth, 2005, p. 138
77   'Death of detainee: Reaction mounts,' *The Star*, 28 October 1971, https://www.ahmedtimol.co.za/downloads/archive/articles/1971Newspaper-Articles/19711028DeathofDetaineereactionmounts28Oct71.pdf, accessed on 15 March 2013.
78   Won two South African Film & Television Awards in 2016: Best South African Short Documentary Award and Best South African Short Documentary Director Award.
79   The newspaper only referred to him by his first name.
80   'Hundreds at the Timol funeral', *The Saturday Star*, 30 October 1971, http://www.ahmedtimol.co.za/downloads/archive/articles/Undatedarticles/SaturdayOct30.pdf, 15 March 2013
81   http://www.ahmedtimol.co.za/downloads/archive/articles/Undatedarticles/SaturdayOct30.pdf, 15 March 2013.
82   *Saturday Star*, 30 October 1971, https://www.ahmedtimol.co.za/downloads/archive/articles/1971NewspaperArticles/19711030DeathofdetaineeAngerrisesathomeandoverseas.pdf
83   Interview with Salim Gabba in 2003. See, Cajee, *Timol: Quest for Justice*, 2005, p 138.
84   Posted on Facebook – date unknown.
85   Salim's father had heard from a journalist that his son had been transferred to a public hospital in Pretoria but when Mr Essop went there, his son's presence was denied. Fortunately, he saw Salim through a fanlight and concluded that he was seriously ill.

He brought an urgent application to the Supreme Court to prevent the police from further torturing his son. On 29 October 1971, Justice Margo granted an interim interdict restraining the police from treating Salim in a manner other than that prescribed or permitted by law or applying any undue or unlawful pressure on him. He made a *rule nisi* incorporating this interdict and according to John Dugard, a Wits law

professor, this was the first successful application for an interdict under Section 6 of the Terrorism Act.
86 Email from Uncle Mohammad in 2004. See, Cajee, *Timol: Quest for Justice*, 2005, p 122.
87 Interview with Arvind on 6 February 2016 in Fordsburg.
88 'They were murdered', *Sechaba*, Vol 6, no 2, 1972, pp 2–3, https://www.sahistory.org.za/archive/sechaba-volume-6-number-2-february-1972, accessed 01 February 2018. Cajee, *Timol: Quest for Justice*, 2005, p 142.
89 'Ahmed Timol, 20th detainee to die in police custody', *Anti-Apartheid News*, December 1971–January 1972, p 7, https://www.ahmedtimol.co.za/downloads/archive/articles/1971NewspaperArticles/197112197201AntiApartheidNewspaper20thdetainee.pdf, accessed on 15 March 2013.
90 'Ahmed Timol, 20th detainee to die in police custody', *Anti-Apartheid News*, December 1971–January 1972, p 7, http://www.ahmedtimol.co.za/downloads/archive/articles/1971NewspaperArticles/197112197201AntiApartheidNewsAhmedTimol20thdetainee.pdf, 15 March 2013.
91 *Anti-Apartheid News*, December 1971. See also, Cajee, *Timol: Quest for Justice*, 2005, p 142.
92 *Anti-Apartheid News*, December 1971. See also, Cajee, *Timol: Quest for Justice*, 2005, p 142.
93 Staff Reporter, *Pretoria News*, 28 October 1971, https://www.ahmedtimol.co.za/downloads/archive/articles/19711028PretoriaNewsSecondDeathDenial.pdf, accessed 15 March 2013
94 They were murdered', *Sechaba*, Vol 6, no 2, 1972, pp 2–3, https://www.sahistory.org.za/archive/sechaba-volume-6-number-2-february-1972, accessed 1 February 2018 https://www.ahmedtimol.co.za/downloads/archive/articles/19711028PretoriaNewsSecondDeathDenial.pdf, accessed 15 March 2013
95 *Anti-Apartheid News*, December 1971, https://www.ahmedtimol.co.za/downloads/archive/articles/19711028PretoriaNewsSecondDeathDenial.pdf, accessed 15 March 2013
96 *Anti-Apartheid News*, December 1971, https://www.ahmedtimol.co.za/downloads/archive/articles/19711028PretoriaNewsSecondDeathDenial.pdf, accessed 15 March 2013
97 *Anti-Apartheid News*, December 1971, https://www.ahmedtimol.co.za/downloads/archive/articles/19711028PretoriaNewsSecond-

DeathDenial.pdf, accessed 15 March 2013

98 *Anti-Apartheid News*, December 1971, https://www.ahmedtimol.co.za/downloads/archive/articles/19711028PretoriaNewsSecond-DeathDenial.pdf, accessed 15 March 2013

99 https://www.polity.org.za/article/nqakula-launch-of-a-book-on-ahmed-timol-290105-2005-01-29, accessed 12 March 2020.

100 South African History Online (SAHO), www.sahistory.org.za/people/helen-joseph, accessed on 20 September 2019.

101 Glenn Moss, *The New Radicals: A Generational Memoir of the 1970s*, Johannesburg: Jacana Media, 2014.

102 Interview with Enver Samuel for SABC documentary, *Indians Can't Fly*.

103 Interview with Karel Maseko in Pretoria in 2017.

104 https://www.ahmedtimol.co.za/wp-content/uploads/2020/03/Untitled4-TOINE-EGGENHUIZEN-HRC-SA-1.pdf, accessed 20 March 2020

105 Founding members of the Human Rights Committee included Prema Naidoo, Murtie Naidoo, Jeanette Curtis, Sheila Weinberg (secretary), Mohammad Timol (chairperson), Rookaya Saloojee, Peter Wellman, Caroline Clark, Toine Eggenhuisen, Aboobaker Ismail, Ian Robertson and Merle Barsel.

106 Abraham 'Bram' Fischer was born on 23 April 1908 into the Afrikaner establishment. Fischer was struck off the roll by the Johannesburg Bar Council in 1965 after he skipped bail on charges under the Suppression of Communism Act. But 294 days later, he was arrested and tried. On 9 May 1966, he was sentenced to life in jail.

107 Human Rights Committee, *HRC Bulletin*, April 1975, p 1, https://www.ahmedtimol.co.za/wp-content/uploads/2020/03/Untitled19-HRC-Bulletin-April-1975.pdf, accessed on 19 March 2020. The HRC Bulletins were brought to my attention by Uncle Mohammad and the surviving copies are uploaded on www.ahmedtimol.co.za

108 Email from Uncle Mohammad, in March 2016.

109 Human Rights Committee, *HRC Bulletin*, 26 June 1975, p 1, https://www.ahmedtimol.co.za/wp-content/uploads/2020/03/Untitled18-HRC-Bulletin-26-June-1975.pdf, accessed on 19 March 2020

110 Human Rights Committee, 'Statement of Policy', *HRC Bulletin*, 5 February 1976, p 2, https://www.ahmedtimol.co.za/wp-content/uploads/2020/03/Untitled17-HRC-Bulletin-5-February-1976.pdf,

accessed on 19 March 2020

111 Human Rights Committee, *HRC Bulletin*, 3 August 1975, pp 6 and 7, https://www.ahmedtimol.co.za/wp-content/uploads/2020/03/Untitled17-HRC-Bulletin-3-August-9-1975.pd, accessed on 19 March 2020

112 https://www.ahmedtimol.co.za/wp-content/uploads/2020/03/Untitled4-TOINE-EGGENHUIZEN-HRC-SA-1.pdf, accessed 20 March 2020

113 https://www.ahmedtimol.co.za/wp-content/uploads/2020/03/Untitled17-HRC-Bulletin-4-December-10-1975.pdf

114 Truth Commission Special Report, http://sabctrc.saha.org.za/reports/volume6/section3/chapter2/subsection8.htm, accessed on 28 March 2019.

115 Ibid.

116 Centre of Applied Legal Studies (CALS), University of the Witwatersrand, https://www.wits.ac.za/news/sources/cals-news/2017/new-report-reveals-shocking-failure-to-uphold-right-of-access-to-information.html, accessed on 28 February 2017.

117 The Federation of American Scientists defines the five-step intelligence cycle as planning and direction, collection, processing, source analysis and production, and dissemination. Collection is done 'overtly and covertly'. Overt intelligence gathering involves obtaining and evaluating information from open sources, while 'covert intelligence is obtained through the penetration of secret agents and informants or by means of special intelligence operations', Federation of American Scientists Operations Security, *Intelligence Threat Handbook*, Section 2 – Intelligence Collection Activities and Disciplines, https://fas.org/irp/nsa/ioss/threat96/part02.htm, accessed on 28 May 2018.

118 James McKillop, 'BOSS: The title that means what it says', *Glasgow Herald*, 11 March 1976. It was supposed to have been named the Bureau for State Security (BFSS) but a bureaucratic error left it as BOSS.

119 The International Defence and Aid Fund (IDAF) was established to support the families of political activists in Southern Rhodesia, Namibia and South Africa and to pay for their defence when they were tried. Its publication, *BOSS: The First Five Years*, provided an in-depth analysis on the formation of the shadowy department.

120 The operational functions of the South African security police were extended to include the occupied area of Namibia, and also possibly the neighbouring states of Lesotho, Swaziland and Botswana. The United

Kingdom and Zambia were two countries where BOSS was undeniably active. It is assumed that its officers worked closely with the Rhodesian Intelligence Services, as they did in Mozambique and in Angola with the Portuguese Directorate-General of Security until independence in 1974.

121 Keable, *London Recruits*, 2012, p 30.
122 E-mail correspondence dated 18 July 2018
123 Institute for Security Studies, 'Organised crime in South Africa: An assessment of its nature and origins', Monograph No. 28, August 1998, https://oldsite.issafrica.org/uploads/Mono28.pdf, accessed on 21 July 2018.
124 Ibid., p 10.
125 Ibid., p 10.
126 International Defence Aid Fund, *BOSS: First Five Years*, 1975, p 23.
127 Submission to the Truth and Reconciliation Commission on South Africa's Illegal and Covert Activities in the United Kingdom, presented by Lord Hughes, TRC Seminar, Cape Town, 10 November 1997, AAM Archives Committee.
128 Truth and Reconciliation Commission of South Africa Report, Volume 2, https://www.justice.gov.za/TRC/report/finalreport/Volume%202.pdf (63), p 16, accessed on 18 June 2018.
129 Gerard Ludi, *Operation Q-018*, Nasionalie Boeke, 1969, p 49.
130 Marius de Witt Dippenaar, *Mobile Units and Radio Communication: The History of the South African Police: 1913 – 1988*, self published, 1988, p 305.
131 Document in Afrikaans, translated by R.M. Maniatis, downloaded from https://disa.ukzn.ac.za.
132 Ken Keable (ed), *London Recruits: The Secret War Against Apartheid*, Merlin Press, 2012.
133 Keable, *London Recruits*, 2012.
134 Handwritten notes made by Captain Gloy, https://www.ahmedtimol.co.za/wp-content/uploads/2020/03/Gloy.pdf, accessed on 6 March 2020
135 *Vrye Weekblad*, No 179, 19–25 June 1992, https://digital.lib.sun.ac.za/handle/10019.2/164, accessed on 2 January 2020
136 Gordon Winter, *Inside BOSS: South Africa's Secret Police*, London: Penguin Books, 1981, p 352.
137 SABC SAHA Truth Commission Special Report, http://

sabctrc.saha.org.za/documents/amntrans/johannesburg/54553.htm?t=%2Banderson+%2Bgavin&tab=hearings, accessed on 18 June 2018.
138 https://www.justice.gov.za/trc/amntrans/2000/201016jh.htm
139 Thokozani Mtshali, 'We need "good, polite, efficient" officials', 13 April 2005, https://www.iol.co.za/news/politics/we-need-good-polite-efficient-officials-238625, accessed on 15 May 2017.
140 Email correspondence dated 22 October 2017.
141 https://www.ahmedtimol.co.za/wp-content/uploads/2020/03/Gloy.pdf, accessed on 6 March 2020
142 Email correspondence dated 14 March 2017.
143 Apartheid-era Security Legislation Directorate Files on Individuals: Timol, Mohamed [sic] 3056, 7 pages translated from Afrikaans titled Memorandum GEHEIM SECRET – From 26 05 1966 – 30 08 1976 when a banning / restriction is recommended. Stored at the National Archives and Records Service: http://www.national.archives.gov.za
144 Email correspondence on 14 March 2017.
145 'Friendship, not torture, is best', *The Sydney Morning Herald*, 10 November 1971.
146 Partial set of 1972 inquest records obtained from Cachalia & Loonat – exhibit in 2017 inquest records. Now accessible at the Ahmed Kathrada Foundation; and Wits Historical Papers – Inventory for AK3388, http://www.historicalpapers.wits.ac.za/?inventory/U/collections&c=AK3388/R/9141
147 http://www.historicalpapers.wits.ac.za/inventories/inv_pdfo/AK3388/AK3388-B5-01-jpeg.pdf, pp 5–12.
148 https://www.ahmedtimol.co.za/wp-content/uploads/2020/03/Gloy.pdf, accessed on 6 March 2020
149 Partial set of 1972 inquest records obtained from Cachalia & Loonat – exhibit in 2017 Inquest Records now accessible at the Ahmed Kathrada Foundation. Wits Historical Papers – Inventory for AK3388; http://www.historicalpapers.wits.ac.za/?inventory/U/collections&c=AK3388/R/9141; TIMOL, Ahmed Inquest, records, 1971–1972; http://www.historicalpapers.wits.ac.za/inventories/inv_pdfo/AK3388/AK3388 B6 01 jpeg.pdf, p 13.
150 South African History Online (SAHO), https://www.sahistory.org.za/people/james-edward-april, accessed on 10 September 2019.
151 http://www.historicalpapers.wits.ac.za/inventories/inv_pdfo/

Endnotes

AK3388/AK3388-B8-01-jpeg.pdf, p 23, accessed on 10 February 2017.
152 Interview with M.H. Desai 2002. See, Cajee, *Timol: Quest for Justice*, 2005, p 105.
153 A/J/1/24/4/70http://www.historicalpapers.wits.ac.za/inventories/inv_pdfo/AK3388/AK3388-B7-01-jpeg.pdf, p 2.
154 https://www.ahmedtimol.co.za/wp-content/uploads/2020/03/Gloy.pdf, accessed on 6 March 2020.
155 A/J/1/24/4/70 http://www.historicalpapers.wits.ac.za/inventories/inv_pdfo/AK3388/AK3388-B7-01-jpeg.pdf, p 2.
156 Vawda was Bahiya's husband.
157 A/J/1/10/11/70, http://www.historicalpapers.wits.ac.za/inventories/inv_pdfo/AK3388/AK3388-B7-01-jpeg.pdf, p 9.
158 https://www.ahmedtimol.co.za/wp-content/uploads/2020/03/Gloy.pdf, accessed on 6 March 2020.
159 Directed by Enver Samuel and winner of a South African Film and Television Award (SAFTA).
160 Christo Davidson and Johan Van der Merwe interviewed by Padraig O'Malley, February 2000, https://omalley.nelsonmandela.org/omalley/index.php/site/q/03lv00017/04lv00344/05lv01353/06lv01354.htm, accessed on 13 September 2017.
161 Ibid.
162 Muriel Horrell, Dudley Horner, John Kane-Berman and Robin Margo (complied), A Survey of Race Relations in South Africa;, Johannebsurg: South African Institute of Race Relations, p. 56, https://www.sahistory.org.za/archive/sairr-1972, accessed on 20 October 2019.
163 Partial set of 1972 inquest records obtained from Cachalia & Loonat, exhibit in 2017 inquest records. Now accessible at the Ahmed Kathrada Foundation and Wits Historical Papers – Inventory for AK3388, http://www.historicalpapers.wits.ac.za/?inventory_enhanced/U/Collections&c=259936/R/AK3388-D9, p 1094.
164 https://www.ahmedtimol.co.za/wp-content/uploads/2020/03/Gloy.pdf, accessed on 6 March 2020
165 http://www.historicalpapers.wits.ac.za/inventories/inv_pdfo/AK3388/AK3388-D9-01-jpeg.pdf, p 1093.
166 Email correspondence dated 27 August 2018.
167 Quentin Jacobsen, *Solitary in Johannesburg*, London: Joseph, 1973
168 https://www.ahmedtimol.co.za/wp-content/uploads/2020/03/Gloy.pdf, accessed on 06 March 2020

169 https://www.ahmedtimol.co.za/wp-content/uploads/2020/03/Gloy.pdf, accessed on 06 March 2020
170 Jacobsen, *Solitary in Johannesburg*, 1973
171 http://www.historicalpapers.wits.ac.za/inventories/inv_pdfo/AK3388/AK3388-D9-01-jpeg.pdf, p 1086.
172 Foundation for Human Rights, 'Timol judgment brings hope to families of victims of torture', https://www.fhr.org.za/index.php/latest_news/timol-judgement-brings-hope-families-victims-torture/, accessed on 15 October 2018; 'Biko: The Quest for a True Humanity", which was an exhibition at the Steve Biko Foundation, lists 114 persons to have died in police detention.
173 Interview with Farouk Bhabha in 2002. See, Cajee, *Timol: Quest for Justice*, 2005, p 148.
174 Israel Aaron Maisels QC (1905 to 1994), affectionately known as Issie or Issy, was a member of the Johannesburg Bar for more than 60 years.
175 http://www.historicalpapers.wits.ac.za/inventories/inv_pdfo/AK3388/AK3388-D9-01-jpeg.pdf
176 Detective Warrant Officer Peter van der Merwe attached to the Photography Division took the pic of room Room 1026 on 27 October 1971 at 17:30, http://www.historicalpapers.wits.ac.za/inventories/inv_pdfo/AK3388/AK3388-B4-01-jpeg.pdf, p 13, accessed on 10 February 2017.
177 Mothle judgment, p 15, http://www.saflii.org/za/cases/ZAGPPHC/2017/652.html, accessed on 26 June 2018.
178 Staff Reporter, 'Timol – Tears at finding of suicide', *Rand Daily Mail*, 1972 https://www.ahmedtimol.co.za/downloads/archive/articles/1972NewspaperArticles /19720623RandDailyMailRealQuestionsstillremain.pdf
179 Muriel Horrell, Dudley Horner, John Kane-Berman and Robin Margo (complied), *A Survey of Race Relations in South Africa*, Johannebsurg: South African Institute of Race Relations, p. 102, https://www.sahistory.org.za/archive/sairr-1972, accessed on 20 October 2019.
180 Interviews with Moe, May 2015 in Durban and May 2016 in Johannesburg.
181 In the Supreme Court of South Africa (Transvaal Provincial Division) Case 323/72 held at the Synagogue Pretoria, Date 8/6/72 and 13/6/72: Volume 7, pp 281–289.
182 In the Supreme Court of South Africa (Transvaal Provincial Division)

Case 323/72 held at the Synagogue Pretoria, Date 8/6/72 and 13/6/72: Volume 7, p 320.
183 In the Supreme Court of South Africa (Transvaal Provincial Division) Case 323/72 held at the Synagogue Pretoria, Date 8/6/72 and 13/6/72: Volume 6, pp 261–272.
184 'Frightened of police, says Essop witness', *The Star*, 18 July 1972, https://www.ahmedtimol.co.za/downloads/archive/articles/1972Newspaper-Articles/19720718TheStarTuesday.pdf
185 In the Supreme Court of South Africa (Transvaal Provincial Division) Case 323/72 held at the Synagogue Pretoria, Date 8/6/72 and 13/6/72: Volume 5, pp. 193–203.
186 In the Supreme Court of South Africa (Transvaal Provincial Division) Case 323/72 held at the Synagogue Pretoria, Date 8/6/72 and 13/6/72
187 Muriel Horrell, Dudley Horner, John Kane-Berman and Robin Margo (complied), *A Survey of Race Relations in South Africa*, Johannebsurg: South African Institute of Race Relations, p 102, https://www.sahistory.org.za/archive/sairr-1972, accessed on 20 October 2019.
188 SADTU South African Democratic Teachers Union, https://www.sadtu.org.za/docs/pe/2014/june26_national_freedom_day.pdf, accessed on 20 November 2019.
189 Case No: I01-2017 Date: 2017-08-14 ef Kadjee – 2017-08-14, p 1025.
190 Dated 29 November 2006, subject matter: Report on the progress made by the task team on TRC cases – 2.2.1 TRC Matters Closed by Priority Crimes Litigation Unit (PCLU).
191 Tymon Smith, 'NPA to re-examine Neil Aggett's death', https://mg.co.za/article/2019-05-07-00-npa-to-re-examine-neil-aggetts-death/, accessed on 20 May 2019
192 Tymon Smith, 'NPA to re-examine Neil Aggett's death' – *Mail & Guardian*, 7 May 2019, https://mg.co.za/article/2019-05-07-00-npa-to-re-examine-neil-aggetts-death, accessed on 20 May 2019.
193 Case no: I01-2017 Date: 2017-08-14 I01/2017– ef Kadjee 2017-08-14, p 1026.
194 The Southern African Legal Information Institute (SAFLII), the reopened inquest into the death of Ahmed Essop Timol (IQ01/2017) [2017] ZAGPPHC 652 (12 October 2017), http://www.saflii.org/za/cases/ZAGPPHC/2017/652.html#_ftn3, accessed on 2 January 2018.
195 https://www.ahmedtimol.co.za/2016/10/26/breakthrough-in-ahmed-timol-case-45-years-after-his-death-in-police-custody/,

accessed on 2 January 2018.
196 Case No: I01/2017 – *mf* Address 2017-06-29, p 195.
197 Case No: I01-2017 – ec Address 2017-06-26, p 3.
198 Case No: I01-2017 – ec Date: 2017-08-14 Address 2017-06-26, p 6.
199 Case No: I01-2017 – ec Date: 2017-08-14 Address 2017-06-26, p 13.
200 Case No: I01-2017 – ec Date: 2017-08-14 Address 2017-06-26, I01-2017 – ec 158 Nel 2017-06-26, p 24.
201 Case No: I01-2017 – ec Date: 2017-08-14– ef Kadjee 2017-08-14, p 1019–1020.
202 Case No: I01-2017 – ec Date: 2017-08-14 Inquest into the Death of: Ahmed Essop TimoL, I01-2017 – ec Nel 2017-06-26, p 35–98; I01/2017 – mvj Essop 2017-06-28, p 100–141.
203 Case No I01-2017 – ec Essop 2017-06-26, p 96.
204 Case No I01-2017 –Essop 2017-06-26, pp 85–86.
205 Case No: I01-2017, Date: 2017-06-27; 2017-06-28, Inquest into the Death of: Ahmed Essop Timol, I01-2017 REC (2017-06-27 TO 2017-06-28) Vol 2.doc, pp 99–100.
206 Sunday Times Heritage Project, http://sthp.saha.org.za/memorial/articles/an_unlikely_way_to_die.htm, accessed on 13 August 2015.
207 Graeme Hosken, 'Father loses race against time for justice – But new hope springs from drive to examine disputed findings in 300 apartheid deaths,' 13 May 2018, https://www.timeslive.co.za/sunday-times/news/2018-05-12-father-loses-race-against-time-for-justice/, accessed on 16 May 2018.
208 Case No: I01/2017 – *mf* Address 2017-06-29 Starts at p 196 and Ends at I01/2017 – *mf* Naik 2017-06-29, p 228.
209 ec Date: 2017-08-14 Inquest into the Death of: Ahmed Essop Timol, I01/2017 – *mf* Naik 2017-06-29, p 206.
210 Starts at I01/2017 I01-2017 Rec (2017-06-29) vol 3.doc – *mf* Naik (Must Read Timol) 2017-06-29, p 228 and Ends at I01/2017 – *mf* Naik (Must Read Timol) 2017-06-29, p 257.
211 Case No: I01-2017 - I01/2017 – mf Naik (Must Read Timol) 2017-06-29, p 232.
212 Case No: I01/2017 – *mf* Naik (Must Read Timol) 2017-06-29, p 237.
213 Case No: I01/2017 – mf Naik (Must Read Timol) 2017-06-29, p 237.
214 Case No: I01/2017 – *mf* Naik (Must Read Timol) 2017-06-29, p 239.
215 Case No: I01/2017 – *mf* Naik (Must Read Timol) 2017-06-29, p 248.
216 Case No: I01/2017 – *mf* Naik (Must Read Timol) 2017-06-29, p 255.

217 Case No: I01-2017 - I01/2017 – *mf* Naik 2017-06-29, p 248.
218 Case No: I01/2017 Started I01/2017-*amn* Jetham 2017-06-30, p 276.
219 Case No: I01/2017 Started I01/2017-*amn* Jetham 2017-06-30, p 292.
220 Case No: I01/2017– ef Kemp 2017-07-24, p 403.
221 Case no: I01/2017-aj, p 159, Discussion 2017-08-04.
222 Case No: I01/2017– ef Vorster 2017-07/27, starts p 591 and ends at p 614.
223 Case No: I01/2017– ef Vorster 2017-07/27, p 603.
224 Case No: I01/2017– ef Vorster 2017-07/27, p 600.
225 Case No: I01/2017– ef Vorster 2017-07/27, p 604.
226 Case No: I01/2017– ef Vorster 2017-07/27, p 605.
227 Case No: I01/2017– ef Matthis 2017-07-24, pp 331–332.
228 https://www.ahmedtimol.co.za/2016/10/26/breakthrough-in-ahmed-timol-case-45-years-after-his-death-in-police-custody/, accessed on 30 July 2016.
229 Case No: I01/2017 – *nh* Thokan 2017-08-03, pp 852–856.
230 Case No: I01/2017 – ef Adam 2017-08-10, p 968.
231 Case No: I01/2017– ef Boffard 2017-07-25 I01/2017– ef, p 428.
232 Case No: I01/2017– ef Boffard 2017-07-25, p 428.
233 Case No: I01/2017 – *nh* Naidoo 2017-07-26, pp 567–568.
234 Case No: I01/2017-aj S Holland 2017-07-26, pp 497–498.
235 Case No: I01/2017– ef Moodley 2017-07-28, p 673.
236 Case No: I01/2017– ef Dutton 2017-07/27, p 623.
237 Case No: I01/2017-aj 2017-06-29. P 664
238 Case No: I01/2017– ef Dutton 2017-07/27, pp 626–640.
239 Case No: I01/2017-aj Dutton 2017-07-27, p 643.
240 Case No: I01/2017 – *mvj* Bizos 2017-06-28, p 145.
241 Case No: I01/2017 – *mvj* Bizos 2017-06-28, p 176.
242 Case No: I01/2017– ef Pahad 2017-07-25, pp 448–467.
243 Case No: I01/2017– ef Pahad 2017-07-25, p 455.
244 Case No: I01/2017– ef Pahad 2017-07-25, p 457.
245 Case No: I01/2017– ef Pahad 2017-07-25, pp 458–461.
246 Case No: I01/2017 – *nh* Kasrils 2017-08-03, p 873.
247 Case No I01/2017 – *nh* Kasrils 2017-08-03, p 878–879.
248 Case No: I01/2017 – *nh* Kasrils 2017-08-03, p 880.
249 Case No: I01/2017 – *nh* Kasrils 2017-08-03, p 885.
250 Case No: I01/2017– ef (673) Els 2017-07-31, p 160 to I01/2017– ef (673) Els 2017-07-31, p xxx.

251 Case No: I01/2017– ef Sons 2017-08-16, pp 1030–1084.
252 Case No: I01/2017 – nh Sons 2017-08-16, p 1067.
253 https://www.ahmedtimol.co.za/2017/08/22/security-policeman-seth-sons-victims-depose-affidavits/, accessed on 1 September 2017.
254 Case No: I01/2017 See exhibits H21 – H26, affidavits of A. Musson; H. Vally; P. Naidoo; I. Momoniat; K. Martin; R. Moosa. These detainees describe how Seth Sons and other members of the SB tortured [by assaulting and humiliating] them during the 1980s. See also *Mail & Guardian* online article dated 17 August 2017 about how Seth Sons and his colleagues tortured Ms Jessie Duarte: https://mg.co.za/article/2017-08-17; https://mg.co.za/article/2017-08-17-timol-inquest-jessie-duarte-helps-apartheid-cop-remember-torture-he-couldnt-recall, accessed on 18 August 2017.
255 Momoniat is now the Deputy Director General of South Africa's Treasury.
256 Duarte further said on Facebook and Twitter: 'He refused my grandmother on the same day entrance to the toilet and she wet herself. He slapped my mother when she wanted to hug her sister who was handcuffed… Your office was on the 9th floor of John Vorster Square. You knew what took place in that space. You stood with folded arms as chair backs were used as racks and as many of us were choked. Smacked. Kicked. You watched as pee ran down our legs because you made us stand for hours.'
Ra'eesa Pather, 'Timol inquest: Jessie Duarte reminds apartheid cop of torture he couldn't recall', *Mail & Guardian*, 17 August 2017, https://mg.co.za/article/2017-08-17-timol-inquest-jessie-duarte-helps-apartheid-cop-remember-torture-he-couldnt-recall/, accessed on 25 August 2017.
257 Case No: I01/2017– ef Kadjee 2017-08-14, pp 1006–1028.
258 The Southern African Legal Information Institute (SAFLII), the reopened inquest into the death of Ahmed Essop Timol (IQ01/2017) [2017] ZAGPPHC 652, 12 October 2017, http://www.saflii.org/za/cases/ZAGPPHC/2017/652.html#_ftn3, accessed on 2 January 2018.
259 Foundation For Human Rights, 'Statement from Advocate Dumisa Ntsebeza SC Following Judgement in the Re-opened Inquest into the Death of Ahmed Timol', https://www.fhr.org.za/index.php/latest_news/statement-advocate-dumisa-ntsebeza-sc-following-judgement-re-opened-inquest-death-ahmed-timol/, accessed on 20 October 2017.

260 Fourth Session, Fifth Parliament Republic of South Africa; Minutes of Proceedings of National Assembly (16) Tuesday, 24 October 2017; No 36 – 2017, https://www.parliament.gov.za/storage/app/media/Docs/min/7f940bca-b6ef-4b41-afed-6bea7d6bf188.pdf, accessed on 10 January 2020.
261 The chairperson of the Islamic Unity Convention (South Africa), Imam Achmat Cassiem has spent his entire life standing up against oppression. At aged 15 he joined the armed struggle against the oppressive apartheid regime in South Africa and at the age of 17 he was one of the youngest people to be imprisoned on Robben Island, http://www.inminds.com/imam-cassiem-talk.html, accessed on 10 January 2018.
262 Lengwadishang Ramphele, 'Hawks to charge security cop in Ahmed Timol murder', 25 October 2017, http://www.capetalk.co.za/articles/277819/hawks-to-charge-security-cop-in-ahmed-timol-murder, accessed on 27 October 2017.
263 Yolisa Tswanya, 'Calls for probe into Ashley Kriel's death', *News24*, 7 February 2018, https://www.iol.co.za/capeargus/news/calls-for-probe-into-ashley-kriels-death-13145977, accessed on 10 February 2018.
264 Andisiwe Makinana, 'NPA to prioritise murders of anti-apartheid activists', 9 May 2018 https://www.timeslive.co.za/news/south-africa/2018-05-09-npa-to-prioritise-murders-of-anti-apartheid-activists/, accessed on 10 May 2018.
265 Interview with Tilana in Cape Town on 6 October 2018.
266 Journalst's Resource, 'Why many sexual assault survivors may not come forward for years', https://journalistsresource.org/studies/government/criminal-justice/sexual-assault-report-why-research/, accessed on 20 October 2018.
267 https://www.aljazeera.com/programmes/tutuschildren/2013/01/20131101357 29653897.html, accessed on 1 August 2018.
268 'We have won dignity for our people', 19 July 2011, http://www.thehindu.com/todays-paper/tp-national/we-have-won-dignity-for-our-people-kathrada/article2248844.ece, accessed on 1 November 2019.
269 'Son of slain Cradock Four activist implicates FW de Klerk in father's murder', 26 November 2019, http://www.702.co.za/articles/368107/son-of-slain-cradock-four-activist-implicates-fw-de-klerk-in-father-s-murder, accessed on 29 November 2019.

270 Member of the Luthuli Detachment who fell in battle in Rhodesia on 15 August 1967 – courtesy of SA History Archives.
271 Niël Barnard, as told to Tobie Wiese, *Secret Revolution: Memoirs of a Spy Boss*, Cape Town: NB Publishers, p 196.

Index

A

Abrahams, Shaun 148, 211
Abrahams, Faizel 9
Academic Staff Association 64
Adam, Abdullah Mohammed 164
Adam, Yacoob 41
Adam, Yusuf 'Chappies' 135
Administration Board 7
African Food and Canning Workers' Union 147
African National Congress (ANC) 9, 13, 15–16, 21, 23, 28–30, 32, 68, 73–74, 76, 77, 79, 80, 85, 87, 90, 92, 95, 96, 101, 104, 105, 117, 131–132, 135, 145, 172–175
Aggett, Neil 147, 168, 187, 211
Ahmed Timol Golf Day 215
Ahmed Timol Memorial Committee 71, 73, 74, 81
Ahmed Timol Secondary School 19
Akhalwaya, Yusuf 80
Alexandra Health Centre (AHC) 16, 34, 159
Algeria 90, 96, 100
Aligarh Muslim University (AMU) 29, 32
ANC Says to Vorster and His Gang, Your Days are Coming to an End 105
Anti-Apartheid Movement (AAM) 65, 89, 117, 145, 159
April, James Edward 106–107
Arbee (Major) 184
Areff, Fatima 215
Argus 211
Arkley 26
Armed and Dangerous 33
Armed Resistance Movement (ARM) 34
Asmal, Kader 34
Assure, Michelle 211
Austria 21
Azaadville 3–7, 17, 19, 107, 195, 214

B

Barnard, Niël 218
Barrell, Howard 24
Barritt, David 43
Basson, Wouter 210
Bean, Richard 18, 125
Bechuanaland 31
Benoni 4
Benzien, Jeffrey 210
Bhabha, G.H. 123

Bhabha, Mohammad 8
Bhagwandeen, I. 67
Biko, Bantu Stephen xi, xii, xxii, 6, 187, 204, 217
Biko, Nkosinathi 204
Billings (Branch Officer) 183
Bizos SC, George xix, 123, 126, 147, 170–171, 204
Black Consciousness Movement xii, 73
Blacking, John 44
Blose, Sicelo 150
Boffard, Ken 165
Botha (Officer) 60
Botha, Pik 74–75
Botswana 81
Bouwer, Frederick 106, 124–125, 200
Bozzoli, G.R. 64
Braamfontein Hotel 16
British Secret Services 87
Brixton Murder and Robbery Squad 47
Browde, J.131, 138–139
Brutus, Dennis 94
Bugwadeen, Durban 131
Bunting, Sonia 94
Bureau of State Security (BOSS) 86–87, 89, 94–95, 97, 115, 116, 164, 218

C
Cachalia and Loonat 123, 131
Cachalia, Azhar 10
Cachalia, Firoz 10
Cachalia, Molvi 23
Cajee, Azhar 8
Cajee, Ebrahim 4, 7, 11, 21, 32
Cajee, Haroon 8

Cajee, Yunus 41
Cajee, Yusuf 'Chichi' 56
Campaign for Nuclear Disarmament 25
Canada 97
Cape Talk 210
Cape Town City Hall 15
Capital Radio 8
Capital Radio 604 11
Cassiem, Achmat 210
Central Committee of the Communist Party 38, 104, 105, 106, 172
Central Intelligence Agency (CIA) xxii, 89
Central Intelligence Service 86
Chalk Farm 117
Chand, Jameel 80–81
Charter of the Organisation of African Unity 78
Chauke, Andrew 211
Chiba, Laloo 'Isu' 163, 174, 199
Chikane, Frank 15
Choonara, Choti 58, 62
Choonara, Ebrahim 58
Chothia, Rashid Ahmed 'Bhai' 11, 32
Chothia, Fatima 32
Chothia, Gadija 163
Chothia, Mahomed 215
Chothia, Zubedia 'Gorikala' 11, 32
Cilliers, S.A. 123
Citizen 6
Clark, Caroline 71
Coaker, J. 131
Coetzee, Stephanus Johannes 'Fanus' 150, 214
Coetzee, Johan 92, 109

Index

Cohen, Martin 118, 120, 121
Coloured Labour Party 66–67
Coloured Representative Council 78
Communist Party of Great Britain 92, 105, 106, 110, 115
Communist Party of the Soviet Union 28
Congress Movement 69, 72
Congress of Democrats 30
Congress of the People of South Africa 77
Convention on the Suppression and Punishment of the Crime of Apartheid 67–68
Coovadia, Cass 16
Coovadia, M. 66
Coronationville 43, 47
Cradock Four xxii, 198, 211, 216
Cronwright (Colonel/Major) 160, 184
Curtis, Jeanette 71, 72
Czechoslovakia 106

D

Dadoo, Yusuf 'Doc' or 'Mota' 23, 24, 29, 34, 91, 92, 99, 100, 101, 104, 107, 117, 119, 173, 174
Davidson, Christo 112–113
Davis, Dennis 162
Dayal, Madan 'Charlie' 12
De Klerk, F.W. 108, 216
De Swardt, J.J. 'Blackie' 103
De Villiers Building 93
De Villiers, J.J.L. 68, 112–115, 119, 120, 123–131, 152, 170, 171, 177, 186, 199, 201, 203, 208
Defence and Aid Fund 34
Department of Bantu Affairs 136

Department of Education and Rapportryers 113
Department of Internal Affairs 98
Desai, Amina 'Mummy' 3, 16, 27, 42, 43, 56, 69, 93, 107, 109, 111, 131, 132, 209
Desai, Bahiya Vawda 42, 109, 110,
Desai, Fatima 107
Desai, Hanief 'M.H.' 107
Desai, Hilmi 32, 42
Desai, Ruwaida 110
Desai, S.M. 42
Desai, Zarina 27, 42
Detention and Torture in South Africa: Psychological, Legal and Historical Studies 162
Deysel, Warrant Officer 125–126, 165, 167, 184
Dindar, Farouk 5, 41, 74
Dindar, Haroon 18, 31, 32, 56, 57, 196
Dindar, Iqbal 'Baboo' 5, 50, 195
Dindar, Jameela 50–51, 194
Dindar, Mohammed 18, 196
Dindar, Nazneen 41
Dirker, Carel Joseph 18, 104
Division N 87
Dollars petrol station 164
Duarte, Jesse 183, 185
Dugard, John 44
Durban gang 88
Dutt, Rajani Palme 25
Dutton, Frank xix, xx, 147–148, 168–170, 200
Dynamos Football Club 134–135

E

Eggenhuisen, Toine 79

Els, Neville 18, 48–49, 104–105, 148, 150, 151, 179–182, 202, 209
Els, Renier 98
Erasmus, Paul 95, 159–160, 163, 184, 200
Essack, Yousuf Hassan 'Moe' 69, 131, 132–140
Essop, Mohammad Salim 42, 43, 48, 61, 64, 66, 69, 109, 112, 121, 131, 134, 137, 148, 152, 163

F
FA Cup Final 6
Fakir, Naseema 150
February, Basil 217
Federal Party 67
Federal Republic of Germany 21
Fick (Major) 157
Financial Mail 74
Fischer, Bram 29, 75, 76, 90, 91, 120, 124
Fisher Street 156
Fordsburg 43, 64, 89, 106, 115, 116, 172
Forensic Pathology Services 166
Foster, Don 161–162, 186
Fouche, Jim 86
Foundation for Human Rights (FHR) xix, 123, 184, 193, 204, 208, 225
Fourie, Stephanus le Roux 18, 48
Freedom Charter 77, 145
Friedman, Roger xix, 203

G
Gabba, Salim 55, 59
Gandhi Hall 75, 76
Gandhi, Mohandas Karamchand 79

General Assembly 67
General Law Amendment Act 130
German Democratic Republic (GDR) 76
Gloy, Johannes Hendrik 'Hans' xviii, 18, 54, 93, 99, 103, 109–111, 115, 118, 124–128, 138–140, 146, 151, 161, 169, 170, 187–190, 197–198, 200, 202
Gluckman, Jonathan 123
Goldstone Commission 168
Goniwe, Matthew 217
Gool, Benny xix, 203
Gous, Police Commissioner General J.P. 91
Grays, The 17
Greyling (Colonel) 18, 49, 128, 158
Groote Schuur Talks 15
Group Areas Act 35, 133
Guinea 67
Gullit, Ruud 14

H
Haffejee, Hoosen 187, 210
Haffejee, Marcia 150
Hare, P.J. 131
Haron, Abdullah 45, 210
Hathorn, Moray xix, 147, 149–150
Heard, Tony 20
Heymans, Hennie 112
High Barnet 26
High Court of South Africa, Gauteng North Division xi
History of the South African Police: 1913–1918, The 49
Hodgson, Jack 24, 30, 31, 91, 99, 100, 104, 115, 173, 175
Hodgson, Rica 91, 94, 104

Index

Holland, Shakeera 165, 166, 167, 190
Hoofstad, Die 189
Horak, John 93–94
HRC Bulletin 76–78
Human Rights 75
Human Rights Commission 203
Human Rights Committee 6, 74–79, 81

I

In Solitary in Johannesburg 117
Indians Can't Fly 27, 55, 112, 149
Inkatha 16
Inkululeko Freedom 115, 112, 127, 132, 135, 137–139, 140, 174, 177
Inside Boss 94
Institute for African Studies, Russian Academy of Sciences 28
Internal Security Act 4
International Defence and Aid Fund 89
Irish Republican Army 11
Irvin, John xxii
Islamic Unity Convention 210
Ismail, Aboobaker 'Baker' (Rashid) 76

J

Jacobsen, Martin 116–117, 169
Jacobsen, Quentin 116–121, 128, 169, 186
Jan Smuts Airport 94–95
Janse van Rensburg, Carel Petrus 53
Jassat, Abdulhay 163, 173–174
Jassat, Sabera 214–215
Jenkin, Tim 175
Jeppe Street Post Office 93, 96, 112

Jetham, Dilshad 158–159, 163
Jiba, Nomgcobo 148
Jinna, Sadique 23
Johannesburg Training Institute for Indian Teachers 108
Johanneson, Albert 6
John Vorster Square 7, 14, 15, 17, 46, 49, 50–51, 54, 69, 76, 92, 94, 106, 1008, 109, 116, 124, 124, 127, 129, 131, 134, 147, 152, 154, 157, 159, 163–165, 169, 170, 180–188, 194, 199, 201, 213, 223
Jooma, Hassen 108–109, 209
Joseph, Helen 69, 72, 75

K

Kader, Abdus-Samad Abdul 32–33
Kader, Shareefah 32–33
Kades, N. 131
Kasrils, Eleanor 91
Kasrils, Ronnie 24, 33, 73, 87, 91, 174, 225
Kathrada, Ahmed 134, 216
Keable, Ken 86, 92
Kei Road police station xii, xiii
Kemp, V.D. 126
Kemp, Stephanie 17, 34–35, 91, 99, 104, 159, 163
Kgoathe, Nicodemus 187, 210
Khan, Mohammed 55
Khan (Sheriff) 88–89
Kholvad 29
Khota, Ahmed 'Quarter' 37, 97
King William's Town xi
Kleyn, Leonard Gysbert 18, 47–49, 153
Kloppers, J.M. 47–48
Kodesh, Wolfie 30

Kotze, P.A.J. 123
Kramer, A.N. 163
Kriel, Ashely 187, 210, 211
Kruger National Park xx
Kruger, Jane 43–44, 46
Kwela, Alan 43

L
Labour Monthly 25
Laher, Ebrahim 'International', 'Hookah', 'Mike Todd' 117–119
Laudium 12
Legal Resources Centre xix, 150, 171, 225
Legodi (Judge) 198
Leicester Polytechnical College 32, 99–100
Lekoloane, Willie 16
Lenin Party School 173
Lenin University 25, 29
Lesotho 95
Lesufi, Panyaza 214
Lion's Head 44
Little Rivonia Trial 90
London Recruits 86, 91–92, 105–106, 174
Long Walk to Freedom xxiv
Longoni, Ruth 25, 37, 100, 151
Louw, Phindi 124, 200, 210
Ludi, Gerard 90
Lusaka 15–16
Luthuli, Albert 187, 210

M
Mabasa, Xitlhangoma 209
Mabelane, Lasch 154, 203
Mabelane, Matthews 154, 210
Mabelane, Phillip 203

Machadodorp 11, 32
Magubane, Peter 43, 163
Main Reef Road 7
Maisels, Issy Aaron 123–124
Maitland Square police station 45
Majija, Goodenough 136
Makhathini, Johnny 96–97
Makiwane, Tennyson 24
Malindi, Gcina 16
Malotwa, Jabulani 150
Mandela, Nelson xxii, 14, 15, 19, 35, 69, 134, 174, 216
Mandela, Winnie 15, 73
Martin, Kevin 183, 184
Martynenko, Vladimir 77
Maseko, Karel 74
Masutha, Michael 148
Mathabatha, Sello Kgoshi 22
Mattera, Don 64
Matthis, Ernest 163–164
Mayfair Jumma Masjid 146
Mbabane 6
Mbeki, Thabo 28–30, 96, 172–173, 174
McCann, Owen 66
McCann, Mike 43
Meer, Fatima 4
Military Intelligence 86, 93
Minnaar, Ben 150, 214
Mitchell, Mike 67
Mlambo, D. 148
Mlangeni, Bheki 16
Modderbee Prison 4
Modipane, Solomon 210
Mogale City 19
Mohapi, Mapetla xi, xiii, 187
Mohapi, Mothiba xiii
Mokoape, Keith 13

Momoniat, Ismail 183–184
Monakgotla, Jacob 210
Moodley, Indhrasen 'Indres' 69, 131, 209
Moodley, Tivesh 167–168
Moosa, Valli 16
Morocco 90
Moss, Glenn 72
Mothle, Billy xi, xii, xx, xxi, 149, 150, 152, 154, 157, 159, 161, 166, 168, 170, 171, 174, 179, 182, 187, 191, 193, 198–199, 201–203, 208, 209, 212, 215
Moumbaris, Alex 175
Mpumlwana, Thoko 204
Msomi gang 88
Msomi, Kukhanya 150
Mthintso, Thenjiwe xiii
Mulaudzi, Hangwani 210
Mulaudzi, Mutondi 150
Musanda Complex 19
Musandiwa, Musatondwa 'Musa' 149
Musson, Alwyn 183–184

N
Naicker, Monty 133
Naidoo, Steve 165
Naidoo, Indres 13, 37, 71, 72, 74, 132
Naidoo, Murtie 71
Naidoo, Prema 71, 72
Naik, Arvind 62, 63
Naik, Dinesh 'Dan' 63, 137, 140
Naik, K.C. 'Kanti' 63, 137
Naik, Kantilal 154, 163, 180
Nanabhai, Abdul Hamid 'Bloms' 13
Nanabhai, Shirish 71

Napier, Prakash 80
Natal Indian Congress 67
National Intelligence Agency (NIA) 19, 21
National Intelligence Service (NIS) 19, 887, 116, 218
National Prosecuting Authority (NPA) xix, xxi, 146, 147, 149, 150, 209, 211, 214
National Union of Students (NUS), United Kingdom 65
National Union of Teachers (NUT), United Kingdom 24, 65
Naudé, Beyers 94
Nayager (Lieutenant) 59–60
NCP 133
Ndlovu, Sifiso 20
Ndou, Sampson 77
Nel, Ben 151
Nelson Mandela International Day 216
New Radicals, The 72
Newclare 43
Newlands Police Station 46
Newtown Mosque 59
Ngakane, Barney 75
Ngcukaitobi, Tembeka 27
Ngoyi, Lillian 75
Ngudle, Looksmart Khulile 123
Nicholson, Ann 28–29
Nimeiry, Gaafar 41
Nirvana High School 64
Nkadimeng and Others versus the National Director of Prosecutions and Others 198
North London Association of the National Union of Teachers (NUT) 24, 65

Nöthling, J.E. 131, 139–140
Ntsebeza, Dumisa 208
Nye, Mark 66
Nzo, Alfred 23

O
O.R. Tambo International Airport 94, 149
O'Brien, Kevin 13
O'Malley, Padraig 112
Old Man Docrat 'Commie Doc' 133
Operation Buttonhole 95
Order of Luthuli 28
Orlando Pirates 136
Orlando West High School 73
Oryx Media 191, 212

P
Pahad, Aziz 24, 31, 44, 91, 100, 117, 172
Pahad, Essop 20, 24, 31, 34, 35, 44, 100, 101, 104, 172–174
Pahad, Meg 20, 24
Pahad, Naseem 'Naz' 134
Pahad, Zunaid 134
Pan Africanist Congress (PAC) 90
Park Station 81
Pattle, Cecil William St. John 18
Pearl Restaurant 43
Pelser, Piet 9, 64
Persad, Harry 183
Pick n Pay 14
Pietermaritzburg Supreme Court 106
Pigou, Piers 146–147
Piliso, Mzwai 76
Pillay, Bobby 13
Playboy magazine 95

Pochee, Essop Bhai 7
Poothawala, Molvi Osman 57
Port Elizabeth 92, 95, 105, 126
Portugal 77
Press, Ronnie 91
Pretorius, Torie 148, 150–151, 154, 182, 183, 191, 209–210
Prinsloo, G.L. 72
Project Coast 210
Promotion of Access to Information Act (PAIA) 85
Publications Control Board 78

Q
Queen's Park 72

R
Rabkin, Dave 175
Rabkin, Sue 13, 175
Rand Daily Mail, The 8, 46, 54, 73, 130
Rapport 113, 168
Republic Intelligence (RI) 86, 115
Republic of Transkei 27
Resha, Robert 24
Rhodesia 103, 106
Richards, Miley 66
Rickard, Donald xxii
Rivonia Trial 90, 124
Robb, David 16–17
Robben Island 15, 64, 71
Roberts, Ronald Suresh 20
Rockey Street 71
Rodionova, Alexandra 'Comrade Shura' 28
Rodrigues, João 'Jan' Anastacio xii, xv–xxi, 18, 54, 124, 127–128, 140, 146, 148, 150, 151, 169–170, 179,

Index

185, 186–192, 199–200, 201–202, 208, 209, 210, 212, 213–215
Roodepoort Club 3, 62, 137–138
Roodepoort Indian High School 23, 32, 41, 48, 57, 62, 64, 69, 100, 101, 125, 136, 158
Roodepoort Moslem Club 135, 137
Roodepoort Muslim Society 58, 99
Roux, L.E. 105

S
Sabra 113
Salisbury Island 37, 42
Saloojee, Ram 10
Saloojee, Rookaya 71, 72
Saloojee, Suliman 'Babla' 17, 41, 58, 61, 71, 210
Saloojee, Yusuf 'Jo Jo' 32, 62
Samuel, Enver 149, 213
Sandler, Diane 162
Sands, Bobby 11
Santayana, George 22
Sastri College 133
Saturday Star, The 57
Savage, Collin Woodall 164
Schepers, Nicholas Jacobus 129, 165
Schoeman, Piet 94–95
Schwartz, Harry 164
Seagal, Stephanie 34
Sechaba 101
Security Branch 148, 153–154, 173, 180, 187, 194–195, 199–203, 215
Security Branch Officer Identity Photograph Album 152
Security Services Special Account Bill 86
Seedat, Mohammad 'Uncle Tony' 20–21

Seedat, Yusuf 'Tara' 59
September, Reg 34
Sexwale, Tokyo 73
Shabangu, Elliot 77
Sharpeville Massacre 30
Sheriff Khan Organisation 88
Shubin, Vladimir 28
Simelane, Nokuthula 198
Sisulu, Walter 134, 158, 176
Sithole, Michelle 150
Skye Products 133–134
Slovo, Gillian 27
Slovo, Joe 16, 24, 27, 34, 73, 91–92, 104, 174
Smith, Ian 75
Snyman (Honourable Mr Justice) 131, 138–141
Sons and Daughters of Africa 105
Sons, Seth 46, 150, 151, 178, 181–185, 193, 202, 209
Sooka, Yasmin 146–147, 149, 168, 204
South Africa House 27
South African Associated Newspapers (SAAN) 43
South African Communist Party (SACP) 99, 100, 104, 116, 117, 126, 131, 132, 152, 159, 172, 174–175, 177, 207
South African Defence Force (SADF) 89
South African Indian Council 67, 78, 184
South African Narcotics Bureau 47
South African Police 11, 14, 47, 49, 86, 87, 103, 129, 147, 152, 165, 168, 170, 176
South African Secret Services

(SASS) 19, 21
South African Student Organisation (SASO) xii
Soviet Union 20, 25, 28, 29, 44, 67, 73, 80, 81, 90, 98, 99, 104, 174
St Mary's Cathedral 66
Stander, Drikus 212
Stander, Tilana 151, 179, 212
Standerton School 8, 10
Stanwest Indian Shopping Complex 7–8
Stanwest Secondary School 9
Star, The 8, 55, 64, 96
State versus Abram Fischer and Thirteen Others 29
Steenkamp (Colonel) 60
Steve Biko Centre 149
Steve Biko Foundation 149
Student Representatives Council 108
Summers, Irene 44
Summers, Joe 44
Sunday Express, The 46, 50
Sunday Times xxii, 59, 67, 71, 117
Super, A.S. 66
Suppression of Communism Act 46, 97, 120
Suttner, Raymond 77, 175
Suttner, Sheila 77
Swanepoel, Pieter 'Oom Swanie' 94
Swanepoel, Theuns 103
Swanepoel, Tj.J. 'Rooi Rus' 103
Swaziland 6, 31, 79, 95

T
Tambo, O.R. 28
Tanzania 90
Taylor, Andy 60

Terrorism Act 46
Thinnies, Adam Alexander Cecil 18, 48
Thokan, Muhammed Ali 164
Thompson, J. Walter 117
Thompson, Douglas 72
Thompson, Ian 64
Timol, Ahmed (son of Uncle Haroon) 215
Timol, Bahiya 42
Timol, Cassim 98
Timol, Haji 4, 19, 29, 55, 195
Timol, Hawa xvi, 3, 6, 15, 17, 31, 41, 50–51, 53–55, 58, 59, 62, 101, 102, 130, 131, 194, 199, 196, 208
Timol, Ismail 5, 32, 59
Timol, Julie 13
Timol, Mohammad 4–6, 8, 9, 11, 13, 59, 62, 71, 73, 74, 76–77, 78, 79, 97–102, 107, 115, 119, 130, 155–158, 163, 196, 204, 207, 215
Timol, Papa Haji 4, 15, 19, 42, 49, 50, 53–55, 57–59, 61–62, 130–131, 195, 199, 204, 208
Timol: Quest for Justice 20, 225
Transvaal College of Education for Indians 64
Transvaal Indian Congress (TIC) 184
Transvaal Indian Youth Congress 172
Treason Trial 30, 72
Tri-Cameral Parliament 10
Truth and Reconciliation Commission (TRC) xv, xvii, 17, 19, 95, 103, 147, 196, 215
Tutu, Desmond 79, 215
Tweedie, Shanti 163

Index

U

UEFA Euro 1988 Soccer Championship 13
uMkhonto weSizwe (MK) 9, 24, 31, 33, 76, , 80, 81, 90, 106, 123, 174–178, 217, 218
UN Committee Against Apartheid 77
Union Castle Line 92
United Democratic Front 184
United Nations International Criminal Tribunal 168
United Nations' Declaration of Human Rights 74
United Party 67
United Progressive Jewish Congregation 66
United States of America 97
University College for Indians 37
University of Cape Town (UCT) 34, 161
University of South Africa 32, 98
University of the Witwatersrand Bursary Committee 42, 44
University of the Witwatersrand Medical School 64
Urban Bantu Councils 78

V

Vally, Hanif Mohamed 183–184
Van den Bergh, Hendrik 46, 86, 116, 218
Van Niekerk, Faan 187
Van Niekerk, Johannes Zacharia xviii, 18, 54, 118–119, 124–125, 127–128, 146, 161, 169–170, 188, 189, 190, 198, 200, 202
Van Rensberg, Roelf 103
Van Wyk, Willem Petrus 18, 105, 106, 113, 118, 120, 124, 125, 127
Vandeyar, Reggie 71
Vania, Fatima 145
Vania, Yusuf 145
Varney, Howard xix, 147–151, 158, 180–181, 183, 190, 193, 225
Vawda, Omar 109, 110
Venter, P.J. 'Tiny' 86, 133
Verster, A.S. 18, 48
Verwey, Dries 103
View from Moscow, A 28
Von Lieres, K. 131, 137–139
Vorster, B.J. 4, 34
Vrededorp 45, 48, 66, 72
Vrye Weekblad 93

W

Wankie Campaign 106
Waterwitch, Robbie 211
Webber Wentzel xix, 147, 150, 225
Weinberg, Eli 71
Weinberg, Sheila 71, 73, 79
Weinberg, Violet 71
Wentzel, E.M. 131
White Suspect Division 94
Williams, Coline 211
Winter, Gordon 94
Wits School of Governance 22
Wrankmore, Bernard 44, 45, 46, 65

Y

Y gang 88

Z

Zikalala, Snuki 163
Zuma, Jacob 13